The Home Office

THE NEW WHITEHALL SERIES

is prepared under the auspices of

THE ROYAL INSTITUTE OF PUBLIC ADMINISTRATION

and is edited on its behalf by Sir Robert Fraser, O.B.E. The purpose of the series is to provide authoritative descriptions of the present work of the major Departments of the Central Government.

THE HOME OFFICE
THE FOREIGN OFFICE

In preparation

THE COLONIAL OFFICE

THE MINISTRY OF LABOUR AND NATIONAL SERVICE

THE MINISTRY OF PENSIONS AND NATIONAL INSURANCE

THE NEW WHITEHALL SERIES

The Home Office

SIR FRANK NEWSAM
K.C.B., K.B.E., C.V.O., M.C.
Permanent Under Secretary of State
for the Home Department

LONDON · GEORGE ALLEN & UNWIN LTD
NEW YORK · OXFORD UNIVERSITY PRESS INC

First published in 1954
Revised Second Edition 1955
(with new analysis of Home Office Staff)

Printed in Great Britain
in 10 point Times Roman type
by C. Tinling & Co. Ltd.
Liverpool, London and Prescot

Preface

*

IT is well known that Government Departments work as a team. The compilation of this book was no exception to that practice, and I gladly take this opportunity to express my thanks to my senior colleagues who have helped me with material and advice on the matters on which they are experts. But I alone am responsible for the contents of the book and in particular for the views and opinions expressed. I have sought in the book to describe the principles, as I see them, which underlie the part played by the Home Office in the preservation of order and the maintenance of civil liberty, and I have also sought to give some account of the nicely balanced relationships which exist between the Home Office and the local authorities in administering the various services with which they are both concerned. It is, however, not possible, and indeed it would not be appropriate, to attempt to describe in detail within the compass of a book concerned mainly with the Home Office these services, or the responsibilities of the local authorities themselves.

The powers of the Home Secretary described in this book do not, in the main, extend to Scotland. Exceptions to this general statement are described in the appropriate parts of the book.

F. A. N.

Home Office
June, 1954

Contents

*

PART ONE

The Home Secretary and his Functions

CHAPTER I

The Business of the Home Office

The range and variety of Home Office business — Why the business of the Home Office is so varied — Two primary duties of the Home Secretary — The basic task of the Home Office.

*

1. THE RANGE AND VARIETY OF HOME OFFICE BUSINESS

MOST people, on being asked to state the Home Secretary's responsibilities, could probably name half a dozen. He is connected in some vague way with the police, the administration of justice, the control of aliens, civil defence, Home Office schools and homeless children. He is also a senior cabinet Minister; and he posts up notices outside his office in Whitehall announcing Royal births and deaths. For the rest, the Home Secretary's responsibilities are little known: so little, that a new incumbent may well remain unaware of the full extent of them through five strenuous years of office. Affairs of state may limit the time he is able to devote to the protection of wild birds, the conduct of charitable collections, and the safe use of hydrogen cyanide; and the realization that he has power to approve the tables of fees to be paid to ministers of religion for their services at burial grounds, and (subject to certain consents) to abolish a fair, may escape him entirely.

The Home Secretary is associated with the appointment of Archbishops, prison governors, children's officers, chief constables, and his own brewers and inn keepers. He is expected to deal with public disturbances of all kinds. He advises the Queen as to the reprieve of murderers under sentence of death, plans the civil defence of the country against atomic warfare, looks to the efficiency of the police, the fire brigades, the electoral system and the probation service, administers the licensing laws, and himself carries on a considerable business as an hotelier and a publican. He controls immigration, grants certificates of naturalization to foreigners, and has a special regard for the affairs of Northern Ireland, Wales, the Isle of Man and the Channel Islands. He is ultimately responsible for the welfare of 90,000 children deprived of a normal home life, 20,000 prisoners,

3,000 boys and girls in Borstals, and a further 10,000 in approved schools, remand homes and probation homes and hostels. And he has many other cares besides.

2. WHY THE BUSINESS OF THE HOME OFFICE IS SO VARIED

All domestic matters not assigned by law or established custom to some other Minister fall to the Home Secretary, so that he has been described as 'a kind of residual legatee.'[1] The nature of the Home Secretary's legacy is in itself sufficient guarantee of variety. The circumstances in which it has been handed down to him enrich the variety still more.

The responsibilities of many Ministers derive only from Parliament, and their Departments are the creations of Statute, sometimes of recent date. Certain of the Home Secretary's responsibilities have likewise been conferred upon him by Parliament, and these are described elsewhere in this book. But centuries before Parliament interested itself closely in the processes of government, the Home Secretary's predecessors had acquired power and influence as advisers to the King in exercising certain of his Prerogative powers. These responsibilities the Home Secretary continues to discharge. Sometimes the ancient Prerogative powers of the Crown have been modified, curtailed, or even superseded by Act of Parliament; but it is ultimately in consequence of his responsibility for advising on the exercise of two of the most important Prerogative powers that the Home Secretary today derives the bulk of his duties. And finally, the Home Secretary derives certain of his responsibilities from still earlier times, when his predecessors in office were secretaries in fact as well as name; private secretaries to the King, lowly officers of his household, and privy to his domestic life. It was in this mediaeval period that the Home Secretary assumed the responsibility for certain purely secretarial functions in relation to the Royal Household which his successor in office performs today, as when, with due ceremony, he announces a Royal birth.

The complex and varied nature of the business of the Home Office is thus due in part to the unique position of the Home Secretary as 'residuary legatee' among his ministerial colleagues, and in part to the threefold origin of the Home Secretary's responsibilities, some being conferred by Statute, others springing from Prerogative powers, and yet others from the humble origins of his first predecessors, the King's private secretaries.

[1] Lowell: *Government of England*, I, 105.

This may suggest that the business of the Home Office follows no clear pattern, and that in an essentially British fashion the Department is the product of casual and haphazard growth, lacking any unifying principle. But this is only partially true; for the form of the Home Office today is largely governed by two primary duties of the Home Secretary which between them embrace the bulk (though far from all) of the Department's business. It is against the background of these duties that Parliament now confers upon the Home Secretary new responsibilities, or hands over to his colleagues responsibilities which have outgrown their origins. Recognition of these two primary tasks is essential to an understanding of the structure and work of the Department today.

3. THE TWO PRIMARY DUTIES OF THE HOME SECRETARY

The two most important of the Prerogative powers which still concern the Home Secretary are the maintenance of the Queen's Peace and the Royal Prerogative of Mercy. The nature of these powers will be discussed later in this book. The present intention is to show how each of them has, over the course of years, attracted other powers and responsibilities of a like kind, generally conferred by Parliament, so that now many of the most important duties of the Home Secretary, baffling alike in their variety and the complexity of their origins, nevertheless conform to an intelligible pattern.

The Queen's Peace

First then, the Home Secretary is responsible for ensuring the maintenance of the Sovereign's Peace, a Royal Prerogative 'as old as the Monarchy itself.' It is the first business of government to maintain order and secure obedience to the laws of the community. Without this there can be no advance of civilization. As Thomas Hobbes put it: in the absence of law and order the life of man is 'poor, nasty, brutish and short.'

But it is no longer enough to keep the Sovereign's Peace. Law and order must be preserved, but the intricate pattern of life in a civilized community, if it is to flourish and grow freely, demands more than this. It demands effective agencies to maintain order, to secure obedience to the law, and to protect the citizen going about his lawful business against physical and moral harm. It demands intervention by the State to ensure public safety and well-being generally, and in particular to provide against the physical danger of fire and bomb and to look to the well-being of children deprived of a normal home life. For social and economic reasons, care is necessary in admitting aliens to this country and in granting naturalization only to those worthy of British nationality. Above all there is need for unceasing vigilance in keeping the delicate balance between the maintenance of law and order on the one hand, and the preservation of the liberties of the subject on the other.

Flowing from his primary responsibilities for keeping the Queen's Peace, the Home Secretary's task today is the wider one of promoting all the conditions precedent to an orderly society. He is concerned with public order in the broadest sense, with the efficiency of the police, with personal liberty, and, among other specific measures for securing public safety, with the efficiency of the fire and civil defence services. Except in so far as agencies of government have special responsibilities in particular fields, he is concerned with the structure, health and well-being of society, and especially with those too young to be able to fend for themselves: and in controlling aliens he must look to the preservation of the national and natural characteristics of that society. In this rôle the Home Secretary acts as a kind of general practitioner, with the whole community as his patient. His ancient instrument, the Prerogative power, has largely been replaced by more modern and effective instruments fashioned by successive Parliaments according to the needs of the time. The wide scope of these 'derivative' powers forms the subject of Part Two of this book.

The Royal Prerogative of Mercy

The Royal Prerogative of Mercy, the second of the two primary powers from which the Home Secretary may be said to derive so many of his present-day responsibilities, now associates him with the administration of great humanitarian services designed on the one hand to protect society against its misfits, and on the other to help these misfits to find their way back into society again. These responsibilities are described in Part Three of this book.

This second group of derivative powers and duties is complementary to the first, and a necessary corollary to it. In 1327, the first year of the reign of King Edward III, an Act was passed providing for the appointment of Justices of the Peace (though the name was not given till later). 'For the better keeping and maintenance of the Peace' the Act said 'the King wills that in every county good men and lawful, which be no maintainers of evil or barrators in the county, shall be assigned to keep the peace.' But these new officers were soon given judicial powers—power to commit for trial in 1334, and power to try offenders and inflict reasonable punishment in 1360. This amounted to recognition that responsibility for keeping the peace should be associated with responsibility for dealing with those who broke it by offending against the law. This is a proposition which no longer holds good, for in modern times the task of keeping the peace is largely in the hands of the police and offenders are dealt with independently by the judiciary. Nevertheless the early association of the two functions continues to be reflected today in the dual nature of the Home Secretary's primary responsibilities. There is, moreover, a logical necessity for this. Impartial enforcement of the law, necessary for maintaining the Queen's Peace, might lead to unreasonable distress were there no power in reserve to mitigate its occasional harshness and to right its occasional wrongs. Humanity may demand interference with the due course of law—exercise by the Crown of the Prerogative of Mercy; and it is appropriate that the Home Secretary, whose duty it is to ensure the maintenance of the Queen's Peace, should have a duty also in this way to temper with mercy the occasional severities of impartial justice, and to put right what the event may show to have been wrong: for only thus can the law command the respect of the community and the Peace be preserved.

These two elementary Prerogative powers are thus inseparably linked in the person of the Home Secretary. Other responsibilities naturally follow. The power of the King to pardon arose from the fact that criminal prosecutions are taken in his name. The Home Secretary used to be (but is no longer) concerned with prosecutions as well as with advising upon the Prerogative of Mercy; and he is now much interested in the administration of justice generally, and in particular in the treatment of convicted offenders. It is true that when sentences of death or transportation were common the Home Secretary had little concern with the treatment of offenders; but in modern times, when prisons (to some extent), Borstals and approved schools are regarded as training centres, the Home Secretary's responsibilities in this field have vastly increased. Again it is from Acts of Parliament, not from Prerogative powers, that the Home Secretary derives these wider responsibilities.

Complementary as these two primary responsibilities are in origin, the wide statutory powers now associated with them have in modern times followed a comparable—and significant—development, similarly guided, no doubt, by the characteristic trend of political thought in the twentieth century. Preservation of the Sovereign's Peace is the basic task of government: in its nature passive, restrictive, inhibitive, and curtailing liberty the better to preserve it; but the wider responsibilities which have evolved from these elementary necessities now compel the Government to reach out actively to guard the citizen against physical and moral harm and to protect the immature—the latter an important social service operated on a vast scale. Similarly the responsibilities associated with the exercise of the Royal Prerogative of Mercy now depict the Government in a creative, purposeful guise, the emphasis here being upon the affairs of tens of thousands of individuals as much as upon the well-being of society as a whole.

In this way the central pattern of the Home Office emerges, a pattern constant enough in its broad lines, but subject to alteration in its details according to the directions of Parliament. It has not always been thus. A century ago, before criminals were thought worthy of reformation or children deserving of protection, the Home Secretary's powers were greater and his duties less. Concerned primarily to preserve the Sovereign's Peace he would be impelled to institute unpopular and perhaps stern and repressive measures. The young thief would be transported to Van Diemen's Land and the defaulting lawyer executed, and neither the Home Secretary nor his officials would have any dealings with either of them. Now changing times reflect the shifting emphasis of the Home Secretary's task. The young thief may be trained in an approved school and the defaulting lawyer in an open prison, and the Home Secretary and his staff will have a close and continuing interest in both. In the change is seen one aspect of the transition from the *laisser faire* state of the early nineteenth century to the welfare state of today.

4. THE BASIC TASK OF THE HOME OFFICE

Ancient in origin, complex in development and many-sided in its present-day activities, the Home Office has been described by a former Home Secretary as 'the last bulwark of liberal opinion.' The description implies no political allegiance, but aptly depicts the basic task of the Home Office in the twentieth century. It is well to recognize at the outset what that task is, so that in the ensuing description of the Department's multifarious functions—important in themselves, but sometimes subsidiary and occasionally irrelevant—it may not be lost to sight.

Discussing the nature of liberty, Dr. Johnson said:

> 'The danger of unbounded liberty and the danger of bounding it have produced a problem in the science of Government which human understanding seems hitherto unable to solve.'

It is true that no complete solution has been stated in an abstract or theoretical form: but the illogical English have, by good luck or good management, hitherto succeeded by a series of practical expedients in maintaining the necessary balance between too much and too little liberty, and it is the basic task of the Home Office, as practical problems come up from time to time, to find a method of keeping that balance. Some of the ways in which this is done are described in the following chapters; but it will be convenient here, at the risk of anticipating what is more fully discussed later, to summarize in general terms the nature of this task as it presents itself to the Home Office.

The object of prohibiting certain activities is to prevent interference with more desirable and important activities. The law which makes it an offence for small boys to throw stones at windows was not passed to deprive small boys of that thrilling pleasure; it was passed in order that householders may not be disturbed in their domestic pursuits and enjoyments. The law that shops shall close at a certain hour was not passed to check the activities of people who want to shop late; it was passed to give greater scope for leisure activities to shop assistants. When Mr. (now Sir Winston) Churchill was Home Secretary a local authority proposed to make a byelaw prohibiting the use of roller skates on London pavements—the object being to protect the peace of elderly people who dislike being bumped into by boys on skates. Mr. Churchill decided that it was more important to protect the London boy against encroachment on his limited opportunities for adventure, and refused to confirm the byelaw. Laws are passed to promote liberty, not to restrict liberty.

These may seem trivial illustrations of the rôle played by the Home Office: manifestations of liberal opinion oddly incongruous in an age disposed to trample heedlessly on civil rights. But they deserve attention; for they depict problems that differ only in degree from what is probably the gravest question—save possibly issues of war and peace—that faces any country today: the question how far liberty can safely be enjoyed without endangering the foundations of government itself.

In recent years Parliamentary systems of government have perished in many lands because Parliaments and Governments which have been anxious to maintain liberty have been too weak to govern, and have allowed so much liberty that their opponents, by abusing that liberty, have been able to overthrow Parliamentary constitutions and to establish despotisms. History has again and again repeated the epitaph: 'Freedom free to slay herself and dying while they shout her name.'

Here we touch upon problems of government that transcend the sphere of any Government Department. Yet the Home Office, because it is intimately concerned with those occasional threats to civil order that from time to time disturb the normal tranquillity of the nation's life, is vitally concerned too with these crucial issues of national security; and in approaching them it is informed by precisely those principles that have already been discussed.

In time of war liberty must be curtailed, and novel methods have to be adopted which sometimes run counter to accepted British traditions. Normally, however, in times of peace Parliament is in the happy position of having to infringe liberty only to a relatively minor extent, because while many people are ready to denounce the government of the day in the strongest language and to fulminate against particular laws or particular institutions, yet very few people really want to overturn the system by which our laws are made and our government is carried on. The few who do have to be carefully watched, and if they should become so numerous or so strong as to be dangerous, it may be necessary to devise new methods of dealing with them. But experience has shown that considerable risks can be taken in Britain without endangering the foundations of government itself.

Probably the main cause contributing to this enviable state of affairs is that the British are instinctively a law-abiding people. They feel that the laws are administered and enforced fairly. They respect the impartiality of the courts and the commonsense and fairness of the police, and are quick to recognize the value of the Prerogative of Mercy in mitigating the harshness of the law. Grievances are freely ventilated, impartially investigated, and frequently redressed. Where liberty is curtailed, the reason for its curtailment is widely understood and accepted, and where liberty is enjoyed it rarely degenerates into licence. The task of the Home Office is consequently less exacting than it might be. Delicate as is the balance which the Home Office holds, it is the British people themselves who largely guarantee its stability: perhaps because the liberal principles which it is the fashion in some countries to deride are deeply ingrained in the British character.

To define shortly, then, the essential task of the Home Office in the mid-twentieth century—it is to maintain, in a world that seems to pay a diminishing regard to such a principle, the widest possible liberty consistent with law and order; and if the Home Office be assailed as an anachronism, the British people stand indicted too.

CHAPTER II

The Office of the Home Secretary

Origin of the Home Secretary — Creation of the Home Office in 1782: its functions then — Later changes: Duties transferred from or added to the Home Secretary.

✱

1. ORIGIN OF THE HOME SECRETARY

THE birthday of the Home Office is March 27, 1782, when Charles James Fox announced, in a circular to foreign representatives in London, 'The King having, on the resignation of Viscount Stormont been pleased to appoint me one of His Principal Secretaries of State and at the same time to make a new arrangement in the Departments by Conferring that for Domestic Affairs and the Colonies on the Earl of Shelburne and entrusting me with the sole direction of Foreign Affairs, I am to request that you will for the future address your letters to me.'

Lord Shelburne was the first Home Secretary: as a peer he took precedence over Fox, the Secretary of State for Foreign Affairs. That precedence the Home Secretary has ever since retained.

But the origins of the Secretary of State's Office extend back far beyond 1782. Indeed all the Secretaries of State[1] hold one office—the ancient office of the King's Secretary. These great offices of the state all derive from one confidential clerk in the Royal household. In the early Middle Ages, the King's private and public affairs were not clearly distinguished: government, in so far as it was carried on, was carried on by the King's household. As the amount of public business increased with the growth of the royal authority, the branches of the household began the process of development into public departments. As each branch became detached from the court another took its place to act as the King's private secretariat and the instrument of his personal authority. Thus, the Chancery with the Great Seal was succeeded by the Wardrobe with the Privy Seal, and they in turn by the Signet Office with the Signet. The Signet had evolved by 1367 from the various secret seals used by Edward II

[1] Home, Foreign, War, Colonies, Air, Scotland, Commonwealth Relations.

and Edward III, but it was not until 1377 that a keeper of the Signet was appointed. In that year the term 'Secretaries,' which for some two hundred years had described a person who enjoyed the King's Confidence, became the title of an office.

The King's secretaries of the 14th and 15th centuries were not men of high standing. The household ordinances of 1478 ranked the Secretary with the Dean of the Chapel, the almoners and the cofferer.[1] Nevertheless his prospects were good: he not infrequently succeeded to the important post of keeper of the Privy Seal and by the end of the century could reasonably hope for a bishopric. The importance of the office varied with the character of the King and the strength of his desire to exercise personal authority. The Secretary was normally in attendance on the King. He conducted the King's personal correspondence, issued bills and warrants in the King's name, and was the channel of approach to the King for those of His subjects who had no right of access to the Sovereign.

That these functions gave great opportunities for power was recognized by the Council which, to control them, laid down in 1442/3 that when the King granted a petition the secretary should direct a warrant to the keeper of the Privy Seal who in turn would send a warrant to the Chancery, unless the matter were in the Keeper of the Privy Seal's opinion one which should be laid before Council

'to the intent that if it be thought necessary to them the King be advertised thereof.'[2]

It is worth remarking that this cumbersome procedure survived for some purposes until as late as 1884, when the intervention of the Privy Seal was abolished by the Great Seal Act of that year.

By the end of the fifteenth century the Secretary had become something more than a confidential clerk. He had recognized functions in the transaction of public business and was normally a member of the Privy Council, but he was still primarily a household official. It was the personal government of the Tudors and their system of using as the chief agents of their policies, not holders of the ancient offices of state, but new men who for rank and office depended wholly on the Crown, that transformed him into a Secretary of State.

[1] Otway-Ruthven: *The King's Secretary and the Signet Office in the XVth Century*, p. 81.

[2] Nicholas: *Proceedings and Ordinances of the Privy Council of England*, Vol. 6, p. 319.

The character of the Secretaryship was transformed by Thomas Cromwell who, in all but name, was Henry VIII's chief minister. He was the first layman to hold the Secretaryship and he had two principal duties with which his predecessors had hardly been concerned at all—the conduct of an extensive diplomatic correspondence and the management of the House of Commons in the King's interest.

The Tudor age saw not only the development of the regal power: it saw the development of the Privy Council as an instrument of that power. Under Elizabeth the Council was the principal organ of government. The influence of the Secretary was the principal influence there, partly because he was the mouthpiece by which the Queen communicated her wishes to the Council and partly because he was the element of continuity in its proceedings. His attention to business was unremitting. It was to him that the Council looked for information and to him that it entrusted the execution of its decisions.

William Cecil enjoyed the Queen's confidence and was able to dominate the Council as Secretary. When he became Lord Treasurer, his successor as Secretary enjoyed an influence second only to his.

At this period the Secretary of State carried the main burden of administration, although he did not of himself directly determine policy. Nicholas Fount, one of Walsingham's confidential clerks wrote in 1592:

> 'Now, amongst all particular offices and places of charge in this state there is none of more necessary use, nor subject to more cumber and valuableness, than is the office of principal secretary by reason of the variety and uncertainty of his employment.'[1]

Variety there certainly was, for he exercised general supervision over domestic affairs, conducted the Queen's tortuous diplomatic correspondence, ran an intelligence service, and organized the defence of the country against enemies abroad and conspiracy at home. Uncertainty there also was, for the Secretary of State had no prescribed function, no legal powers except as a privy councillor. His authority depended on his relationship with the Crown; and the office might lapse altogether as it did on Walsingham's death when Burleigh took over the Secretary's work.

Under James I and Charles I lesser men were employed and royal favourites exercised much of the influence that had been the Secretary's. But Thurloe, appointed under the Protectorate, by a combina-

[1] Quoted in Evans: *The Principal Secretary of State*, p. 9.

tion of firmness of character and outstanding administrative ability restored the Secretaryship to its earlier pre-eminence in the state.

In the seventeenth century it became the established practice to appoint two Secretaries of State with equal powers and to divide foreign business between them. A second secretary had been appointed on occasions in the sixteenth century. On the first occasion in 1540,

'it was laid down that they were to be in every way equal, that each should keep a signet seal and also "a book containing all such things as shall pass by either of their hands and th'one to be made privy to th'other's register." In every way they were both to have, enjoy, and use the place of the principal secretary as heretofore hath been accustomed.'[1]

The title 'Principal Secretary' came into use at this period to distinguish its holder from the subordinate French and Latin Secretaries.

The division of work prescribed in 1640 preserved this principle. English ambassadors abroad were told that they would in future receive instructions from only one of the Secretaries, but they were to continue to send dispatches to both. The line of division was primarily religious and political: one Secretary dealt with the Protestant powers; the other with the Roman Catholic powers. Later, this arrangement was regularized when the spheres of authority were known as the Northern and Southern departments. After the Revolution it was the custom for the Irish and Colonial business to be taken by the Senior of the two Secretaries while domestic business continued to be equally divided between them; each Secretary was informed of the affairs of the other's province and could intervene in it. Some problems were common to both. The arrangement probably only worked because, in practice, the stronger of the two made his influence felt in the affairs of both departments.

Under Charles II and James II the Secretary's importance continued to depend on his relationship with the King. After the Revolution power passed from the Crown to the leaders of the emerging political parties and the importance of the Secretary was determined by his relationship with the leaders of the dominant party. The change was masked under William and Mary, but under their immediate successors real power came to be transferred from the Crown to the Ministry, and the Secretary of State absorbed the not inconsiderable powers hitherto exercised directly or indirectly by the King. So strong was his power that for considerable periods the senior Secretary was the principal power in the Ministry.

[1] Evans: *op. cit.* p. 103.

This increase in the Secretary's authority was counterbalanced by the gradual development of cabinet government, and of the doctrine of collective responsibility. It received a decisive check when in 1766 the House of Commons declared general warrants to be illegal. In Elizabeth's reign it had been customary for the Secretary, because he was responsible for the security of the realm, to issue warrants for the arrest of suspects, to examine them either with or without other Privy Councillors, and if necessary to commit them to prison. He similarly seized seditious books and examined their authors and publishers. In the seventeenth century warrants for the seizure of papers were authorized first by the Star Chamber in 1637 and later by the Licensing Acts. But they continued to be issued after these Acts had expired; and warrants continued to be issued for the arrest of persons suspected of conspiracy against, or later on behalf of, the Stuarts. By the middle of the eighteenth century it had become the custom to issue general warrants, i.e. warrants for the arrest of unnamed persons alleged to have committeed a named offence or for the seizure of unspecified papers of a named person, so that a number of persons might be available for examination by the Secretaries of State. The cases of *Wilkes v. Wood* and *Entinck v. Carrington* declared general warrants for the seizure of papers illegal and doubt was thrown on the legality of warrants for arrest. It was admitted that the extraordinary jurisdiction of the Secretaries of State, the existence of which was undeniable,

> 'was so dark and obscure in its origin that Councel have not been able to form any certain opinion whence it sprang.'[1]

The significance of the declaration of the House of Commons is that thereafter the Secretaries of State issued warrants for committal only in cases of treason; they ceased to investigate political offences and a line of development which might have led to a Ministry of Justice or Police was closed. The Secretary of State was not above the law: the continental system of 'lettres de cachet' could not become part of the English system. No English Minister could on his own will and by his own act commit a man to prison. He could not tell the police whom to arrest or the justices what sentences to impose. The law was supreme.

After the Act of Union in 1707 a third Secretary of State was appointed for Scottish affairs. This appointment was dropped in 1746. Thereafter, until 1885 when the Secretary for Scotland was

[1] *State Trials*, XIX, par. 1046, quoted in Evans *op. cit.* p. 253.

appointed and a Scottish Office was established, the responsibilities for the conduct of Scottish affairs, which before 1707 had been exercised by the Scottish Privy Council, were discharged first by the Lord Advocate and after 1828 by the Home Secretary with the assistance of the Lord Advocate.

The Home Secretary still retains certain functions in matters not related to any one part of the United Kingdom such as naturalization, or in which uniform administration is important, such as the control of aliens and dangerous drugs.

2. CREATION OF THE HOME OFFICE IN 1782: ITS FUNCTIONS THEN

In 1782 the division of foreign business between the Northern and Southern Departments was abolished. It had long ceased to serve its original purpose, and it did not bear any relation to the organization of the staff which worked in one or other of the offices in Whitehall and St. James's. The Records of the Northern Department were in 1760 divided into 'Domestic, Colonial and Foreign."[1] It was characteristic of the office of Secretary of State that the change was made without formality. There was no royal warrant; no legislation; the King on a change of government signified his wish that business should be redistributed between his Principal Secretaries of State.

What were the duties of the Home Secretary in 1782? At that time he possessed practically none of the vast statutory powers which subsequent legislation has conferred on him. With a few unimportant exceptions his only powers were those which had arisen from a long line of predecessors as Secretaries to the King, and long before 1782 it was recognized that the Secretary of State had three constitutional functions.

First: He was the sole channel by which the subject might approach the King. All petitions from subjects and even Addresses from Parliament must pass through his hands.

Secondly: He was the King's adviser in the exercise of his prerogative powers, such as the Prerogative of Mercy.

Thirdly: He issued on behalf of the King His Majesty's instructions to officers of the Crown, Lords Lieutenant, Magistrates, Governors of Colonies and others, and sometimes to local authorities.

[1] *Calendar of Home Office Papers*, Vol. 1: Preface p. v and cf. *Domestic Entry Book*, p. 16.

The work of the Department was described in 1785 by the Chief Clerk of the Home Office.

'The business of the Secretary of State's office for the Home Department comprises whatever relates to the internal Government of Great Britain, Ireland, Jersey, Guernsey, Alderney, Sark, the Isle of Man, the Colonies in North America, the West Indies, the East Indies, Africa, and Gibraltar. Revenue and Admiralty business are, of course, excepted: but all other matters, such as Crown grants, Army commissions, Church preferments in His Majesty's Gift, Approbation of Lords Lieutenants' appointments in the Militia, and business relative to criminals, pass through this office and are laid by the Secretary of State before His Majesty for His Royal Signature or approbation.'[1]

It has to be remembered that although there were no police in 1782 there were police duties. Public order had to be maintained—not a particularly easy matter when there were no police. That was why Lords Lieutenant had to be supplied with instructions; magistrates to be stirred into activity; and when things became serious, troops moved. It was the Secretary of State, not the Secretary *at* War, who directed the movement of troops. As Anson puts it: 'The Secretary of State was ultimately the exponent of the King's Pleasure in matters relating to the government and disposition of troops.' His functions included many duties that were not associated with home affairs. Some he lost quite soon. In 1794 under the stress of the French War a new Secretary of State, the Secretary of State for War, was created and took over the Home Secretary's powers over the army, except that of moving troops to maintain public order. In 1801 the new Secretary of State took over responsibility for Colonial business as well.

3. LATER CHANGES: DUTIES TRANSFERRED FROM OR ADDED TO THE HOME SECRETARY

Since 1801 the Home Secretary has been responsible for all domestic affairs which are not the direct responsibility of some other Minister of the Crown. The history of the Home Office during the past 150 years consists first, of the *extension* of its jurisdiction to new subjects by a long series of Acts of Parliament, and secondly of the *removal* from its jurisdiction of certain subjects which have grown to such importance that new Departments had to be created to deal with them or were more appropriate to deal with them. In some cases the child has become larger than the parent. It is because for many years after 1801 there was no other Minister with

[1] Appendix to the First Report of the Commissioners to inquire into Fees in Public Offices appointed by Act 25 Geo. 3. No. 2.

any considerable interest in domestic matters that the Home Secretary acquired a miscellany of statutory functions whose only unifying principle was their relation to the order, safety and well-being of the King's subjects. Criminal law reform, prison and penal reform, factories and workshops, mines and quarries, reformatories and industrial schools (now approved schools), prevention of cruelty to children, employment of children, explosives, aliens, cinematographs, probation, shop hours, intoxicating liquor, dangerous drugs, civil defence—these are but a few of the subjects in connection with which Parliament has imposed new duties or conferred new powers on the Secretary of State. His functions were further enlarged in October, 1951, when he was appointed Minister of Welsh Affairs.[1] Some of these duties the Home Secretary has in the past 80 years surrendered to other Ministers, such as Scottish criminal business to the Secretary of State for Scotland, mines and quarries to the Minister of Fuel and Power, infant life protection to the Minister of Health, advertisement regulation to the Minister of Housing and Local Government, factories and workshops to the Minister of Labour and National Service, freshwater fisheries to the Minister of Agriculture and Fisheries, and workmen's compensation to the Minister of Pensions and National Insurance.

These transfers of work to other Departments of State have not reduced, permanently or materially, the work of the Home Office. Although the Home Office from time to time surrenders to other Departments some of its functions it remains, like the widow's cruse, always full; and today it is still the Home Secretary's duty as it was centuries ago to advise the Sovereign on the exercise of many of her Prerogative powers, to be the channel of communication between the Sovereign and her subjects, to maintain the Queen's Peace, and to discharge the Crown's ultimate responsibility for the internal safety of the realm.

[1] In this capacity the Home Secretary represents Welsh opinion to his Ministerial colleagues, although he has no executive responsibility in matters which are their concern.

PART TWO

The Queen's Peace

CHAPTER III

Maintaining the Queen's Peace

What is the Queen's Peace? The rôle of the Home Secretary — Order and liberty — Emergencies.

*

1. WHAT IS THE QUEEN'S PEACE?

DESCRIBING the Gordon Riots of 1778, the Annual Register for that year records: 'For six days successively the Cities of London and Westminster were delivered into the hands of an armed and nameless mob to be plundered and burned at its discretion.' 'These tumults,' the Register continues, 'threatened the very existence of the Metropolis.'

It is easier to describe what is not the Queen's Peace than what is. Stephen put it tersely:[1] 'The King's Peace is the legal name for the normal state of society.' It is more than the mere prevention of crime and disorder and is, rather, the maintenance of conditions under which the normal functions of civilized government can be carried on, where obedience to the law is adequately secured, and the people are free to pursue their lawful ends without threat of interference.

The Home Secretary is the Minister on whom rests the primary responsibility for ensuring that the Queen's Peace—the normal state of society—is maintained.

2. THE RÔLE OF THE HOME SECRETARY

Historically the Crown has always been responsible for maintaining the Sovereign's Peace. Maitland, writing of the Middle Ages, said: 'It is for the King to keep the peace, the peace is *His* peace.' In medieval times the strengthening of the Central Government led to the extension of the King's Peace to include the 'peace' of other authorities; in the 17th and 18th centuries the restriction of the personal power of the Crown left to other authorities much of the preservation of the King's Peace; and later the extension of the power of the Crown acting in accordance with the wishes of Parlia-

[1] Stephen: *History of the Criminal Law*, I, 185.

ment—the Commons being elected on an increasingly democratic franchise—put an end to the abuses and inefficiencies of various organs of government, local and central, in order to meet the needs of a new age. One result of this progress was the creation of the modern police system, with which the Home Secretary is intimately concerned.

The primary responsibility for preserving the peace rested originally on the individual. He still has a duty to help the police and the power to arrest a felon caught red-handed. As Lord Haldane put it:

> 'Every citizen is bound to come to the assistance of the civil authority when the civil authority requires his assistance to enforce law and order.'

Quite early it became the custom for the common duty to be discharged by an elected constable who had at common law certain powers not possessed by the private citizen. In the 14th century the King, in the interests of a more effective organisation, appointed justices of the peace. Their primary function was to be responsible for the maintenance of the peace in each county, and until the introduction of the regular police force in the 19th century it was the justices, the parish constables or the watchmen appointed under Local Improvements Acts, who were responsible for the maintenance of order. But the responsibility for dealing with threats to the peace which were beyond the capacity of the justices devolved on the King's Secretary. In the 16th century he was considered especially responsible for the peace of the Kingdom and the safety of the Sovereign. The Tudor Secretaries devoted much of their energies to the detection and suppression of what the Book of Common Prayer, with a particularity born of experience, calls 'sedition, privy conspiracy and rebellion.' For the next two centuries it was with political threats to the King's Peace that the Secretary was primarily concerned. Civil disorders he left for the most part to the magistrates, merely taking the precaution, if dangerous assemblies were expected, of seeing that troops were available in case of need. He has always had the right to call in troops within his jurisdiction for that purpose.

The arrangements for the prevention of crime which devolved upon the parish constable in the country and on the watchman in the cities and boroughs were, as the experience of the Gordon Riots showed, woefully inadequate; and in the fifty years between 1770 and 1829 no fewer than seventeen Parliamentary Committees investigated the problem of maintaining law and order. Even in 1822 a committee appointed by Sir Robert Peel reported:

'It is difficult to reconcile an effective system of police with that perfect freedom of action and exemption from interference, which are the great privileges and blessings of society in this country; and your committee think that the forfeiture or curtailment of such advantages would be too great a sacrifice for improvements in police or facilities in detection of crime, however desirable in themselves if abstractedly considered.'

Despite public opinion against any form of police force it was because the Home Secretary of the period felt that something better was required than the inefficiency of local magistrates and the incompetence of parish constables and watchmen, supplemented when the situation had got out of hand by the calling in of troops, that the modern police service was born in 1829, when the Metropolitan police force was created by the Metropolitan Police Act of that year. The later development of the police service, and its present organization, are described more fully in the next chapter. The point which should be emphasized in this context is that, with the exception of the Metropolitan police force, every police force is under local control, and that there is no danger of the police being used as the servants of the central authority. The principal agents for preserving the Queen's Peace today are the police, and successive Home Secretaries have played a large part in the developments and improvements which have brought the service to its present high state of efficiency. It is the Home Secretary's duty to see that the local police authority maintains a force capable of preserving law and order; but he has no authority to give directions to police officers as to how they should exercise their powers to enforce the law.

3. ORDER AND LIBERTY

It is not enough that the means of maintaining law and order are adequate and effective; there must be both obedience to the law and respect for the law.

In this country, notwithstanding the post-war increases in various types of crime, it is still true to say that the community as a whole is law-abiding. The reasons for this are complex, but include the following.

In the first instance this country is fortunate in having a homogeneous population, with a tradition of order and high standards of public conduct which for over a long period have not been disturbed by invasion, foreign conquest or civil war.

Then all men are equal before the law, and the courts administer justice without fear or favour. In 1948 the Criminal Justice Act wrote a further chapter of English history by abolishing the privilege of the peers to be tried for their felonies by their own Order in Parliament or by the Court of the Lord High Steward, and in recent years Parliament has concerned itself with making increased provision for the assistance of those who appear before the courts so as to make the processes of law the same for all, regardless of their financial status. It is also important that the police officers who are the agents of the law are not vested with any autocratic powers but are themselves answerable to the courts for the way in which they exercise their powers and carry out their duties.

Also important is the fact that the individual citizen has a right to petition the Crown for the mitigation of a grievance; and that after the criminal courts have done with the case it is still possible, where the circumstances warrant it, for the harshness of a punishment to be mitigated by the exercise of the Royal Prerogative of Mercy. Long ago Absalom was able to start an insurrection by standing beside the gate and calling to any man who had a controversy: 'See, thy matters are good and right; but there is no man deputed of The King to hear thee.'[1] In this country, whatever the grievance, there is someone 'deputed of The King' to hear the petitioner, and in many instances it is the Home Secretary who is the appropriate Minister to consider such complaints.

In this country it has long been fundamental that the law should allow wide liberty to be enjoyed by people of all creeds and opinions, unimpeded either by official interference or by those who disagree with them, but it is a consequence of that wide liberty that the authorities responsible for law and order have constantly to strike a balance between the freedom of the few to propagate opinions which do not themselves constitute an incitement to break the law or are otherwise unlawful, and the freedom of the many to express their disapproval of, or objection to, those same opinions. Order without liberty we think intolerable; but liberty without order is impossible. Legitimate agitation must not be allowed to degenerate into violence; but if the law has to be strengthened it must be strengthened no more than circumstances require. To give one illustration: when in the 1930's the development of the Fascist movement menaced the King's Peace, it was the Home Secretary's duty to consider what needed to be done to meet the threat, and in pursuance of this duty he introduced the legislation which became the Public Order Act, 1936. Among other provisions that Act pre-

[1] II Samuel, chapter 15, verse 3.

vented the creation of private armies for political purposes, and by giving the police special powers to control processions, made it possible to curb those activities that were most likely to cause disturbance, without depriving anyone of the right to express his opinion in public.

An essential feature in the discharge by the Home Secretary of his duties for the preservation of law and order is close and continuous co-operation between the Home Office and the police. The police have the primary responsibility for preserving order, and in this respect they have the advantage of a certain singleness of purpose. The Home Secretary has a more complex function, since he must seek to ensure that the order which is preserved is that which best ministers to liberty. There is a point to which, for the sake of order, he must support the curtailment of absolute freedom, but beyond which, for the sake of liberty, he may be ill-advised to go. Where that point lies is a matter for his judgment.

4. EMERGENCIES

The Home Secretary has certain powers for dealing with serious threats to the Queen's Peace.

The Emergency Powers Act, 1920, which was enacted to assist the authorities in dealing with serious threats to the life of the community by large-scale action such as strikes in essential industries and services, does not in itself confer any power on the Home Secretary, but regulations which have been made by Order in Council on the occasions when the Act has been invoked have supplemented his other powers. He has, for instance, been given power to give general or special instructions for the employment of members of police forces outside their usual areas, to prohibit specific meetings or processions, and to prohibit wholly or partially dealing in firearms or explosives, or their carriage or use.

The use of the military in aid of the civil power where normal measures are insufficient to cope with a threat to the Queen's Peace has happily become less frequent with the development of a more efficient police organization. The use of the military in such circumstances is a matter which concerns the Home Secretary closely. It is sometimes supposed that magistrates have a legal right to call for the aid of soldiers from any military station, but this is not so. A magistrate may call on soldiers within his jurisdiction, as on other citizens, to aid in suppressing disorder, but soldiers not within his area of jurisdiction, or as an organized body with lethal weapons, can be called upon only by permission of the Crown. Existing arrangements under which, in response to a call from a magistrate, a body of soldiers may be sent from the nearest military station depend on orders from the Government. These are now embodied in the Queen's Regulations for the Army, and so avoid the need for permission being sought from higher authority on every occasion, as had formerly to be done. Movement of troops from a distance requires the sanction of the War Office, which would not be given without consultation with the Home Secretary.

In time of war, in the interest of the security of the State, it may be necessary to restrict the normal liberties of the subject, because evilly disposed persons might endanger the safety of the realm at a time of acute national danger. When in such crises restrictions on liberty are required, it has fallen to the Home Secretary in two wars to discharge the difficult task of administering those regulations in such a way as to place the minimum of restraint on liberty while taking precautions necessary for the safety of the realm and the preservation, in the domestic community, of the Queen's Peace.

There are also emergencies which are not man-made. When the sea flooded the East coast on the night of 31st January, 1953, with heavy loss of life and damage to property, the Home Secretary was the Minister responsible for co-ordinating the efforts of all concerned to deal with this emergency; and, on the spot, the police did invaluable work in the immediate crisis and in helping the more specialized agencies to do what they could to make good the loss.

CHAPTER IV

Police Administration

Introductory — Organization of the police — Statutory functions of the Home Secretary — Non-statutory functions of the Home Secretary — Some current problems — The Metropolitan police.

*

1. INTRODUCTORY

FIRST in importance in maintaining the Queen's Peace are Her Majesty's own law-abiding subjects. Second are the professional policemen and policewomen who compose the organized and trained police forces which have now existed in much their present form for a century.

The duties of the police in the modern community are considerably wider than their traditional duty to prevent and detect crime, and include a number of miscellaneous functions arising from their general responsibility for the protection of life and property and the preservation of public tranquillity. Any attempt to define strictly the limits of police duties would be controversial, but there can be no doubt that in almost any emergency it is the police to whom the ordinary citizen looks, in the first instance at any rate, for assistance.

The policeman is given limited protection by the law to enable him to carry out his duties, but he is also subject to certain restrictions on his activities so as to make sure that he is free of any suspicion of partiality or bias. Thus, it is an offence to wear a police uniform without permission, and the law provides special penalties for those convicted of assaulting police officers; on the other hand a police officer is prohibited by statute from being a member of a trade union,[1] and the conditions of his appointment preclude him from being concerned with the carrying on of any business.

But, notwithstanding this special protection conferred on police officers, and these special restrictions imposed upon them, they are not a class set apart from the rest of the community. The police

[1] The Police Act, 1919, which made this prohibition also provided for the setting up of the Police Federation as the representative body for constables, sergeants and inspectors.

officer, who is the descendant of the old township constable, is no more than a citizen acting on behalf of his fellow citizens, although he is armed with certain special powers, notably powers of arrest. Policemen in this country do not carry arms (save in the most exceptional circumstances when they are sent out on dangerous missions), and their success depends in the last resort on the maintenance of good relations between police and public. The police can carry out their responsibilities for maintaining the Queen's Peace only if they preserve the regard and esteem of the community, and remember that they are the servants, and not the masters, of their fellow citizens.

The police service in this country is not a national service. It is made up of a considerable number of self-contained local police forces, in all of which (with the single exception of the Metropolitan police district) the police authority is a local body. The Home Secretary, however, with his general concern for the preservation of the Queen's Peace, has responsibilities for seeing that the local police authority maintains a force capable of preserving law and order and for ensuring that there is co-operation between the different forces and that a common standard of efficiency is maintained. The Home Secretary has always had a special relationship with the police and is dependent on them for help and information in carrying out a number of his functions—for example, in inquiries about applications for naturalization, in keeping watch over the activities of subversive organizations, in establishing the facts in cases where he has to consider the possible exercise of the Prerogative of Mercy, and in a whole variety of the day-to-day functions of the Home Office he must look for information to the police and must depend in large measure on their impartiality and accuracy.

The relationships between the central Government and the local authorities, who are thus jointly responsible for the police service of the country, will be further considered in this chapter; but it is necessary at the outset to make it clear that the powers necessary for the preservation of law and order are vested in the individual policeman, and that in enforcing the law he is subject to the orders neither of the police authority nor of the Home Secretary. As explained in chapter XII, the Home Secretary now has no responsibilities for prosecutions. The policeman of today has inherited the common law powers of his medieval predecessor, and has been judicially described as 'a Ministerial officer of the Crown.'[1] At the same time, the policeman himself is not above the law; and if he exercises more force than is both reasonable and necessary in the

[1] McCardie J. *Fisher v. Oldham Corporation* (1930).

execution of his duty, if he wrongly arrests an individual, or if he otherwise misuses his authority, the processes of law can be invoked against him.

2. ORGANIZATION OF THE POLICE

It has been explained in the previous chapter that the modern police service dates from 1829, when the Metropolitan Police Act of that year provided for the setting up of the Metropolitan police force. The Municipal Corporations Act, 1835, required borough councils to establish paid and permanent police forces, and the counties were empowered in 1839, and required in 1856, to establish similar forces. The Police Act, 1946, abolished nearly all the non-county borough forces and merged them into the counties, and it also provided machinery for the amalgamation of county and county borough forces. But it left untouched the basic principle that, except for the Metropolitan police district, the maintenance of the police force is primarily a local responsibility and the police authority is a local body. There are at present 126 police forces in England and Wales—the Metropolitan police force; 42 county police forces; 74 city and borough forces (including the separate City of London force); and 9 amalgamated police forces. They vary considerably in size. The biggest is the Metropolitan police force, with an authorized establishment of just over 20,000 men and women, and an actual strength, at the time of writing, of just over 16,000. The biggest county force (Lancashire) has an authorized establishment of over 2,800 and the biggest city force (Birmingham) one of over 2,100. The smallest county force (Cardiganshire) has an establishment of 64 and the smallest borough force (Wakefield) an establishment of 84. Throughout England and Wales there is a total establishment of about 72,000 men and 2,000 women.

In counties, the Standing Joint Committee, composed half of county councillors and half of justices, is the police authority, and in boroughs the Watch Committee, a committee of the borough council, is the police authority.[1] The powers of the Watch Committee are greater than those of the Standing Joint Committee—the Watch Committee, for example, is the appointing and disciplinary authority for the force, whereas in a county the chief constable exercises these responsibilities. Each force is fully responsible for its own district, and there is no overlapping of jurisdiction. The Metropolitan police force is in exactly the same position in this

[1] In amalgamated forces the combined police authority follows the county or the borough pattern according to which is the preponderant element in the make-up of the amalgamated force.

respect as any other force. The notion that in some way it has a sort of general jurisdiction in police matters is mistaken.

The police service then is made up of a number of separate units. As has already been indicated, however, the Home Secretary is much concerned with its general efficiency. He has a general concern for ensuring the maintenance of the Queen's Peace, and therefore an interest in seeing that the principal agents for the maintenance of the Queen's Peace are efficient; and to this end he has had conferred on him certain statutory functions with regard to the administration of the police. A brief explanation of these functions will be given in the next section, but the picture would be incomplete if there did not also follow a section giving some account of the functions he exercises in this connexion which do not derive from statute.

3. STATUTORY FUNCTIONS OF THE HOME SECRETARY

The County and Borough Police Act, 1856, provided for the payment of a grant from the Exchequer towards part of the cost of administering local police forces; and it also provided for the appointment by the Crown of Inspectors of Constabulary. The payment of the grant to any police force was to depend on the Inspector being satisfied that that force was efficiently maintained and administered. The police grant is now 50 per cent of all approved police expenditure (in the City of London, less the proceeds of a fourpenny rate) and the Police (Grant) Order, 1951, makes payment of the grant conditional upon the Home Secretary being satisfied that the area is efficiently policed, that adequate co-operation is afforded by the police force to other police forces, that the police force is efficiently maintained, equipped and administered, and that the rates of pay and allowances of the force follow the prescribed scales. If these conditions are not satisfied, the grant may be withheld in whole or in part. It is not often that the grant is withheld, or that even the threat to withhold it is made; but the existence of the power is one which police authorities are not likely to forget.

There are now four of Her Majesty's Inspectors of Constabulary, together with a woman Assistant Inspector. Each force, except the Metropolitan police force (for which the Home Secretary is himself the police authority), is inspected at least once a year, and it is on the Inspectors' reports that the Home Secretary must mainly depend in deciding whether the Exchequer grant may properly be paid.

The power of inspection and the payment of grant are not the only statutory functions of the Home Secretary in connexion with the police service. The Police Act, 1919, empowered the Home Secretary to make regulations as to the conditions of service of the members of all police forces in England and Wales; any regulations which the Home Secretary proposes to make have first to be submitted to a Police Council[1] consisting of representatives of all ranks of the police service, the local police authorities and the Home Secretary. Various codes of regulations have been made under these powers—there are two sets of regulations dealing with discipline, a set of regulations dealing with promotion, and general regulations which deal with various aspects of conditions of service, including appointment, hours of duty, annual leave, uniform, and pay and allowances. It is unnecessary here to go into any detailed exposition of these regulations, but there are two aspects which are important in this context. First, the regulations apply equally to all members of the police forces throughout England and Wales, so that, for example, all constables are paid the same in whatever force they serve.[2] Secondly, the regulations themselves put certain specific responsibilities on to the Home Secretary; for example, every appointment to the post of chief constable is subject to his approval, as is the authorized establishment of each force.

Police pensions are also dealt with by regulations which apply equally to all police forces. These regulations are made by the Home Secretary under the Police Pensions Act, 1948; before making them he is obliged to consult the Police Council, and the regulations have to be laid before Parliament and are subject to affirmative resolutions.

The Police (Appeals) Acts, 1927 and 1943, provide that a police officer in any force who is found guilty of an offence against discipline and is punished by dismissal, requirement to resign, reduction in rank or reduction in pay may appeal to the Home Secretary.

4. NON-STATUTORY FUNCTIONS OF THE HOME SECRETARY

This summary of the Home Secretary's statutory powers must be supplemented by some account of his non-statutory responsibilities and of the manner in which the Home Office plays its part as the central co-ordinating authority in administering to the efficiency of the nation's police service.

The Home Office, over the years, has come to act as a general

[1] A new Police Council for Great Britain has recently been set up, by agreement, for the negotiation of pay and other conditions of service—see page 44. The Statutory Council remains in being pending legislation.

[2] The regulations provide for sergeants and constables in London to be paid an extra allowance of £10 a year.

clearing house for the exchange of ideas and experience, and to make its contribution to fostering the well-being and sense of common purpose that invests the whole police service. Much is achieved by personal discussion, either between senior police officers and Home Office officials, or more formally at sessions of the Central Conference of Chief Constables. General guidance is given to chief constables, frequently by circular letter, on general questions of principle concerned with the administration of justice, on matters of operational interest or on new legislation affecting the duties of the police. The Inspectors of Constabulary, with their detailed knowledge of local conditions, play a valuable part in co-ordinating the work of the whole service and in making available to all the experience of individual forces. The Home Secretary often avails himself of the advice of representative chief constables when considering whether legislative proposals creating new offences are appropriate for enforcement by the police.

In operational matters, the Home Office acts as a reservoir of experience, an advice bureau and a general research agency serving the needs of the whole police service. It takes the greatest pains not to attempt to derogate from the local administrative control of the force or from the personal responsibility of its members; and to enable it to serve a useful purpose as a central co-ordinating body, it is essential that the Home Secretary and his advisers should preserve good personal relationships not only with chief constables, but also with representatives and officers of the various local authorities.

It is not fanciful to regard the following passage from John Stuart Mill as illustrating the essence of such a relationship between central authority and a locally controlled service:

'I need not dwell on the deficiencies of the central Government in detailed knowledge of local persons and things . . . In the details of management the local bodies will generally have the advantage; but in comprehension of the principles even of purely local management the superiority of the central Government, when rightly constituted, ought to be prodigious . . . The knowledge and experience of any local authority is but local knowledge and experience, confined to their own part of the country and its mode of management, whereas the central Government has the means of knowing all that is to be learned from the united experience of the whole kingdom, with the addition of easy access to that of foreign countries . . . The principal business of the central authority should be to give instruction, of the local authority to apply it. Power may be localized, but knowledge, to be most useful, must be centralized; there must be somewhere a focus at which all its scattered rays are collected, that the broken and coloured lights which exist elsewhere may find there what is necessary to complete and purify them.'[1]

The Home Office owes any effective authority it possesses in its dealings with the police themselves and with police authorities less to the ultimate sanction of the law than to its experience, patiently acquired and recorded over many years, of police problems.

The Home Office has taken a prominent part in recent years in the consideration which, by force of circumstances, has had to be given to ways of coping with problems which are outside the range of an individual police force. Criminals no longer confine their activities within the restricted range of a local community, and have at their disposal all the resources of communications and science which modern civilization provides. There are also emergencies, such as the floods on the East coast at the beginning of 1953, which put a greater strain on the local forces than they can carry with their own resources, and more pleasurable events, such as the Coronation of Her Majesty, where again the forces of the areas primarily concerned have to look for help from elsewhere. Machinery has been devised to deal with problems of these kinds whilst preserving the local character of the modern police system.

There have for a number of years been arrangements for mutual aid between the different forces, and a force which has to cope with an emergency or a special ceremonial occasion has no difficulty in borrowing men from other forces.

Since 1871 the Commissioner of Police has, by statute, maintained a central register of persons convicted of crime, and particulars in this register (the Criminal Record Office) are collected from, and made available to, police forces throughout the country. In 1903 arrangements were made under which provincial chief constables could ask the Commissioner of Police to lend them detectives from the Metropolitan police force for the purpose of investigating serious crime, and although each force now maintains its own criminal investigation department, calls are still made on this service. More recently, a specialized department of detective officers drawn from the Metropolitan and City of London police forces has been set up to assist chief constables anywhere in the country in investigations of difficult cases involving the possibility of commercial frauds.

In the last twenty years, there has been a new development in the provision of certain common services for the police which are provided in the first instance by the Home Office, half of the cost

[1] J. S. Mill: *Representative Government*, 282-4.

being met by the local police authorities. These common services are essential to the efficient working of the police in modern conditions, but too expensive to be provided by each separate force.

The first of these services was the forensic science laboratories. A Committee appointed in 1933 to inquire into the whole field of detective work found that England and Wales lagged behind some other countries in the use of scientific aids in the detection of crime. Some Chief Constables had established small forensic science laboratories as adjuncts to their criminal investigation departments, but this arrangement was uneconomic for individual forces and could not justify the permanent employment of scientists capable of dealing with every kind of material. Six laboratories have now been established by the Home Office, each serving all the forces within a particular area of the country. A similar laboratory is maintained by the Metropolitan police force, and is available to some of the other neighbouring forces. The services of the laboratories are freely available to all police forces, half of the cost of the laboratories being recovered from the local rates in proportion to the authorized establishment of the force, so that a force pays the same however much or little use it makes of the facilities provided.

Similar arrangements have been made to provide the police forces with wireless facilities. The Home Office carries out the technical work of surveying areas and siting transmitting stations, buys the equipment, and rents it to local police authorities. The equipment is maintained at nine Home Office depots which are charged as a common service in the same way as the laboratories.[1]

An important development since the war has been the setting up of district training centres for recruits. Before the war some forces provided initial training for their own recruits and sometimes helped their smaller neighbours, but the arrangements varied a good deal, and in some places little or no training was provided. After the second world war there was a large intake of new recruits; and police authorities agreed that, to cope with their training, the Home Office should undertake temporary responsibility for providing a residential thirteen-week course of basic training for all recruits to all the provincial forces. It has since been agreed that this system should be made permanent, and, at the time of writing, eight district training centres are functioning. The syllabus at these centres

[1] These wireless facilities are available to all police forces in England and Wales other than the Metropolitan, Lancashire and Birmingham police forces, which maintain their own schemes, and the City of London which is comprised in the Metropolitan police scheme.

emphasizes from the very first the essential principles on which policemanship in a democratic community must be based.

Before the war there was a Police College in the Metropolitan police force which accepted a small number of students from forces overseas. Consultation with police authorities and with chief constables themselves showed that there was generally agreed to be a need for a national institution which would give higher training to police officers destined for higher ranks, and would enable the police service to train its own leaders. The Metropolitan Police College was not therefore revived after the war; but there was set up a national Police College to serve the needs of all police forces in England and Wales. The setting up of this College is perhaps the most important development in the police service since the war. Its management is in the hands of a Board of Governors, half of whom are nominated by the Home Secretary (and include representatives of the police service as well as Home Office officials) and half representatives of police authorities. The Police College is at present in temporary premises at Ryton-on-Dunsmore, Coventry, but a permanent home has been acquired for the College at Bramshill, Hampshire, and the College will move to Bramshill when the new buildings which will be necessary can be erected. A certain number of officers from police forces in the Colonies are trained at the College.

The Home Secretary is helped in the administration of these common services by a committee representing the local police authorities, called the Common Services Committee. This committee is consulted on questions of policy, and examines the estimates in detail. Although therefore the Home Secretary must take prime responsibility for the administration of these common services, they are administered in full co-operation and partnership with the local authorities. If there should be an impression that in administering these common services the Home Office is taking an unduly large part in the direct administration of the police system, it should perhaps be borne in mind that of the total cost of over £60 m. of the police services in England and Wales, the share of the special services amounts to less than £1 m.

5. SOME CURRENT PROBLEMS

This section briefly discusses one or two problems of current concern to the police.

The Police Council, which was set up in 1919, has come to be increasingly criticised in the police service because it does not give representatives of the police service full negotiating rights. Although the Home Secretary is obliged to consult the Council, he has the last word, and there is no right to independent arbitration. This was one of the questions considered by a committee set up in 1948 under Lord Oaksey to consider the whole range of police conditions. This committee recommended that the insulation of the police service from industrial negotiations should continue, but proposed a new form of negotiating procedure which would secure to the service much the same rights as if they were given access to some such tribunal as the Industrial Court. After considerable discussion a new form of Police Council has been set up, in anticipation of legislation, to cover Scotland as well as England and Wales, consisting of an Official Side and a Staff Side. There are an independent chairman and three independent arbitrators, to whom any dispute between the two sides of the Council on certain specific subjects, such as pay, allowances and hours of duty will be referred. For the time being effect will be given to agreements of this new body by Regulations under the Police Act, 1919. The new Police Council for Great Britain held its first meeting in November, 1953.

The great expansion of road traffic has considerably affected the duties of the police, who have a vital concern in the regulation of this traffic and in road safety. When the general speed limit was first removed by the Road Traffic Act, 1930, motor patrol sections were organized in all police forces to secure a reasonable standard of road behaviour, and some financial contribution was made to these sections by the Ministry of Transport. Vehicles are increasingly being used by the police themselves; but there is general agreement in this country that the prevention and detection of crime must still depend in large measure on policemen walking their beats. The question of how far police resources can be allocated to traffic control, possibly at the cost of depleting the resources available for dealing with ordinary crime, is a difficult one; and it is particularly in this field, where police officers are likely to have to deal with respectable citizens for what are sometimes only minor infringements, that difficulties arise in securing the full co-operation of the public.

From the figures quoted earlier in the chapter it will have been seen that the Metropolitan police force is at present considerably under its authorized establishment, and there are a number of forces, particularly in the larger cities, which also find it difficult to obtain enough recruits. It is true that over the country as a whole there are now more police officers in post than there were before the war, that the average annual intake of recruits since the war has been much greater than it was before the war, and that most police forces are now up to establishment or nearly so: but in those forces where the deficiency persists the problem is serious, and the central and local authorities are conscious of the necessity for doing all that they can to secure that there are adequate numbers of police officers.

One other current problem should be mentioned—that of police building. Great efforts have been made by police authorities since the war to provide houses for the police, and in the past four years more police houses have been built than were in existence in 1939. The waiting lists are still there, but the end of this particular problem is in sight. This unfortunately is not true of the problem of providing adequate police stations in new centres of population and replacing old and unsatisfactory buildings which are still in use. Problems of capital investment and finance have so far prevented this problem from being tackled on any large scale, conscious though the authorities are of the bad effect on efficiency and morale of working in dismal and crowded buildings.

6. THE METROPOLITAN POLICE

The Home Secretary is himself the police authority responsible for the Metropolitan police force, the largest police force in the country. The Commissioner of Police of the Metropolis, the Deputy Commissioner and the Assistant Commissioners, who are in executive control of the force, and the Receiver for the Metropolitan police district, who is responsible for financial matters, are appointed by the Crown on his recommendation. The Home Secretary cannot give orders to the Commissioner or to other members of the force with regard to their duty of enforcing the law; but he has some measure of responsibility for the executive action of the Commissioner. By statute 'all such orders and regulations as the Commissioner shall from time to time deem expedient' are 'subject to the approbation of the Secretary of State,' and the Commissioner must 'execute such duties as shall be from time to time directed by him.' As Mr. Henry Matthews put it, 'it is quite plain that the intention of the legislature was to put the police force under the authority of the Secretary of State, and to hold him responsible, not for every detail of the management of the force, but in regard to the general policy of the police in the discharge of their duty.'[1]

The Metropolitan police force is no different from any other force in that (subject to the arrangements described in the next paragraph) its jurisdiction extends only within the limits of the Metropolitan police district. This applies to all branches of the force, including the Criminal Investigation Department, and when detective officers from New Scotland Yard investigate crimes outside the Metropolitan

[1] *Parliamentary Debates,* 330 (1888), 1174.

police district they do so on the invitation of the local chief constable, who retains his full responsibility for the case.

Officers of the Metropolitan police force provide personal protection for members of the Royal Family and certain Ministers of the Crown, and are responsible for looking after distinguished visitors to the country; and in consideration of these and other special functions the force has for a number of years received a special Exchequer grant of £100,000 a year and a contribution towards certain salaries in addition to the ordinary 50 per cent grant.

The Receiver for the Metropolitan police district is responsible to the Home Secretary for an expenditure amounting to some £18 million a year. He holds the police stations and other property used for police purposes in the Metropolis and is responsible for all disbursements and for raising any loans under the Metropolitan Police Acts. The estimates and appropriation accounts for the Metropolitan police are presented to Parliament and the accounts are subject to audit by the Comptroller and Auditor-General. The Receiver submits his estimates annually to the Home Secretary and appears before the Public Accounts Committee of the House of Commons to answer for his financial transactions. The ultimate division of the cost between the Exchequer and rates, subject to one minor exception, is similar to that in any other force, the police rate being levied over the whole of the area on the basis of a precept issued on the authority of the Home Secretary. The local authorities in the area have no police functions; informal arrangements have, however, been made under which a representative committee on their behalf may go into the financial position in detail with the Receiver and raise and discuss appropriate points with the Home Secretary.

The Commissioner's Office at New Scotland Yard is staffed by a mixed establishment of policemen and civilians and the Receiver's Office is staffed exclusively by civilians. These civil officers are recruited and derive their pension rights under the authority of special Acts of Parliament. They are not civil servants in the normal sense, but their conditions are similar to those of the Civil Service. There are Whitley Councils in both the Commissioner's and Receiver's Offices.

CHAPTER V

The Fire Service

Development of the fire service — The Home Office and local fire authorities — Firemen and firewomen — Training, research, and fire prevention.

*

1. DEVELOPMENT OF THE FIRE SERVICE

THE development of the nation's fire service provides an example, in some respects comparable with the development of the police service, of the way in which the Home Office has been able to exercise a unifying influence; but in this case the influence owed its origin not to statutory powers, but to the gradual building up in the Home Office of a body of experience and knowledge of fire problems. Indeed the Home Secretary had no statutory responsibility for the fire service before the passage of the Fire Brigades Act, 1938, although the Home Office had for many years been offering advice on fire problems, and unobtrusively encouraging fire brigades to co-operate to their mutual advantage.

The need for encouragement of this sort was strikingly indicated by Sir Edward Troup, who found it necessary to write, as late as 1925,

'... with [certain] exceptions the maintenance of fire brigades and fire appliances has been left to the local fire authorities alone, with the result that there is often much lack of co-ordination and that a fire brigade will sometimes even refuse assistance to extinguish a fire if it lies just outside its own boundary.'[1]

The Home Secretary, with his general responsibility for public safety, could scarcely disregard such a state of affairs. Although he enjoyed no statutory authority, a Royal Commission on Fire Brigades had recognized in 1923 that the Home Office 'deals with many important fire problems and has acquired considerable experience of such topics through its Inspectors of Factories and Explosives. It is in touch with the organization of police fire brigades and was responsible for the war-time schemes for the co-operation of fire brigades ... it is the Department concerned with problems of fire pre-

[1] Sir E. Troup: *The Home Office*, p. 194.

vention in general.'[1] The Royal Commission recommended that the Home Office should be the Central Fire Authority for certain purposes. They expressed the view that:

> 'What is required is, in essentials, a clearing house for information and experience . . . provision should be made for [county councils] to transmit to the Home Office the tentative schemes arrived at after consultation with the local fire brigade authorities and to take into consideration any suggestions that that Department may be able to offer as the result of experience of similar problems gained elsewhere.'[2]

Fifteen years were to pass before any of the recommendations of the Royal Commission were embodied in legislation; but in the meantime the Home Office, with varying co-operation from local authorities, had pursued its ends as best it could in the absence of statutory powers.

What were these ends? The fire brigades, like the police, were a local service. Their pattern had changed little for many years; their loyalties were local, and in this lay both their strength and their weakness. The times demanded greater efficiency, especially as the shadow of war deepened; and with the technical progress made in producing more effective and standardized fire-fighting appliances greater efficiency was becoming attainable—but only if neighbouring fire brigades could be persuaded to co-operate and avail themselves of modern methods. The problem was to widen loyalties without undermining them; to propose standards of efficiency without power to enforce them; and to influence without derogating from local control. Such were the ends pursued by the Home Office until the Fire Brigades Act, 1938, conferred the authority that had hitherto been absent.

The joint parent of that Act was the report, published in 1936, of a Departmental Committee.[3] The report re-affirmed many of the recommendations of the Royal Commission, noted that the fire service had 'grown up without any general co-ordinating agency' and that there was 'no central supervision nor any recognized standard of efficiency,' and asserted that there had been 'an increasing realization of the need for co-operative arrangements between neighbouring brigades.' The 1938 Act went a long way to meeting these needs. It gave the Home Secretary power to prescribe standards of efficiency

[1] *Report of the Royal Commission on Fire Brigades and Fire Prevention*, 1923, p. 212.

[2] *Ibid* p. 171.

[3] *Report of the Departmental Committee on Fire Brigade Services*, 1936. Cmd. 5224.

and to appoint inspectors to enforce them; to set up fire service boards in any area in which he was satisfied after enquiry that an efficient fire service did not exist; to appoint a Central Advisory Council; and to establish a training centre.

Much of this legislation was rendered abortive by the war; for in 1941 the thousand local fire brigades which then existed in England and Wales were merged in the National Fire Service. This provided the Home Office with its first large-scale excursion into the direct control of the lives of a great army of men and women.[1] Problems of feeding, clothing, training, quartering, and equipping some 300,000 persons were tackled; and at the same time an opportunity was at last presented of standardizing the equipment, raising the efficiency, and broadening the loyalties of the whole service.

The opportunity was seized. After the war the National Fire Service was disbanded, but the lessons so hardly won were taken to heart. The largely abortive Fire Brigades Act, 1938, was repealed by the Fire Services Act, 1947, which settled the post-war pattern of the service. It preserved and extended the powers of the Home Secretary, authorized an Exchequer contribution of twenty-five per cent of the cost of local fire brigades, provided machinery to secure standard conditions of service in all brigades, and by appointing counties and county boroughs (or a combination of two or more of them) to be the local fire authorities, it reduced the number of brigades from well over a thousand to 135.

2. THE HOME OFFICE AND LOCAL FIRE AUTHORITIES

Uppermost in the minds of the members of the Royal Commission of 1923 was the problem of reconciling central authority with local responsibility. Commending its lucidity of exposition and noting its relevance to their problems they quoted in their Report the passage by John Stuart Mill to which reference has already been made in a similar context.[2] But as we have seen, the Department's influence, born of experience, was later extended by legislation, further broadened by the direct experience of administering a unified fire service in war time, and finally affirmed by the Act of 1947. What has been the effect of this on local administration?

As already stated, one of the chief benefits of the National Fire Service was a quickened appreciation of the need for more unifor-

[1] The Scottish units of the National Fire Service were administered by the Scottish Home Department.

[2] Page 40.

mity, and it was the intention of the Act of 1947 to combine this with the advantages which, in time of peace, flow from a decentralized organization. This intention is fulfilled by the Home Office partly by directions in the form of statutory regulations, partly by the work of the Inspectors, and partly by guidance in the form of departmental circulars. The most important result has been the adoption by all brigades of uniform 'standards of fire cover' for areas of similar fire risk, measured in terms of the time taken for the brigade to respond to a call and the number of fire appliances to be sent. Similarly, standard specifications have been prepared covering a wide range of fire-fighting equipment; model syllabuses of training have been laid down, and regulations have been made prescribing qualifications for appointment and promotion in all brigades.

It would be a mistake to think of these activities as the imposing by the Home Office of exacting standards on unwilling local authorities. Before giving general guidance on any matter of importance, the Home Office first discusses it with the Central Fire Brigades Advisory Council, and before any statutory regulations on these matters can be made consultation with (but not necessarily the consent of) the Council is required by the Act of 1947. This Council consists of representatives of Government Departments, of local authorities, and of all ranks of the fire service under a chairman appointed by the Home Secretary. Its advice is generally unanimous, and on any matters on which it fails to agree the differing points of view are reported to the Home Secretary. The Council can also offer advice to the Home Secretary on any matter within its scope without awaiting a reference from him. There is a separate Council for Scotland and joint committees have been set up to consider the design of uniform and equipment and certain other matters.

Co-operation on these lines results in a partnership between the Home Office on the one hand and the local fire authorities on the other, similar to the relationship between the Home Office and the local police authorities in administering the police service. So far as his statutory duties permit, it is the Home Secretary's policy to interfere as little as possible with local discretion; but in one respect—the size of the brigade—he is closely concerned. The number of firemen required at any given station depends on the hours of duty, and the number of fire stations and fire appliances in any brigade depends largely on the standards of fire cover; but it is not possible (even if it were desirable) to devise standards of such arithmetical accuracy as to leave no room for discretion. Present economic conditions, in any event, render perfection unattainable. Generally no difficulty arises in settling establishments, but a few authorities are disposed to be either niggardly or extravagant, and in these cases the Home Office has to intervene.[1]

Seventy-five per cent of the cost of the fire brigades falls on the local rates, and their day-to-day management is vested in the local fire authorities. It is a condition of the twenty-five per cent contribution from the Exchequer that the Home Secretary shall be satisfied that a fire brigade is efficiently run. The main instrument through which the Home Office discharges this supervisory responsibility is the Inspectorate, a body of experienced officers appointed by the Crown on the recommendation of the Home Secretary.[2] Any serious defects are the subject of formal reports and are followed up by the appropriate administrative division of the Home Office, but minor matters are dealt with less formally by the Inspectors on the spot. Their object is not so much to criticize shortcomings as to make generally available the lessons of practical experience throughout the country, and relations between them and the local fire authorities are uniformly cordial.

Fundamentally the task of the Home Office is to ensure the adoption of a sufficient degree of administrative, technical and operational uniformity of practice among all brigades.

3. FIREMEN AND FIREWOMEN

To-day the firemen and firewomen, though properly proud of their own brigades, are conscious of a wider loyalty to a service which covers the whole country. In most towns they serve as whole-time local authority employees at fixed weekly or annual rates of pay, but the country areas are served by what are known as 'retained' firemen, who comprise all kinds and conditions of men, turn out when required, and are paid by fees.

Before the second world war the recommendations of the Middlebrook Committee (appointed by the Home Secretary in 1919) that firemen should, as long as their hours of duty were substantially

[1] An additional reason for bringing in the Home Office as arbiter in the case of counties is to protect the rights of the district councils to be consulted on the proposals of the county council and to make representations to the Home Office. Under the earlier Act of 1938 the district councils had been independent fire authorities and when, for the purpose of enlarging the units of organization, Parliament in 1947 substituted the county council for the district councils it not only gave them the right just mentioned, but also provided for their individual or collective representation on the county councils' Fire Brigade Committee and imposed on the Home Secretary the duty of seeing that satisfactory schemes for this purpose were made in every county.

[2] Assistant Inspectors are appointed by the Home Secretary himself.

longer than police hours, have the same rates of pay as the police, and like the police, have free quarters or rent allowances, had been adopted by most of the larger brigades. The Committee's recommendation that the rate of pay should be standard throughout the country had not however been implemented, and a substantial minority of professional firemen were paid less favourably than the police.

During the last war the professional firemen formed a small nucleus of the very much expanded Fire Service. The rates of pay in the Auxiliary Fire Service were settled by the Government (upon whom the cost fell in full), the basic rate being the same as that in the Civil Defence General Services and corresponding approximately to the rate of a married soldier with one child. This basic rate—later increased on account of the rising cost of living—became the basic rate in the National Fire Service, with appropriate rates for the ranks above fireman. Negotiations after the war with the representative organizations of the members of the National Fire Service resulted, in December, 1946, in an arbitration award by the Industrial Court giving all firemen the current police scale of pay, and similar rent allowances. By a later award of the Industrial Court in January, 1950, this link with police pay and allowances was severed. The former emoluments of free quarters or rent allowances in lieu, were abolished, and a consolidated scale of pay, not related to that of the police, was substituted.

Other negotiations with the staff organizations resulted in an agreement that the 60 hour week should, as soon as practicable, replace the prevailing system of 24 hours on, and 24 hours off, duty.

One result of the National Fire Service had therefore been that in these and other respects the members of the fire service enjoyed uniform conditions of service throughout the country. One of the objects of the Act of 1947 (in line with the general policy of uniformity) was to ensure the continuance of a reasonable degree of uniformity of conditions of service in the different fire brigades. It was the intention of the Act that so far as possible those conditions should be settled by negotiation in the same way as conditions of employment in industrial occupations, but the Home Secretary's responsibilities to Parliament were specially safeguarded. Section 17 of the Act gives him the power to make regulations prescribing pay and other conditions, but also requires him before exercising that power to take into consideration any recommendations made as a result of negotiations between the fire authorities, as employers, and the employees. A National Joint Council was accordingly set up comprising on the Employers' Side representatives of the London County Council and the local authority associations and, on the Employees' Side, representatives of the organizations for all ranks below Chief Officer.[1] The Council is a negotiating body, but there is provision (as in corresponding industrial councils) for arbitration in the event of disagreement. On rare occasions the Home Secretary has exercised his right of referring back the Council's proposals, but in general its recommendations are embodied in statutory regulations made by him without question. The Home Secretary can also initiate proposals but must first submit them to the Council for consideration. In addition to the formal correspondence arising from these proceedings, the Home Office maintains close informal relations with both the Employers' and the Employees' Secretaries of the National Joint Council. The successful operation of this machinery, which seeks to combine industrial practice with the needs of a disciplined service, calls for the exercise of mutual restraint and discretion. If the machinery were to break down the Home Secretary would be faced with a new problem. He would no doubt use his good offices with the Minister of Labour and National Service to restore the normal machinery and he would certainly consult representatives of the interests concerned; but in the last resort the powers conferred by the Act of 1947 are wide enough to enable the Home Secretary himself to prescribe conditions of service.[2]

Another respect in which the Act of 1947 ensures uniform conditions of service is that the Home Secretary is empowered (subject to the approval of the Treasury) to make an order governing the award of pensions; an order of general application was made in 1948, and amendments are made from time to time after consultation (as the Act requires) with the Central Fire Brigades Advisory Council.[3]

4. TRAINING, RESEARCH AND FIRE PREVENTION

The need for 'a clearing house for information and experience' to which the Royal Commission of 1923 drew attention has now been

[1] There is a separate National Joint Council for Chief Officers.

[2] Since 1952, the constitution of the National Joint Council was enlarged to enable it to deal with conditions of service in Scottish Fire Brigades on which it reports to the Secretary of State for Scotland. At the time of going to press the Home Secretary had under consideration representations addressed to him by the National Joint Council that the system under which their recommendations are given effect by regulations should be abolished.

[3] It will be recalled that the Regulations governing the award of police pensions must similarly be laid before the Police Council before they are made (page 39).

met, and the Home Office serves as a nucleus for training, research, study and guidance.

The Home Secretary has authority under the Act of 1947 to establish a central training institution and one or more local training centres. The latter have not been found necessary, as efficient arrangements for training recruits are made by the larger brigades for the smaller brigades as well as for themselves. But the Fire Service College which was set up by the Home Office for the National Fire Service has been continued, under the general direction of a Board, to serve the needs of Scotland as well as England. Half the Board is appointed by the Home Secretary and the Secretary of State for Scotland and half by the local authority associations of England and Scotland; the former half includes representatives of all ranks of the fire service. Half the cost of the College is borne by the local authorities and is shared between them in proportion to the size of their brigades. At this College there are courses of general instruction for senior and junior officers (both whole-time and retained) and courses in fire prevention for specialist officers.

Reports of all fires, in a standard form, are sent to the Home Office, partly to serve as the raw material for the research and statistics of the Joint Fire Research Organization for which the Department of Scientific and Industrial Research and the Fire Offices Committee[1] are jointly responsible, and partly to ensure that the Home Office is informed of all fires of special interest so that it can decide whether any inquiry into the circumstances of any particular fire, or the steps taken to deal with it, is necessary. The reporting system also makes it possible for the Home Office to get a clear picture of the causes, the incidence, and the consequences of fires over the country as a whole. This is of great value in assessing the need for legislative changes to cover new fire hazards and in drawing up codes of fire precautions for individual risks.

Much of the information obtained from this central study of fire problems is circulated to fire brigades to help them to carry out their obligation under the Act of 1947 to advise industry and the general public on how to prevent outbreaks of fire. In this way the experience of each brigade is made available to all.

For prevention, particularly here, is infinitely better than cure; and fire brigades are now giving increasing attention to measures for preventing fire. To this end the Home Secretary set up in 1946 an Inter-Departmental Committee 'to review, collate and correlate informa-

[1] The Home Office also makes material available to the Fire Protection Association, an organization which was set up by the Fire Offices Committee to disseminate advice on fire protection and allied subjects.

tion on fire prevention matters within the scope of various Departments . . . and generally to develop consistent action as between Departments, and effective contact with other agencies operating in the fire prevention field.' A parallel will be noted between the Home Secretary's initiative in setting up this committee and (in the following year) the Inter-Departmental Committee on Accidents in the Home[1]: each represents one facet of the Home Secretary's far-reaching concern for the safety of Her Majesty's subjects.

[1] Page 93.

CHAPTER VI

Civil Defence

Development of the Civil Defence Department — The purpose of civil defence — Civil defence planning — Duties of the Civil Defence Department — The protection of the public.

*

1. THE DEVELOPMENT OF THE CIVIL DEFENCE DEPARTMENT

THE Air Raid Precautions (now Civil Defence) Department of the Home Office was created in 1935. Its first task, to send to local authorities a circular setting out the Government's policy on air raid precautions, with an invitation to members of the public to volunteer for air raid precaution duties, was oddly reminiscent of one of the first acts of the first Home Secretary one hundred and fifty years earlier: in 1782, when France and Spain joined in America's war with Britain, Lord Shelburne issued a circular directing Mayors of English towns to enrol volunteers for the national defence.[1]

Tradition and practical convenience, rather than theoretical considerations, dictated the choice of the Home Office, 'the recognized guardian of the public safety', as the seat of the new administrative agency. But at that time the Home Secretary had no statutory powers; the object was to create a channel between the central Government, the local authorities and the public on all air raid precaution matters, and to supervise the preparation of local schemes, without derogating from the responsibilities of other Ministers.

The immediate pre-war years saw the rapid expansion of this small Division of the Home Office, the appointment of Inspectors (without accepted standards to enforce or statutory powers to enforce them!), the establishment of an anti-gas school, the publication of training manuals, and, after the first Air Raid Precautions Act in 1937, the creation of a regional organization. In this early formative period the Department's work was, in its own phrase, 'of a missionary character.'

[1] T. H. O'Brien, *Civil Defence*, History of the Second World War (Civil Series). This contains a full account of the growth of the Civil Defence Department of the Home Office.

The immense range and variety of problems tackled by the Civil Defence Department before and during the second world war cannot be described here; nor is there space to outline the legislative changes that, *inter alia,* enabled the functions of the Home Secretary under the Civil Defence Act, 1939, to be performed by him as Minister of Home Security—a post created at the outbreak of war and abolished in 1945. Much of this legislation remains in force: the Air Raid Precautions Act, 1937, and the Civil Defence Acts of 1939 and 1948 constitute the present statutory background.

2. THE PURPOSE OF CIVIL DEFENCE

The admirable work during the second world war by the men and women in the various civil defence services earned for them the title of 'The Fourth Arm of Defence.' The title, and the comparison with the fighting services which it implies, is helpful towards an understanding of the civil defence duties of the Home Office, but in some respects it is misleading.

It is helpful because it throws into relief the peacetime problem of manpower and emphasizes the contrast with the fighting services. The latter have not only standing armies, fleets and air squadrons, partly maintained by conscription, but also highly organized reserves from which to expand in war. On the civil defence side there is nothing comparable. There are, it is true, the regular police, fire, and hospital services, but their strengths are only sufficient for peacetime needs, and they have no large reserves for war; civil defence operations outside their scope would in war time be carried out by the civil defence corps, which in peacetime relies on voluntary recruitment for part-time service.

The title of 'Fourth Arm of Defence' is misleading to the extent that it obscures the many administrative problems which make civil defence planning difficult and complex. However successful the fighting services may be in frustrating attacks on civilians, any modern war must inevitably entail some casualties and damage at home. The task of the civil authorities is to devise measures to mitigate these effects, to succour the injured and homeless, to put out fires, to mend broken mains and cables, to repair houses and factories, and to keep the activities of the nation going in spite of heavy attack: a wide range of tasks whose ultimate success, vital to the war effort, demands not only the courage and devotion of trained civil defence workers, but also the patient and far-sighted planning of officials. There are limits to what can be done, and the public are not unreasonable judges of where they lie; but any failure within these limits would have unpredictable effects on civilian morale.

In essence therefore the purpose of civil defence is to maintain the national morale, and the planning of the necessary measures is a continuing process in peace and in war.

3. CIVIL DEFENCE PLANNING

The task of planning measures for civil defence is an intricate one, requiring the co-ordination of a great variety of organizations, not only in central and local government, but in the essential services, such as transport, power and water, in industrial and commercial undertakings, and indeed in almost every branch of the national life. It would be foolish to seek to replace the organizations which are accustomed in peace to minister to the needs of the community by new machinery set up to do the same, or similar, work in war. Accordingly, from the earliest days of civil defence, the first principle has been to allocate war-time functions to those organizations or authorities which have analogous functions in peace. In time of war this may involve some minor adjustments, the contraction of some activities and the expansion of others, but with one exception it has not so far been found necessary to set up any completely new organization.

The exception is the Regional Commissioners' organization which was planned by the Home Office before the second world war. It was feared at that time that enemy attack might be so severe that the central Government might not be able to keep in touch with all parts of the country. A number of 'regions' were therefore created, for each of which there was to be a 'Regional Commissioner', appointed by the Crown and provided with an administrative and operational staff. If communications with the central Government had been broken, he would have exercised in his region all the powers of government. Fortunately this did not happen; but a secondary object, described in the warrants of appointment of the Regional Commissioners as 'the co-ordination of measures of civil defence', was fully achieved. Indeed the success of the organization was so complete that its re-creation in war is now taken for granted. Nucleus regional organizations are maintained in peace by the Home Office and other Departments, and they play a valuable part in the planning and development of civil defence services.

This regional organization provides at the same time for decentralization and for co-ordination. At the centre of affairs, no single Department is responsible for the whole field of civil defence; and the multiplicity of organizations involved creates a need, in peace as well as in war, for some authority to exercise a general oversight and prevent the chaos which would result from an uncontrolled scramble for manpower, materials and money. In the last resort major questions of policy can be decided only by the Cabinet, but some organization is needed at a lower level to reconcile differences, co-ordinate action, and arrange for the exchange of information. Since before the second world war the Home Office has acted as a clearing-house of information on civil defence problems; it has assimilated the lessons of the war; and its archives and records are available for consultation. Consequently the Home Office, in addition to carrying out its specific Departmental duties, acts as a kind of central authority on civil defence, providing machinery for planning and co-ordination, and thus serving the needs of all Departments concerned with civil defence problems.

For this purpose two organizations have been created within the Home Office—a Civil Defence Joint Planning Staff and a Civil Defence Joint Supply Staff. The latter is concerned with the material requirements of civil defence, such as stores and equipment, and the former with all other aspects of planning. These organizations have a common chairman, who is an Assistant Under-Secretary of State in the Home Office, with a small permanent organization in the Home Office to assist him. Other members of the two 'Staffs' are representatives of the various interested Departments, civil and military. A programme of work has been mapped out and periodical reports from Departments enable the Staffs as a whole to keep an eye on progress. By these means the Home Secretary is able to maintain responsibility for the oversight of civil defence preparations over the whole field without infringing the principle that departmental Ministers are responsible to Parliament for the work of their own Departments.

This planning organization deals also with the early stages of problems for which the Home Office has specific departmental responsibility, and carries them to the point at which they can be handed over for action to one of the administrative divisions of the Civil Defence Department, but before passing to that side of the Department reference should be made to the post of Chief Scientific Adviser, which serves the needs of all the Ministries concerned with civil defence.

Civil defence gives rise to many technical and scientific questions, not by any means confined to those connected with atomic energy. The Chief Scientific Adviser does not himself conduct original research, but he has access to various research organs and serves as a link between them and the Departments interested, either individually or through the Civil Defence Joint Planning Staff. He also has a small branch which continues the valuable work known as 'operational research.' This was started by the Research and Experiments Department of the Ministry of Home Security in the second world war. It consists in essence of the application of the methods of the trained scientist to estimates made by competent authorities of probable methods and scales of attack for the purpose of evaluating them, e.g. in terms of casualties and damage. The results do not purport to represent mathematical accuracy, but they are of immense value to all concerned with plans and preparations.

4. DUTIES OF THE CIVIL DEFENCE DEPARTMENT

The Civil Defence Department has many specific duties of its own, in addition to its general responsibility for co-ordinating and encouraging the work of others. It would be tedious to list them all. Certainly, if the amount of work is any criterion, the most important problem is that of building up an organization of men and women for dealing with the immediate consequences of air attack. Apart from the expansion of the peace-time police and fire services men and women are required in war (some to serve whole-time and others part-time) for reconnoitring and reporting incidents or areas of damage, for rescuing trapped casualties and getting them to hospital, for ministering to the first needs of the bombed out, and generally for serving as a focus for the organization by the community of measures of neighbourliness and self-help. The plans which were made before 1939 were based on the principle (already well recognized in the police and fire services) of local services organized so as to provide for mutual aid or reinforcement of one area by another. During the war small mobile forces under regional control were superimposed on the local services, but it was not found necessary (as it was with the fire service) to nationalize the civil defence services. Present indications are that the general pattern of organization will remain much the same, with heavy responsibilities resting upon the shoulders of local authorities, although the 'regional' or 'national' element will need enlargement. But whether the services are local, regional or national, they are bound to need many men and women: the task of balancing this need against the needs of other claimants is primarily one for the Ministry of Labour and National Service. Upon the Home Office lies the onus of initiating proposals for solving the many problems of organization and administration which arise in peace-time (volunteers have to be equipped and accommodated as well as recruited and trained) and the Home Office discusses these problems with representatives of local authorities and other organizations (such as the W.V.S.) whose advice and co-operation are needed.

It will be seen that the partnership between the Home Office and local authorities in administering the police and fire services is carried a stage further in the development of the civil defence corps; although the essential rôles of the central and local Government vary significantly in relation to each of the three services. The duties of local authorities derive from regulations made by the Home Secretary, or other Ministers, under Section 2 of the Civil Defence Act, 1948; these regulations are always discussed in principle, and usually in detail, with representatives of the local authorities before they are made. The complementary regulations under Section 3 of the Act as to the payment of Exchequer grant in aid of the expenditure of local authorities were made, after very full discussion, towards the end of 1953. The Act provides for the reimbursement of the remainder, and the regulations give effect to this requirement.

Another Home Office responsibility is to provide training for those concerned with civil defence. Programmes of specialized training are settled by other Departments (e.g. the Ministry of Health advises upon ambulance duties) but all the syllabuses and manuals of instruction are prepared and issued by the Home Office. The Department maintains technical training schools, one of which is in Scotland, and a Civil Defence Staff College. The schools, as their name implies, provide courses of technical instruction in such matters as the rescue of trapped casualties, anti-gas precautions, and the detection and measuring of atomic radioactivity; these courses are attended mainly by men and women selected by the local authorities as instructors for the services for which they are responsible, but they include also members of the W.V.S., representatives of industrial organizations, and a regular flow from the British Commonwealth, the United States of America, and other friendly countries. The schools were started before the second world war as anti-gas schools; they adjust their curriculum according to changing knowledge and requirements, and they have been taken as a model by other countries.

The purpose of the Staff College is different. It was designed not so much as an institution for the dissemination of orthodox doctrine as to serve as a laboratory of ideas. The students who attend it are those concerned with the higher levels of organization and administration (officers of Government Departments and the fighting services, senior local government officials, police and fire brigade officers, officials from the voluntary organizations and so on) and certain foreign students are also welcomed. Discussions at the Staff College courses have been proved to be of value not only to the students but also to the Home Office and other Departments. During 1952 the College was expanded to enable it to provide courses, intermediate in character between its present courses and those of the technical training schools, in the tactical problems arising from the operation in war of the civil defence corps and other organizations.

5. THE PROTECTION OF THE PUBLIC

How far is all this going to protect the public against the physical consequences of enemy attack?

In the second world war precautions were taken, and successfully taken, against various weapons known to be in possession of the enemy. Shelter was provided which gave reasonable and effective protection against the blast effects of near bursts of high explosive; services and equipment were provided for fire fighting on a large scale; and the country-wide distribution of respirators may have played a decisive part in preventing gases from being used against us. We should, however, not fail to note that these measures by themselves would have been powerless to protect us without the simultaneous successes of the armed forces in keeping the enemy's air attack within manageable limits and finally defeating it.

In any future war we might be called upon to face not merely developments of the weapons with which we were attacked in the last war, but the effects of nuclear weapons of a new order of power. But our survival would, as before, depend upon the joint effort of our active and civil defences, and indeed upon the powerful and combined resources of all the North Atlantic Treaty powers. To secure this co-ordination at home with the Armed Services, a Director-General of Civil Defence at the Home Office is in the closest and constant touch with the Chiefs of Staff and Commanders-in-Chief, designate, of the fighting forces allotted for Home Defence, and the Home Office also provides for national representation on the Civil Defence Conferences of N.A.T.O. The civil defence of the United Kingdom must therefore be regarded as one part of a massive defence organization primarily designed to prevent another world war by its vigilance and readiness to defend itself and retaliate if attacked.

Many of the civil defence measures of the last war would still find a place in our defences if war should come again. A warning system is still needed to cover the United Kingdom and is a joint concern of the Air Ministry and the Home Office, each with their separate responsibilities for warning the defence services and the public, but both using the same system. Any policy for the provision of shelter, and its co-ordination with an evacuation plan, is also a responsibility of the Home Office, and here the problems to be resolved need the closest co-ordination with the appropriate bodies concerned with nuclear weapons and research, for shelter is no longer concerned only with the effects of blast and fire and falling debris, but also with the far less calculable effects of possible radioactivity.

Over the whole field of civil defence these problems, many as yet unresolved anywhere in the world, are vast and complicated, but this much is certain: the possession of voluntary trained civil defence services, available, ready, and willing to back up the Armed Services in the skilled defence of the country, is as essential as ever. Above all the determination of the Government, central and local, and the people, to defend themselves against any aggressor is today, as it has always been in our history, still the greatest factor in the preservation of our freedom.

CHAPTER VII

The Children's Department

The Home Secretary's responsibility for child care — Local authorities and the Children Act — Developments since 1948: Boarding out — Local authority children's homes — Voluntary organizations and voluntary homes — Training for child care work — Children neglected in their own homes — Adoption — Emigration — Juvenile delinquency — Juvenile courts — Remand homes — Approved schools — Attendance centres — Financial arrangements.

*

1. THE HOME SECRETARY'S RESPONSIBILITY FOR CHILD CARE

THE partnership between the Home Office and local authorities in developing and administering the police, fire and civil defence services is directed ultimately to maintaining the Queen's Peace and protecting the public safety. This partnership, widened now to embrace a great number of voluntary organizations, is also found in the administration of measures designed to promote the welfare of children for whose upbringing some degree of public responsibility is accepted. But now there is a difference. The services discussed in preceding chapters are means to an end—the maintenance of the Queen's Peace and the protection of her subjects. In a sense they are impersonal: vigilant but unobtrusive. The Children's Department of the Home Office, on the other hand, concerns itself ultimately with the personal well-being of tens of thousands of boys and girls, those who, unfortunately, cannot be brought up in their own homes, and the errant who need training to give them a chance to become good citizens—an end in itself as well as a means to the end of promoting the Queen's Peace by fostering the welfare of these among her subjects.

The interest of the Home Office in the welfare of children dates from the beginning of the nineteenth century, when a series of protective measures designed to prevent the abuse of child labour in factories and mines was passed. It has also been concerned for long with the care and training of children in approved schools, in remand homes, and in some of the voluntary homes; and with children committed by a court to the care of a local authority. A great expansion of the work occurred in 1947 when the Government accepted the recommendation of the Curtis Care of Children Committee[1] that one Department should have central responsibility in England and Wales for the care of children deprived of normal home life, and decided that this Department should be the Home Office. The present-day responsibility of the Children's Department of the Home Office consequently covers a wide field, extending to the care of children deprived of normal home life, the law governing the adoption of children, juvenile courts and methods of treating juvenile delinquents, and to approved schools and remand homes, and attendance centres for persons who have reached twelve but not seventeen years of age: to these subjects must be added a joint interest with the Prison Commission in the conduct of detention centres[2] and (when these are established under the Criminal Justice Act, 1948) of remand centres, for persons who have reached fourteen but not seventeen years of age.[3]

This responsibility, far-reaching as it is, does not require the Home Office to provide children's homes, approved schools or remand homes. Children who cannot be brought up in their own homes are looked after by a local authority, or by a voluntary organization. Remand homes and some approved schools are provided by local authorities, but most of the schools are managed by voluntary managers who may be religious bodies, voluntary organizations concerned nationally with the welfare of children, or interested local people. Nor, except to a minor extent, does the Home Office carry out what may be termed the operational side of the work—the extensive and detailed fieldwork incidental to any major social service. That is done by a small army of devoted workers in all parts of the country in the employ of local authorities or voluntary organizations, and by foster parents who give invaluable service by taking as members of their families children who cannot be brought up in their own homes. The responsibility of the Home Office is the wider one of co-ordinating the multifarious activities of those engaged in child care, of inspecting and advising, of setting standards, giving

[1] Cmd. 6922.

[2] Chapter XIV.

[3] The main statutes affecting the work of the Children's Department are the Children and Young Persons Act, 1933, and the amending Act of 1952, the child life protection provisions of the Public Health Act, 1936, the Children Act, 1948, the Criminal Justice Act, 1948, and the Adoption Act, 1950. The term 'child' is variously defined in different statutes; for simplicity, the word is used throughout this chapter to mean a person under the age of eighteen.

guidance, and in general acting as a clearing-house for the exchange of ideas upon child care and the problems of juvenile delinquency.

These are general terms. In practice, the main responsibilities of the Children's Department are to ensure that proper standards are maintained in children's homes, approved schools and remand homes, to allocate among them the available capital investment resources, and to promote developments in methods of child care, and in the treatment of juvenile delinquents. Statutory rules made by the Home Secretary govern the conduct of these homes and schools. General guidance is given to local authorities and voluntary organizations by circulars, visits are paid by inspectors to their establishments and reviews are carried out of the arrangements made by local authorities for the boarding out and subsequent supervision of children in their care.[1] The contacts in the field are made mainly by the Children's Department Inspectorate, which (apart from the Chief Inspector and two deputies and certain specialist inspectors, including medical inspectors, who work from the Home Office in London) is organized in six territorial groups covering England and Wales, with headquarters in London (two groups), Birmingham, Leeds, Manchester and Cardiff. The Inspectors maintain friendly contact with the local authorities and voluntary organizations and managers of approved schools, and are able to convey information of value from one area to another. The Children's Department receives important help from the Advisory Council on Child Care and the Central Training Council in Child Care. Assistance is given by the Ministry of Labour and National Service, the Ministry of Health, and the Ministry of Education in dealing with subjects of common interest. There is frequent communication on a variety of subjects with the local authority associations. The Children's Department has continuing contacts with other countries, bringing interchange of information and experience; and programmes of study and observation of the methods employed in this country are arranged for many social science students and other persons from abroad.

The size of the task can be judged from the numbers of children in care or under supervision. At the end of November, 1953, there were in England and Wales 65,309 children in the care of local authorities under the Children Act. Large numbers of children come into care for short periods because their parents are unable to look after them for the time being, commonly because of the mother's temporary incapacity; during the twelve months to the end of

[1] The Children's Department Inspectors also review the arrangements made by local authorities for the supervision of children under the child life protection provisions of the Public Health Act, 1936.

November, 1953, 39,300 children were received into care by local authorities and 38,600 went out of care. In addition, there were in care some 24,000 children for whose upbringing voluntary organizations had taken sole responsibility. In November, 1953, some 6,500 children placed privately for reward in foster homes, 8,000 placed without reward in foster homes including those placed for adoption, 2,000 in private children's homes, and children in independent schools were being visited by local authorities. At the end of 1953, there were some 8,100 children (6,800 boys and 1,300 girls) in approved schools.

2. LOCAL AUTHORITIES AND THE CHILDREN ACT, 1948

Until 1948, when far-reaching measures of new social legislation came into operation and the Poor Law was brought to an end, children in public care were maintained by local authorities under the Poor Law or by voluntary organizations. Local authorities also looked after children committed by order of a court to their care.

The Children Act, 1948, which put into effect the main recommendations of the Curtis Committee, brought about marked administrative changes, requiring among other things the appointment by every local authority (the council of a county or county borough) of a children's committee and a children's officer. These measures were recommended by the Curtis Committee to secure that, just as responsibility was placed centrally on one Department, so responsibility should rest locally with one committee, assisted by a chief officer whose sole concern should be with the work of that committee. The children's committee, aided by the children's officer, administer the local authority functions described in this chapter.

The Children Act puts a local authority under a duty to receive into care, if they consider this to be necessary in the interests of his welfare, any child in their area under the age of seventeen who has no parents or guardian, who is abandoned or lost, or whose parents or guardian are unable, for any reason, to provide for his proper upbringing. A local authority is also under a duty to receive a child committed to their care by a court under the Children and Young Persons Act, 1933. The Children Act requires the local authority to board out children in their care, except where this is not practicable or desirable for the time being. Most of the children who are not boarded out live in a local authority children's home or in a voluntary home. The Act requires use to be made of the facilities and services available to children in the care of their own parents, and empowers local authorities in certain circumstances to give financial assistance to persons over the age of eighteen who have been in care and who need help while taking further education or training for employment.

3. DEVELOPMENTS SINCE 1948: BOARDING OUT

The local authorities can fairly claim that much has been accomplished since 1948, though the restriction on capital investment has limited the material improvements which would be made in children's homes. On the other hand, the proportion of boarded out children among those in the care of local authorities rose from 35 per cent at the end of 1949 to 41 per cent (37 per cent of the boys and 49 per cent of the girls) at the end of 1953: this is an encouraging development, since boarding out in the right foster home is the form of care—short of adoption—nearest to that enjoyed by a child brought up in his own home by good parents.

Perhaps the most important single development since 1948 is the general recognition that a child who, unhappily, has to be brought up away from his own parents needs not only decent material conditions, but a home of the right kind where he can find understanding, interest and affection and the security that these bring. The aim is to ensure that each child in care is brought up in the spirit of the Children Act, which requires the local authority to exercise their powers with respect to every child 'so as to further his best interests and to afford him opportunity for the proper development of his character and abilities.' But, when all is said, the right place for a child is his own home with his own parents, if he can reasonably remain there; thus increasing emphasis is placed on the need to take all practicable steps, at a sufficiently early stage, to arrest neglect of children in their own homes and to improve the home conditions rather than to take children into public care. When a child is in care, it is a continuing duty of the local authority to restore him, whenever it is consistent with his welfare, to the care of his parents or guardian or of a suitable relative or friend.

4. LOCAL AUTHORITY CHILDREN'S HOMES

Most of the children who are not boarded out are cared for in children's homes of various types—residential nurseries, family group homes, grouped cottage homes, large institutional homes, and hostels. The number of local authority children's homes is about 1,100. The grouped cottage homes (consisting of numbers of cottages sharing the services of a sick block, chapel, recreation hall, and in a few cases a school) were built mostly towards the end of the nineteenth century and in the early part of this century by enlightened authorities of that day to replace the large barrack homes and workhouses in which the children had previously been housed. Now the aim is to make a children's home as much as possible like an ordinary home, and the preference is, therefore, for the family group home situated in a street or on a housing estate and indistinguishable from the surrounding houses, and taking up to twelve children of a wide age range and both sexes. In the charge of a good housemother, or of a suitable married couple, the husband following ordinary employment in the neighbourhood, the children enjoy the advantage of being brought up in the midst of the local community, in company with other children living in their own homes and attending the same schools. While some young children on coming into care need the expert attention which can be given best in a nursery, boarding out or, failing that, placing in a family group in a children's home is for most to be preferred to residence in a nursery. Progress is being made with the establishment of reception centres, where children coming into care stay for a time while their physical, emotional and mental condition is assessed with a view to determining the right form of care for each one of them.

Regional inspectors of the Children's Department visit the children's homes periodically, and visits are made as necessary by medical and other specialist inspectors.

There still remain large homes of institutional type whose size and construction make a homely atmosphere difficult to achieve; even where this can be done, such homes have the disadvantage of congregating in one place a block of children who cannot easily identify themselves sufficiently closely with the life of the neighbouring community. The Home Office advocates the reservation of the larger home as far as possible for children likely to be in care for short periods, and for special purposes such as reception centres and residential nurseries.

Children, particularly those in the larger homes, are greatly helped by members of voluntary agencies and others who interest themselves in their welfare and undertake a wide variety of personal services. Especially valuable are the 'Uncle' and 'Aunt' schemes organized in many parts of the country by Women's Voluntary Services and other bodies whose members invite children to their homes or take them for outings or holidays. In this way the children make valuable contacts outside the home and often gain permanent friends and sometimes foster homes.

5. VOLUNTARY ORGANIZATIONS AND VOLUNTARY HOMES

The care of children by private charity is traditional in this country; the work of religious orders in medieval times was continued and developed by philanthropists, especially in the eighteenth and nineteenth centuries. The voluntary organizations include religious bodies, national and local societies and charitable trusts, of whom many were pioneers in work for children and continue to give a lead in devising and testing new methods of child care. The Children Act recognizes their importance: much good comes from their initiative and willingness to experiment.

The diversity of types of children's homes provided by local authorities is found equally in voluntary homes, about 600 in number. The homes vary widely not only in size but also in their scope and aims. About seventy of these homes provide education on the premises, a practice which is not favoured now unless the place is similar to a boarding school from which the children go in the holidays to their homes or to foster homes. Most of the voluntary homes, however, are similar in kind to those provided by local authorities, and all are run with the same desire to care properly for the children. The children in voluntary homes (apart from those placed there by local authorities) are maintained entirely from voluntary funds. The Children Act enables the Home Secretary to make grants towards the expenses of voluntary organizations in certain circumstances for improving the premises or equipment of their homes, or for securing that the homes are better provided with qualified staff; these grants, which are intended to assist those homes which have the right perception of child care but lack funds to make necessary improvements, do not represent any substantial contribution towards the expenses of voluntary homes.

The Children Act makes it unlawful for anyone to carry on a voluntary home unless it is registered by the Home Secretary, who is empowered to remove a home from the register if he considers the conduct of it unsatisfactory, or to refuse registration of a new home, subject in either case to a right of appeal by the persons concerned to an independent tribunal established under the Children Act. So far, the need to take formal action to remove a voluntary home from the register has arisen only once.

Inspectors of the Children's Department visit voluntary homes in the same way as local authority children's homes. Regulations governing the conduct of children's homes which were made by the Home Secretary in 1951 apply to voluntary as to local authority homes.

Most of the children in the care of voluntary organizations are provided for in voluntary homes, but some organizations also board out children in foster homes.

6. TRAINING FOR CHILD CARE WORK

The Curtis Committee attached so much importance to the subject that they made an interim report urging the need to provide training for child care work. A few of the voluntary organizations were already running training courses in residential work for their own staffs. The Central Training Council in Child Care was appointed by the Home Secretary in 1947, and the first Home Office courses started towards the end of that year. Experience has shown increasingly their value.

There are two main types of course: one for persons to be employed as visiting officers in boarding-out, adoption and after-care work, and the other for housemothers and housefathers to be employed in children's homes. Successful students are awarded the Training Council's certificate in child care. The courses for visiting officers are provided by the social science departments of certain universities, and those for housemothers and housefathers by local education authorities and voluntary organizations. Students are eligible for grants to cover tuition fees, maintenance, travelling and incidental expenses. Those who have completed training successfully find employment readily, and are doing good work in the child care service. Refresher courses for staff employed in child care work, in approved schools and in remand homes are also provided. These courses are popular, providing as they do opportunity for those employed in the work to exchange ideas and experience, as well as to acquire fresh knowledge. The Home Office, in co-operation with the Ministry of Health and the Ministry of Education, is concerned also with the arrangements for training nurses for work in residential and day nurseries.

7. CHILDREN NEGLECTED IN THEIR OWN HOMES

Although removal from home, with the attendant risk of emotional injury to the child, is sometimes necessary, neglect can often be remedied by guidance and help to the parents. In a circular issued jointly by the Home Office, the Ministry of Health and the Ministry of Education in July, 1950, local authorities were asked to ensure that the most effective use was made of the local statutory and voluntary services; and it was suggested that to this end there should be regular meetings of representatives of the services concerned. Most local authorities have made arrangements on these lines. Officers of the statutory services are in touch with many of the homes, and give what help they can. A main object of the National Society for the Prevention of Cruelty to Children is to improve conditions in the homes visited by their inspectors, and so to enable the children to remain at home. Women's Voluntary Services assist by giving practical help in house management and child care to mothers who are in need of it. The Family Service Units do intensive work with problem families in certain areas.

The 'Mayflower' Salvation Army Home in Plymouth is an interesting development in the treatment of neglectful mothers. It was opened at the beginning of 1948 for the purpose of training mothers found guilty of child neglect and placed on probation on condition that they stay in this home for four months. Children under the age of five accompany their mothers. The training is on simple, practical lines, and includes instruction in the upbringing of children, in household management and in elementary citizenship. While the mother is at 'Mayflower', the probation officer does what is possible to improve the conditions at home, and supervises the mother on her return home. The results so far are encouraging.

8. ADOPTION

Adoption, where it can be arranged successfully, is generally recognized to be the best provision that can be made for a child (meaning here a person under the age of twenty-one) who has no parents or who cannot be brought up by his parents and whose circumstances make adoption possible.

The Home Office, when consulted, advises courts, local authorities, adoption societies and others on questions of procedure; enquires into complaints of irregular procedure; inspects the work of local authorities in placing for adoption children in their care and in regulating voluntary associations registered with them as adoption societies; and studies the general operation of the law with a view to suggesting amendments which experience may show to be advisable.

Legal adoption was first introduced into England and Wales in 1926; and the Adoption Act, 1950, is a consolidation of earlier legislation. The importance of ensuring as far as possible that adoption will be for the child's good is reflected in the requirement on a court in every case to appoint a *guardian ad litem*, that is, a person (who may be a local authority) charged with the duty of safeguarding the interests of the child throughout the proceedings; a person who undertakes to act as *guardian ad litem* is under obligation to enquire into all relevant circumstances and to report to the court. An additional safeguard for the child is the provision that an adoption order may not be made until the child has been in the care of the prospective adopters, and under the supervision of the local authority, for at least three months.

The making of an adoption order in England and Wales transfers to the adopter all rights, duties and liabilities of a parent in relation to the custody, maintenance and education of the child. An adopted child is treated for almost all purposes, including succession to property, as a child born to the adopter in lawful wedlock and not as the child of any other person. Marriage with an adopter is prohibited, but not with a relative of the adopter or with another person adopted by the same adopter. A copy of every adoption order is sent by the court to the Registrar General who enters it in an Adopted Children Register; copies of entries in this register, which does not record the natural parentage of the child, have the force of birth certificates. Adopted persons, like any other person, can obtain a 'short birth certificate' which does not disclose the fact of adoption. 12,874 adoption orders were made in England and Wales in 1952, comprising 65 in the High Court, 4,026 in the County Courts, and 8,783 in Juvenile Courts.

Early in 1953 the Home Secretary and the Secretary of State for Scotland appointed a Departmental Committee to consider the law of adoption, and to report whether any changes were desirable in the interests of the welfare of the children.

9. EMIGRATION

Emigration may be in the best interests of some children who are being brought up in public care, for example, a child with no parents or unsatisfactory parents who is healthy and self-reliant and likely to be able to adapt himself to a new life abroad.

A local authority, with the consent of the Home Secretary, may arrange for the emigration of a child in their care. Not many such children emigrate: the number in the twelve months to the end of November, 1953, was 41. The emigration of children apart from their parents is arranged, in the main, by voluntary organizations.

10. JUVENILE DELINQUENCY[1]

The importance of remedying conditions resulting in neglect of children in their own homes has already been mentioned. Those

[1] Juvenile delinquency is dealt with in this chapter because the subject is mainly the concern of the Children's Department. It has been thought convenient, however, to describe here only the services for which the Children's Department is solely responsible, and to deal in Chapter XIV with detention centres for persons aged 14-17 years, as well as for those aged 17-21, as all the centres are provided by the Prison Commission. Similarly, remand *centres,* which may take in certain circumstances persons aged 14-17 years, are also dealt with in Chapter XIV.

dealing with maladjusted children are familiar with the harm that is done to them by family conflicts, neglect, and lack of affection and of parental interest; others whose work brings them into contact with juvenile offenders are aware that unsatisfactory home life is at the root of a great deal of delinquency. Among other main causes are insufficiently early diagnosis and treatment of children of sub-normal intelligence or unstable character, and lack of training and opportunity for the use of leisure. Some children find their way into the juvenile courts through irresponsibility, but most get there because they have not learned to control themselves or to respect the rights and property of others. Fortunately, most of them grow out of their anti-social attitude; for them, the need is to provide for a time a steadying and correcting influence.

Statistics of juvenile delinquency are to be found in the Home Office Criminal Statistics for England and Wales, published annually by H.M. Stationery Office. The following figures are given to indicate the numerical extent of the problem. In the year 1952, 24,189 boys under the age of fourteen and 17,093 who had reached fourteen but not seventeen years of age were found guilty of indictable offences by all courts in England and Wales; for girls, the corresponding figures were 2,023 and 1,773. The numbers in 1952 found guilty of indictable offences per 100,000 of population in the same age group were 1,336 boys under the age of fourteen and 1,981 aged fourteen but not seventeen years; for girls, the corresponding figures were 117 and 210: on this index, the peak age of offenders among boys was fourteen years and among girls thirteen.

The Home Secretary deals with representations and complaints received on behalf of children who have been before a juvenile court. This duty arises from his constitutional function to advise the Crown on the exercise of the Prerogative of Mercy (Chapter XI), and also because he is entrusted with various statutory powers, including the power to discharge a child from the care of the managers of an approved school.

Trends of juvenile delinquency and results of treatment are studied. Local problems of juvenile delinquency are being considered in many areas in response to a memorandum sent in 1949 to local authorities by the Home Secretary and the Minister of Education. The memorandum discussed measures for the prevention of delinquency, and suggested that representatives of the local services and agencies concerned should meet at regular intervals to act as a focus of practical experience and local knowledge, and to encourage the local services to take executive action where necessary to improve the facilities for young people in the area.

The value of scientific inquiry into causes of delinquency and the results of treatment is recognized, but it is not possible at present to arrange for any extensive investigation. Several limited projects are being undertaken by certain universities in co-operation with the Home Office.

11. JUVENILE COURTS

Juvenile courts were established originally by the Children Act, 1908, and are now constituted under the Children and Young Persons Act, 1933. They are courts of summary jurisdiction formed for the purpose of dealing with any charge, except homicide, against children (boys and girls under the age of fourteen) and young persons (boys and girls who have reached fourteen but not seventeen years of age). They are not solely criminal courts: they hear also applications in respect of children and young persons in need of care or protection or beyond control, truancy cases, and most applications for adoption orders.

Outside the Metropolitan Magistrates' Courts area, the justices in every petty sessional division elect from among their number justices specially qualified to deal with juveniles. Under rules made in 1950, a justice may not be a member of a juvenile court panel after reaching the age of sixty-five. In the Metropolitan Magistrates' Courts area, the Home Secretary himself appoints justices to the juvenile court panel.

Education and training, not punishment, are the governing considerations in the treatment of the juvenile offender, numbers of whom are educationally retarded or sub-normal. Every court in dealing with a person under the age of seventeen is required by statute to have regard to his welfare and, in a proper case, to take steps to remove him from undesirable surroundings, and to secure that provision is made for his education and training. A court of summary jurisdiction may not send a person under the age of seventeen to prison.

12. REMAND HOMES

Remand homes are the successors of the 'places of detention' provided by police authorities under the Children Act, 1908, for juveniles remanded in custody. The Children and Young Persons Act, 1933, requires local authorities to provide remand homes for the detention of boys and girls under the age of seventeen who are remanded in custody while awaiting trial, or while enquiries are being made after a finding of guilt, or pending admission to an approved school. They are used also as 'places of safety' for, among others, children about to be brought before a court as being in need of care or protection. By section 54 of the Act, courts may also order up to one month's detention in a remand home as a punishment. About sixty remand homes are provided by local authorities, some of whom arrange also for the use of a small number of voluntary homes for remand and 'place of safety' cases.

In recent years, courts have tended increasingly to remand children in custody for examination and report by a psychiatrist or psychologist before deciding on treatment, and the Criminal Justice Act, 1948, empowers local authorities to provide observation facilities in their remand homes to enable adequate reports to be prepared. The superintendents of the homes commonly provide reports for the courts on the behaviour and character of the children while in the home. The influence exercised by the staff of the remand home on the children is of importance, particularly as for many of them it will be the first separation from their parents.

Inspectors of the Children's Department visit remand homes regularly to see that proper standards are maintained and that there is compliance with the Remand Home Rules.

13. APPROVED SCHOOLS

Approved schools are boarding establishments approved by the Home Secretary under the Children and Young Persons Act, 1933; in origin, they date from the industrial schools for destitute children and the reformatories for errant children. The courts commit to them boys and girls under the age of seventeen, whether guilty of offences or found to be in need of care or protection, to give them the residential education and character training of which they stand in need. The period of detention authorized by an approved school order is ordinarily three years. The school managers are under a duty to release children on licence as soon as they have made sufficient progress.

At the end of 1953, in England and Wales there were some 8,100 children in 130 approved schools (91 for boys and 39 for girls). 27 of these schools were administered by local authorities, and 103 by voluntary managers. The schools are graded according to the sex and age of the pupils; schools within each age group are reserved for Roman Catholics. Three 'classifying schools' for boys and two for girls, serving the greater part of England and Wales, have been established in recent years. It is intended eventually to extend the system to cover all areas. A boy or girl goes to a classifying school for a short period of observation and assessment of character, aptitudes and requirements, and is then allocated to a suitable training school. The classifying system has already proved its value, but some features call for further experiment and development, among them the classifying techniques and the possibility of some integration of the work of the classifying schools with that of the remand homes.

The boys and girls in approved schools are subject to discipline and rules, but not to physical restraint. Habits of self-reliance are encouraged, to prepare them for their return to life outside the school. Those who fail to settle or to make satisfactory progress in one school can be transferred to another.

In junior approved schools for boys, the education is similar to that given in the secondary modern schools except that the proportion of practical work is high and classes are smaller than in outside schools. Junior girls generally go out to local schools. Older boys and girls are given vocational training which is increased in extent when they reach school leaving age; backward pupils get continued help by means of special classes in basic subjects. Most children go on home leave for a few weeks each year. Religious instruction and attendance at a place of worship are features of school life. The provision of suitable education and varied occupation and recreation is essential to the training, but of greatest importance is the influence of the head and staff of a school on the boys and girls.

Every boy or girl leaving an approved school on licence is liable to recall until the legal period of detention expires; and afterwards remains under the managers' supervision for a period which varies according to age but is not less than three years, subject to termination at the age of twenty-one. During the periods on licence and under supervision, the managers must see that the boy or girl is visited, advised and befriended, and given assistance, if necessary, in maintaining himself. Boys and girls leaving the schools are found employment, and, if they have no suitable homes, are placed in lodgings or hostels. Supervision is sometimes undertaken by the school staff, but when a boy or girl is living at a distance from the school, supervision is usually exercised by a local agent, who may be a probation officer or officer of a local authority children's department, or, for boys resident in certain areas, a welfare officer attached to an approved school.

The Home Secretary has extensive statutory responsibilities towards approved schools and the children in them. He is responsible for seeing that proper standards of care, health, education, training, accommodation and equipment are maintained. Inspectors of the Children's Department visit the schools regularly and, in addition to examining the general arrangements for the welfare of the children and for the conduct of the school, have to see that there is compliance with the Approved School Rules, including such matters as the licensing of children and provision for their after-care. There are regular meetings at the Home Office of the Approved Schools Central Advisory Committee, on which school managers and heads are represented.

The Home Office has to see that the types of approved schools, as well as the amount of accommodation, match the need as far as possible. Provision of special types of schools is impracticable for all the categories of children committed, while some (for example, those found to be mentally defective or to be suffering from severe epilepsy) cannot be dealt with in approved schools, and have to be provided for elsewhere. Many children who are educationally retarded reach an approved school, and the policy has been to improve the teaching facilities for such children within the existing approved schools rather than to establish approved schools of the character of the residential special schools provided for under the Education Acts. A school for selected girls aged fifteen and over who require psychiatric treatment under residential conditions was opened in 1949.

14. ATTENDANCE CENTRES

The Criminal Justice Act, 1948, empowers the Home Secretary to establish attendance centres as a new form of treatment for persons who have reached twelve but not twenty-one years of age and who, in the opinion of the court, could be dealt with suitably by being deprived for a time of part of their leisure. A person may be ordered to attend a centre for not more than twelve hours in all, and a maximum of three hours on any day. As an experiment, centres are being provided for boys under the age of seventeen. The first centre was opened in London in July, 1950. At the end of 1953, there were twenty-two centres, and more were in prospect. All serve large centres of population, where the demand is likely to be sufficient to enable group activities to be organized. A scheme of instruction for each centre is approved by the Home Office, and usually includes physical education, some form of practical work, and instruction in such subjects as first-aid. While there is firm discipline at the centre, the aim is to educate the boys in the proper use of leisure and to develop their sense of responsibility. Attendance is on Saturdays, the younger and older boys coming at different times. With the exception of a centre at Hull, which is provided by the local authority at their remand home, the centres started so far are run for the Home Office by police officers interested in the welfare of young people and experienced in organizing youth activities.

15. FINANCIAL ARRANGEMENTS

The cost of the child care service of local authorities under the Children Act, and of approved schools and remand homes, is a charge on public funds, half being paid by the local authorities and half by the Exchequer. The parents of a child under the age of sixteen who is in care under the Children Act, or in an approved school, are liable to contribute according to their means towards the cost of the child's maintenance. The cost of maintaining children for whose upbringing a voluntary organization takes responsibility is not a charge on public funds, but is met from voluntary sources.

The financial control exercised by the Home Office over the child care expenditure of local authorities incurred under the Children Act is on broad lines, leaving wide discretion to the authorities within the limits of approved policy stated in circulars issued by the Home Office. Staff complements do not require the approval of the Home Office, and there is no detailed control of expenditure on the running of children's homes. All proposals for new building construction, and for other minor adaptations of existing premises, require the approval of the Home Office in principle; where the estimated cost of a project exceeds £5,000 detailed information is submitted for Home Office approval. The same arrangements apply to remand homes.

Local authorities determine the amount spent on any child boarded out by them with foster parents, provided that the authority's average expenditure per child in a financial year does not exceed a specified sum (at present forty shillings weekly).

The cost of maintenance of approved schools varies from school to school, but it is arranged that, in each financial year, the local authorities pay at a uniform rate (known as the flat-rate and fixed annually at about half the average maintenance cost over all the schools) for children for whose maintenance they are responsible, in whatever school the children are placed other than in a school provided by the paying authority. By means of an equalization fund, the cost of maintaining the schools over a period of years is borne equally by the local authorities and the Exchequer.

CHAPTER VIII

Public Well-being and Public Safety

Protective legislation and public services — The Explosives Department — Safety in cinemas and theatres — Public entertainment and censorship — Sunday entertainment — Liquor licensing — State management of the liquor trade — Betting and lotteries — Dangerous drugs and poisons — Obscene publications — Theatrical employers registration — General responsibilities of the Home Secretary.

*

1. PROTECTIVE LEGISLATION AND PUBLIC SERVICES

LEGISLATION in the field of public well-being dates from very early times, and many of the first statutes, such as the 16th and 17th century gaming laws and the 17th and 18th century laws on Sunday observance and places of public entertainment, are still in force. Most of the early statutes are wholly negative—they prohibit some activity which is regarded as injurious to the public well-being. The same principle is to be found in some of the later legislation, such as the Betting Act, 1853, or the Street Betting Act, 1906, which entirely prohibit cash betting elsewhere than on a racecourse. But in most of the legislation from the nineteenth century onwards, a new principle is at work—the regulation of activities which are potentially dangerous to the public well-being by a system of licensing, or some other form of control. Later still an even more positive approach is found, as for example, in the actual management of public houses by the State or the conduct of totalisator betting at horse racecourses by the Racecourse Betting Control Board, a body set up by statute for whose activities the Home Secretary has a limited responsibility; and recent times have seen, in the development of the child care service, the outstanding example of the Home Secretary's concern with the public well-being.

In the field of public safety, too, there is the same general distinction between the older restrictive legislation, coupled with licensing and inspection (as in the control of explosives and other dangerous substances), and the more recent organization of large services to meet particular dangers, such as the fire service and the civil defence service.

2. THE EXPLOSIVES DEPARTMENT

The oldest specialist branch of the Home Office concerned with public safety is the Explosives Department, which came into being with the Explosives Act of 1875. This was not the first act dealing with explosives. An Act of William III which forbade the firing of squibs and serpents in the streets was the first: more recent was the Nitro Glycerine Act of 1869 passed after an explosion on Town Moor, Newcastle upon Tyne, which killed the Sheriff, the Town Surveyor and five others who were engaged in destroying a confiscated consignment. An explosion in a barge on the Regent's Canal in October, 1874, destroyed a bridge over the canal, the barge and its crew. Subsequent inquiry showed that all safety regulations had been neglected, benzoline had been carried with gunpowder, and its vapour had probably been ignited by the cabin fire or by a bargee lighting his pipe. This explosion convinced the authorities that legislation on explosives without inspectors to enforce it was not enough—despite the statement in the report[1] of Major Majendie, who conducted the enquiry and who was afterwards the first Chief Inspector of Explosives, that 'all State interference in industrial life is absolutely contrary to the first principles of economical science.'

The Explosives Act, 1875, which authorized the appointment of Inspectors of Explosives, required the manufacturing and keeping of explosives to be licensed, and divided the tasks of licensing and of enforcing the Act between the Home Secretary and the local authorities. The Home Secretary appoints the Inspectors of Explosives, licenses explosives factories and magazines, and is responsible for the general administration of the Act and for advising the local authorities, who are responsible for registering shops in which smaller quantities of explosives are kept. The Act gives power to make Orders in Council laying down requirements for the construction of buildings, the precautions to be observed by workers and the classification, packing and conveyance of explosives. This power has been frequently used. Notice of accidents causing injury to life or limb has to be given to the Home Secretary, who is empowered to order enquiries to be held into them. The Inspectors of Explosives are also the Home Secretary's technical advisers on other matters relating to public safety, for which he has a statutory responsibility, such as the storage and transfer of petroleum spirit and other dangerous substances, and the use of hydrogen cyanide for the fumigation of ships and buildings. The inquiry into the fire at Avonmouth Docks in September, 1951, when two people were killed and 2,000,000 gallons of petrol lost, was conducted by the Chief Inspector

[1] Cmd. 977, 1874.

of Explosives, and one of the Inspectors assisted the Chief Magistrate of the Metropolis in the inquiry into the explosion at a Bristol garage in November, 1951, when 11 people lost their lives.

During the war the Inspectors took on many responsibilities in addition to their usual tasks. Thus, they carried out inspections and enquiries into accidents at Government explosives factories (which are exempt from the Explosives Acts) and acted as consultants to other Departments on such diverse questions as the securing of a quicker turn-round of tankers at the docks, and the safeguarding of large stocks of whisky, a valuable export.

These subjects do not however exhaust the duties of the Explosives Inspectors: they carry out many other tasks in connection with explosives. Some of these are highly dangerous, as when they are asked to dismantle bombs designed for criminal purposes. The gallantry of Her Majesty's Chief Inspector of Explosives in this field was recognized in 1948 by the award of the George Medal. The Inspectors are also the technical advisers of the Home Secretary and of other Ministers in connection with the transport of dangerous objects by land, sea and air, ranging from radio-active substances to compressed gases.

3. SAFETY IN CINEMAS AND THEATRES

The introduction of the motion picture with its use of a highly inflammable celluloid film brought very grave possibilities of serious threats to public safety because of the risk of fire in crowded halls. The Cinematograph Act of 1909 regulated the use of inflammable film by requiring premises where films were shown to be licensed by the local licensing authority and by empowering the Home Secretary to make regulations for the safety of the public and of the staff. During the past 10 years the film industry has developed a new type of film with an acetate base, which is claimed to be non-inflammable. But fire from the film used in the projection room is not the only danger that may arise in a crowded assembly and the need for strict safety conditions in such premises remains. Accordingly the Cinematograph Act of 1952 extended the system of control over commercial exhibitions of films to non-inflammable, as well as inflammable, films.

The Celluloid and Cinematograph Film Act, 1922, places on local authorities the duty of enforcing precautions in connection with the storage of this highly inflammable material. Changing habits and the development of new substances and materials have so reduced the uses of celluloid by private individuals as to make it unnecessary for the Home Secretary to use his power to make general regulations.

Occasionally, however, he is called on to advise local authorities on their problems under the Act.

The Home Secretary has for many years advised on safety matters the local licensing authorities under the Theatres Act, 1843, the Public Health Act, 1890, and under a number of local Acts of Parliament under which premises used for public music and dancing and like entertainment have to be licensed.

4. PUBLIC ENTERTAINMENT AND CENSORSHIP

Reference to cinemas and theatres leads naturally to the point that if public safety is to be secured and public order to be preserved it is not enough merely to endeavour to control physical sources of danger or suppress disorder: the moral health of society must be protected. The Home Secretary has no statutory responsibility for the censorship of stage plays or films or for ensuring that proper standards of decency are observed in the music halls. The Lord Chamberlain is, under the Theatres Act, 1843, responsible for the censorship of stage plays published since 1843; the local licensing authorities under the Cinematograph Acts, 1909 and 1952, for the censorship of films. The latter authorities avail themselves in discharging this responsibility of the assistance of the British Board of Film Censors, an unofficial body established by film producers, exhibitors, distributors and manufacturers of cinema instruments, but entirely independent of the industry and paid for by fees based on the footage of film examined. The licensing authorities who grant licences for places used for public music and dancing and public entertainment of the like kind are responsible for ensuring that decency is maintained in the field of variety entertainment.

Nevertheless Parliament would look to the Home Secretary to submit proposals to it if there were signs that the existing methods of control were failing in their purpose. He has, when there has been public concern on the question of nudity on the stage, conferred on that matter with the Lord Chamberlain and the local licensing authorities. He has also advised licensing authorities under the Cinematograph Act on the exercise of their powers of attaching conditions to licences to cinematograph exhibitors to prohibit the exhibition of objectionable films, or to prohibit or restrict the admission of children when films considered to be unsuitable for children were being shown.

It was increasing public concern as to the influence of the cinema on children which led to the appointment in 1947 of the Committee on Children and the Cinema, over which Professor Wheare presided, to enquire into the effects of attendance at the cinema on children under sixteen with special reference to attendance at children's cinema clubs and to consider, in the light of these effects, what steps if any it was desirable to take. In their Report[1] the Committee made a number of recommendations, some of which have been carried into effect by the Cinematograph Act, 1952, which has done much to extend and improve the means whereby control can be exercised over commercial cinematograph exhibitions in the interest of the health and welfare of the children who attend them.

5. SUNDAY ENTERTAINMENT

The Home Secretary's concern with the moral health of society in the field of public entertainment extends also to the field of Sunday entertainment. From the passing of the Sunday Observance Act, 1780, up to 1932, all forms of entertainment or amusement to which the public were admitted on payment were illegal on Sundays. Soon after the Cinematograph Act, 1909, was passed, however, cinemas in many areas began to open on Sundays, often applying the profits to charity, and in 1916 the London County Council began to grant permission for Sunday opening subject to the payment of the profits to charity. In 1930, at the instance of the promoters of certain rival entertainments, who had failed to obtain similar permission from the London County Council, a case was taken to the High Court, who held that, in view of the provisions of the 1780 Act, the Council had no powers to make any arrangement by which cinemas might be opened on Sundays to the public on payment. The Government of the day thereupon decided, in view of the change in public opinion on the question of Sunday entertainment which had clearly taken place since the early years of the century, to introduce legislation to legalize those forms of entertainment which had, in fact, been generally accepted by public opinion for many years.

It fell to the Home Secretary to take charge of this legislation which became, after not a little controversy, the Sunday Entertainments Act, 1932. Under this Act cinemas may be allowed by the appropriate licensing authorities to open on Sundays in areas where public opinion has expressed itself in favour of Sunday opening, by means of a prescribed procedure which, in urban areas, usually involves the taking of a poll of local government electors. Musical entertainments may be given on Sundays if duly licensed, and the prohibition on the Sunday opening, on payment, of museums, picture galleries, zoological or botanical gardens or aquaria, and on the holding of any lecture or debate was wholly removed. It remains

[1] Cmd. 7945.

illegal on Sundays, if the public are admitted on payment, to open theatres, music halls or dance halls, or to hold sporting events such as professional football or cricket matches or boxing or wrestling contests. In January, 1953, a Private Member's Bill which sought to repeal the Sunday Observance Acts and to extend the provisions in the Sunday Entertainments Act, 1932, to theatres and music halls was rejected by the House of Commons by a large majority.

The Home Secretary's functions under the Sunday Entertainments Act, 1932, are limited to those of its provisions which deal with the Sunday opening of cinemas; and it does not rest with him, even in that connection, to decide whether power to allow Sunday opening in any particular area shall or shall not be conferred. If a draft order is submitted to him by a borough or county district council who desire that Section 1 of the Act shall be extended to their area and such power thereby conferred, he has a duty under the Act to lay the order before Parliament if he is satisfied that the statutory requirements have been complied with. The order cannot come into operation until it is approved by resolutions passed by both Houses. His other functions under the Act are to make regulations governing the conduct of the polls which may have to be held in urban areas in connection with proposals to submit draft orders, to appoint persons to hold the local enquiries which may be needed in connection with similar proposals in respect of rural districts, and in connection with the contributions which exhibitors who open their cinemas on Sundays are required to pay to charity and the Cinematograph Fund in pursuance of Section 1(1)(b) of the Act, to prescribe the percentage (at present 5 per cent) of such contributions to be paid to the Fund.

6. LIQUOR LICENSING

Another instance of restrictive legislation designed to protect the health of society is to be found in the liquor laws, which have a very long and varied history. In their present form they are designed to restrain the abuse of intoxicants by placing those who sell them under public supervision, and by limiting the opportunities for over-indulgence. Broadly speaking, a person may not sell liquor retail without a justices' licence; the hours for selling it are limited; a licensee must obey other legal restrictions—for instance he must not permit drunkenness; his premises are open to inspection by the police, and he may lose his licence if they are not properly conducted.

The Home Secretary takes practically no part in the day-to-day administration of the law. That is the business of the justices and of the police. Between them and the Home Office there is a two-way traffic of consultation and information, but they are not answerable to the Home Secretary, nor he for them.

The Home Secretary has, however, a general responsibility for the efficacy of the law. He obtains and publishes information—statistics of drunkenness, for instance—which may throw light on the success or failure of the law. If drunkenness increases, it is his duty to seek evidence of the possible causes, and to consider whether any remedy within the reach of law and administration can be found. Again, if some defect appears in the law, it is the Home Secretary's responsibility to find a cure. The bottle party provides a recent example. This was a profitable device for meeting, without technical infringement of the law, the demand for liquor outside the hours permitted by law. It was based on the fiction that the sale of the liquor took place when the bottle was ordered on licensed premises during permitted hours, not when it was delivered and its contents consumed on unlicensed premises after permitted hours. The cure provided by the Licensing Act of 1949 was to prohibit the supply or consumption of intoxicating liquor outside permitted hours at any party organized for gain in premises habitually used for the purpose. At the same time the legitimate demand for liquor after permitted hours was provided for by enabling clubs and restaurants in the West End of London which satisfied certain requirements to supply liquor up to 2 a.m.

The difficulty must be obvious of securing a proper balance in this field between reasonable personal freedom and legitimate indulgence on the one hand, and the restrictions necessary in the public interest on the other. Essentially this is the Home Secretary's problem. The inherent difficulty is multiplied by the existence of so many irreconcilable differences of strongly held opinion in and out of Parliament. The liquor question is always alive and always controversial because there are involved in it deep moral convictions, strong prejudices and powerful interests, as well as some part of the comfort and convenience of great numbers of ordinary people. It is a subject as politically unrewarding as it is unavoidable. The Home Secretary has to see to it that sooner or later any needed adjustment is made in the law to meet changes in public opinion or in social conditions, because in the long run, if this is not done, either abuse will follow, or the law will be found so irksome that it will tend to fall into contempt.

7. STATE MANAGEMENT OF THE LIQUOR TRADE

The Home Secretary's responsibility for the liquor laws led him to become, after the Postmaster-General, a pioneer of State trading.

Nearly all the public houses in the City of Carlisle and a large area surrounding it are owned by him and managed by his servants. There are also a State brewery, a small mineral water factory and a State brand of blended whisky.

During the 1914-1918 war, a great munitions factory was erected at Gretna. This attracted a large new working population. Social conditions were bad and much drunkenness resulted. Here was an evil which called for urgent remedy; but the ordinary forms of supervision were not sufficiently effective or swift to effect a cure. So the State intervened, in the shape of a war-time creation called the Central Control Board (Liquor Traffic), by assuming direct control of the liquor trade throughout what became the Carlisle and Gretna State Management Districts on either side of the Border. The Board closed many public houses, improved the remainder and raised the standards of management. The cure was effective; and the State Management Scheme was soon a successful concern, socially and financially.

In 1921 the Board was wound up and the Home Secretary took over direct responsibility for the Carlisle scheme. It has continued ever since. Its avowed object has been and is to satisfy the legitimate needs of the public for liquor and associated amenities in the best possible conditions under disinterested management. In its earlier years the scheme was examined and not found wanting, in both its social and its economic aspects, by a Departmental Committee and a Royal Commission. It has had many critics, but it has also achieved widespread recognition as a valuable social experiment; and some of its new public houses have been favourably noticed by critics of public house design and architecture.

Its administrative features are simple. The progress of the scheme is watched over by an Advisory Council appointed by the Home Secretary and the Secretary of State for Scotland, which includes, besides officials, prominent members of the brewing trade and others with wide experience of public life. This Council functions very much like the Board of a commercial company, but without impairing the Secretary of State's ultimate responsibility. The day-to-day management is in the hands of the General Manager and his staff at Carlisle. Formal contact with local opinion is maintained through a local Advisory Committee, on which the local authorities and magistrates are represented. The Scheme's public houses are run by managers who are disinterested, not in any pejorative sense, but solely in the sense that the amount of their pay does not depend on how much liquor they sell.

For reasons very different from those which led the State to intervene at Carlisle, the Licensing Act of 1949 provided for the extension of State Management to new towns established under the New Towns Act, 1946. It was thought that this would be a good way of securing the provision of public houses of a high standard according to a proper plan. The advisory State Management Districts Council was enlarged to include representatives of the Development Corporations of the new towns, and local advisory committees were set up in most of the new towns; but before plans could be translated into pubs, or the difficult exercise could be performed of setting up and furnishing a satisfactory organization to supervise and service small groups of public houses in a dozen widely separated small towns, a change of policy followed a change of Government, and by the Licensed Premises in New Towns Act, 1952,[1] it was decided to leave it to the Development Corporations, the licensing justices and private enterprise between them to ensure that the new towns have public houses worthy of them in character and right in number and distribution.

8. BETTING AND LOTTERIES

The danger that a law that is out of touch with public opinion may fall into contempt has already been mentioned; this danger is very apparent in another field—namely that of gambling—where the Home Secretary has a general responsibility for the efficiency of the law. A Royal Commission was appointed in 1949 to examine the law and to recommend what changes were desirable and practicable. It made a number of recommendations, of which the most important was that the existing statutory prohibition of cash betting elsewhere than on a racecourse should be replaced by the provision of licensed facilities for cash betting off the course.[2] The system of licensing proposed by the Commission resembles in many ways the licensing system under the liquor laws. At the time of writing no decision had been announced about the implementation of the Commission's proposals.

9. DANGEROUS DRUGS AND POISONS

Drug addiction has existed in this country for a long time—there are well known references to opium smoking in Victorian literature —but it was not until the beginning of the present century that the Government of the United Kingdom began to take a serious interest in the matter and then it was primarily in its capacity as a Colonial Power. In 1909 an International Opium Commission was set up in Shanghai to devise means of suppressing the opium traffic which had

[1] Repealed and re-enacted in the Licensing Act, 1953. [2] Cmd. 8190.

become very serious in some parts of the East, particularly China; the ultimate result was the Hague Convention of 1912, the first international instrument for the control of the drug traffic.

The outbreak of the first world war prevented this convention being brought into force. When it was found during the war that cocaine was being hawked among soldiers in London with serious consequences, a Defence Regulation was made in 1916 making it an offence for unauthorized persons to possess, sell, give or supply opium or cocaine.

After the war the League of Nations assumed the task of co-ordinating international action in the sphere of narcotics control. The Hague Convention, ratification of which was made a condition of the Treaty of Versailles, was followed by a series of international agreements designed primarily to restrict the manufacture of dangerous drugs (including ultimately synthetic drugs) to legitimate requirements for medical and scientific purposes and to regulate their distribution. To give effect to these agreements two international bodies were set up: the Permanent Central Opium Board (a body of eight experts now appointed by the Economic and Social Council of the United Nations) and the Supervisory Body (which consists of four experts, two being appointed by the World Health Organization and one each by the Commission on Narcotic Drugs[1] of the Economic and Social Council and by the Permanent Central Opium Board).

To implement these agreements several Dangerous Drugs Acts were passed from 1920 onwards. They were consolidated in the Dangerous Drugs Act, 1951. The system of control is based on the licensing of the import, export and manufacture of dangerous drugs. Each Government sends to the Permanent Central Opium Board every year an estimate of the drugs it will require for medical and scientific purposes in the following year. This estimate is scrutinized by the Supervisory Body who may ask for further information and where appropriate may, with the consent of the Government concerned, amend it. Statistics of imports and exports are sent quarterly to the Permanent Central Opium Board, and if it appears to the Board that a country has exceeded its estimate the Board notifies this to all other contracting states, who are bound to prohibit further exports of the particular drug to the country which has exceeded its quota (unless a supplementary estimate is submitted).

The control of imports and exports in this country is maintained by a system of licences issued by the Dangerous Drugs Branch of the Home Office. No one may import into the United Kingdom a

[1] The work of this international body is discussed in Chapter XVI.

consignment of dangerous drugs without an import licence or export one without an export licence, the latter only being granted on production of proof that the Government of the importing country has authorized the import. Control is also maintained over dangerous drugs while they are in this country. Thus no one may manufacture, sell, supply, process or procure dangerous drugs without authority and all who handle them must keep available for inspection precise records of drugs in their possession and must be prepared to account for them.

The trade in dangerous drugs is subjected to a control more stringent than any likely to be found in any other form of commerce. The control begins before the drug reaches the United Kingdom, and remains in force throughout its stay here right up to the moment of re-export where that occurs. The Dangerous Drugs Branch is responsible for the issue of all licences and authorizations, and for preparing and submitting information generally to the United Nations including estimates and returns, e.g. reports on illicit traffic. It is their constant preoccupation to ensure that no drugs are imported or manufactured except for medical or scientific purposes, that the estimates are kept as low as is consistent with medical and scientific needs and are not exceeded, and that drugs are only exported in accordance with international obligations. The Dangerous Drugs Inspectorate further have the task of ensuring that drugs are not diverted to illicit purposes within the country. They inspect manufacturers' premises and records and maintain close liaison with the police, who are primarily responsible for inspecting retail pharmacies in this connexion, and with Regional Medical Officers who also assist in maintaining control as regards doctors. There is the closest liaison with Customs. There is much work involved in the preparation of licences and reports and in the scrutiny of returns which all licensees are required to furnish. The Dangerous Drugs Branch further examines estimates, reports and returns from the colonies, the Isle of Man and the Channel Islands, and transmits them to the United Nations.

Thanks to the strictness of this system of control, and no doubt in part to the fact that we live in an island, there is no sign of any widespread organized illicit drug traffic in this country at the moment, and it is particularly noteworthy that the troubled years following the second world war produced no drug problem comparable with that which existed after the first world war. But drug addiction is a most terrible scourge, and the experience of other countries shows that once it gains a foothold on any appreciable scale it spreads rapidly bringing with it widespread misery, and is then most difficult to suppress. Although this country is comparatively free from this evil no one can be sure that this immunity would continue if the control were relaxed. Indeed there are signs—rare and slight but very real—that if no control were exercised the risk of widespread addiction could arise, and there can be no question of relaxing the present system of stringent supervision.

The retail sale of poisons is governed by the Pharmacy and Poisons Acts, 1852 to 1933. Under these Acts the Home Office has the duty of ensuring that poisonous substances which the general public require for legitimate purposes are sold only with safeguards designed to protect the public from careless or improper use. For example, poisons may only be sold to authorized persons, and there are provisions as to their storage, and the labelling of containers. In his administration of these Acts the Home Secretary has the advice of the Poisons Board. This is a statutory body consisting of a Chairman and eighteen other members. The present Chairman is a Metropolitan Magistrate. The remaining members are all experts with qualifications in science, medicine or pharmacy, except for two officials who have experience of the types of problem that arise. The Home Secretary is required to appoint one member; he may, and normally does, appoint three additional members. He also selects the Chairman. Other members are appointed by the Secretary of State for Scotland, the Minister of Health, the Minister of Agriculture and Fisheries, the Council of the Pharmaceutical Society of Great Britain (one of whose nominees must be a person engaged in the manufacture for sale by way of wholesale dealing of pharmaceutical preparations), the Royal Colleges of Physicians of London and Edinburgh, the General Medical Council, the Council of the Royal Institute of Chemistry of Great Britain and Ireland, and the British Medical Association. The Government Chemist is a member ex-officio but may be represented by a member of his staff.

10. OBSCENE PUBLICATIONS

All governments have to guard against the corruption of public morals by obscene publications, and in England and Wales the Home Secretary is the Minister primarily responsible for keeping a watch on this problem and for seeing that the law is enforced.

In England and Wales the publication of any obscene book, picture, print, etc., and the procuring for sale of such publications, are misdemeanours at common law, punishable on indictment by fine or imprisonment. There are also several statutory provisions on the subject. The principal of these, so far as the Home Office is concerned, is the Obscene Publications Act, 1857, which empowers magistrates on sworn information to issue a search warrant to search for and seize any obscene book or other article kept for sale, exhibition, etc., and, if they are satisfied that the books or other articles are obscene, to order their destruction. There is no statutory definition of obscenity but Chief Justice Cockburn in *Regina v. Hickling*, 1868, said that 'the test of obscenity is whether the tendency of the matter published is to deprave and corrupt those whose minds are open to such immoral influences and into whose hands the publication might fall.'

If a work is brought to the Home Secretary's notice which seems to him to be obscene he normally brings it to the attention of the Director of Public Prosecutions. It is not for the Home Secretary to decide whether the work is obscene: that is a matter for the courts. The Home Secretary has no power to prohibit publications, to demand the removal or alteration of offending passages, or to approve manuscripts or draft publications, although he is not infrequently pressed to do this.

Two other Departments are concerned in the suppression of this traffic. It is an offence under the Post Office Act, 1908, to send or attempt to send obscene matter through the post, and the Customs Consolidation Act, 1876, prohibits the importation of obscene publications. The Post Office and Board of Customs and Excise are respectively responsible for the enforcement of these provisions, but it is obviously desirable that they and the Home Office should act in conformity with each other and there is close consultation between all three Departments.

The work has an international aspect since there is some international traffic in obscene wares. As long ago as 1910 an international agreement was signed in Paris pledging the signatories to co-operate in the suppression of this traffic. For this purpose the contracting parties undertook each to designate a central authority which would maintain direct communication with other central authorities with a view to the rapid exchange of information. The Home Office is the designated central authority, and in this capacity takes up directly with the central authorities of other countries cases of obscene matter of foreign origin, and conversely investigates complaints about obscene matter originating in the United Kingdom. A further international Convention, designed to improve international arrangements for the suppression of the illicit traffic in obscene matter, was signed at Geneva in 1923 under the auspices of the League of Nations.

11. THEATRICAL EMPLOYERS REGISTRATION

An example of the concern of the Home Office with the well-being of a particular group of persons is seen in the Theatrical Employers Registration Act, 1925, which was designed to prevent such abuses by a theatrical employer as leaving his company stranded without payment of their wages or expenses. The Act requires all theatrical employers, with certain minor exceptions, to register with the registration authority (the county or county borough council) of the area in which they normally live. Copies of the register entries and particulars of any subsequent amendments have to be sent to the Home Office, where they are open to inspection by the public on payment of a small fee. The Home Secretary has made rules prescribing the forms to be used for the purpose of the Act.

12. GENERAL RESPONSIBILITIES OF THE HOME SECRETARY

In 1925 a serious disaster occurred by the breaking of the dam of a reservoir in Dolgarrog, North Wales. Parliament by the Reservoirs (Safety Provisions) Act, 1930, provided that large reservoirs must have their construction and design supervised, and after construction must be periodically inspected, by a qualified engineer; and placed on the Home Secretary the duty of constituting panels of qualified engineers for the purpose of the Act.

But the Home Secretary's responsibilities to discharge the ultimate responsibility of the Crown for the safety of Her Majesty's subjects extend far beyond his statutory duties. It is he who must take action to find the cause of accidents involving loss of life or serious danger to the public which arise in fields in which no other Minister of the Crown has a direct responsibility. Thus it was the Home Secretary who ordered the Inquiry into the Holborn Gas Explosion in 1928, when a Post Office worker was fatally injured when an explosion of gas underground badly damaged the surface of several streets in and around High Holborn, and the Inquiry into the Bolton Football Ground accident in 1946, when a large crowd broke into an already crowded ground and 33 people were killed. Again it was he who established in 1947 the inter-Departmental Committee on Accidents in the Home to co-ordinate the activities of the Government Departments with some measure of interest in trying to devise ways and means of reducing the heavy loss of life and man hours due to domestic accidents; and to maintain contact with unofficial organizations interested in the subject. The Committee has concentrated on two main lines of approach: first, to make the public more aware of the dangers of home accidents and how to prevent them; secondly, to encourage the development of safer designs in domestic equipment.

It was as the Queen's Minister responsible for the general safety of her subjects that he commended to the House of Commons the Bill which became the Heating Appliances (Fire Guards) Act, 1952, which, by making compulsory the guarding of certain kinds of domestic fires, carries into effect one of the most important safety precautions recommended by the Standing inter-Departmental Committee, and should help to solve an urgent problem on which the Committee did much to focus public attention.

CHAPTER IX

The Control of Aliens

The need for controlling aliens — Admission of aliens — Aliens in this country — Deportation — The work of the Aliens Department.

*

1. THE NEED FOR CONTROLLING ALIENS

THE Home Office is concerned not only with the public well-being as a whole, but also with the intimate personal affairs of individuals— in this case men, women and children of every race, colour and creed. A Sovereign State must reserve the right to protect the well-being of its citizens against the risks which the uncontrolled entry of foreigners might bring. Control of immigration is necessary not only to keep away from our shores people undesirable in themselves, but in the present state of the world for economic and social reasons as well. Yet it is only within the last fifty years that systematic restrictions have been imposed on the entry of aliens to this country and on their residence here. The Plantagenet and Tudor monarchs claimed a prerogative right to exclude or to admit aliens, and when they needed loans from Hanseatic merchants or Lombard money-lenders to carry on their wars, found reasons not only for admitting them but for granting them special privileges. In the eighteenth century the right to exclude had fallen into abeyance, and aliens enjoyed entire freedom until in 1793, when war broke out with France, legislation was passed giving power to exclude or expel aliens. After Waterloo, when peace was restored, milder requirements were gradually substituted[1] and even these fell into desuetude.

It was not until towards the end of the nineteenth century that the need again arose for restricting the admission of aliens to this country. At that time the pressure of poverty or racial persecution on numerous people in Eastern Europe, a great expansion and improvement of the means of transport, and the imposition of restrictions on admission to the United States of America combined to bring to the East End of London large numbers of aliens whose competition lowered the wages in some of the unorganized trades to starvation point, and

[1] By Acts of 1816, 1826 and 1836.

whose habits had a demoralizing effect in the crowded areas in which they settled. A Royal Commission was set up and its report led to the Aliens Act, 1905, the broad effect of which was to give powers to exclude alien steerage passengers who were potential paupers or were diseased or criminals, and to expel from the country aliens who had become paupers or criminals.

When war broke out in 1914 wider powers of control were needed, and were given by the Aliens Restriction Act, 1914, which enabled Orders in Council to be made regulating the landing of aliens, controlling their residence and movement in this country, and providing for their deportation when necessary. After the war the need for these more rigorous controls was reviewed, and the Aliens Restrictions (Amendment) Act, 1919, was passed. This continued for a further year the powers which had originally been granted for the purposes of the war. Since then conditions at home and abroad have made it necessary to renew these powers each year by the Expiring Laws Continuance Act. In 1920 an Order in Council was made under the Acts of 1914 and 1919 and a number of amending Orders were made subsequently. The Home Secretary's existing powers are conferred by the Aliens Order, 1953, which consolidated and revoked all previous Orders.

Briefly the Order requires an alien to obtain leave to land, which may be granted subject to conditions, such as a time limit on the period of stay or a condition as to the taking of employment; and empowers the Home Secretary to exercise control over aliens in this country, e.g. by varying the conditions imposed on entry, and to bring their stay to an end, by deportation if necessary.

In exercising these powers in the case of temporary visits for business, holiday or educational purposes, which are freely allowed, the object of the Home Office is to reduce the formalities to the minimum necessary to exclude undesirables and those whose real though undisclosed intention is to stay here permanently. When an alien asks to be allowed to settle here the problem is to consider his request against the background of economic and social considerations which forbid an unlimited influx of aliens, but to avoid hardship to those whose claim is based on compassionate grounds.

No other section of the Home Office has more direct or more frequent contacts with the public than the Aliens Department. Each month some 30,000 letters, reports and other communications are received and some 4,000 callers interviewed by staff at headquarters. Inevitably, there is a large volume of correspondence from Members of Parliament on individual cases. Inevitably, too, there are complaints from those dissatisfied by the Home Secretary's decisions who are unable or unwilling to understand that the Home Office must weigh the circumstances of each particular case against wider considerations of national policy. For reasons which will be obvious few Departments have wider contacts in the Government machine.

2. THE ADMISSION OF ALIENS

In 1953, 770,000 aliens (excluding resident aliens returning from abroad) were given leave to land in the United Kingdom. About 620,000 of these were business visitors or tourists, who are freely admitted, usually for three months. Longer periods of stay are permitted to genuine students, who are usually given permission to stay for a year in the first instance subsequently extended if necessary to cover their period of study; and to Ministry of Labour permit holders.

The Ministry of Labour permit system, applied to aliens who seek employment in this country, is a method of safeguarding the interests of British workpeople. The prospective employer must obtain a permit from the Ministry of Labour and National Service,[1] who before granting it will satisfy themselves that there is essential work to be done, that British labour will not be displaced or excluded, and that there will be no undercutting of British wage standards.[2] An alien in possession of such a permit is granted leave to land or to remain here unless he is for some personal reason undesirable. Permits are normally granted for twelve months but they may be, and often are, renewed for further periods. The alien may not change his employment without the consent of the Ministry of Labour and National Service; but after four years in this country he may apply to the Home Office to be accepted as a resident, and if so accepted he is free to take any form of work.[3] About 35,000 Ministry of Labour and National Service permits are granted each year, but many of the aliens (e.g. entertainers) to whom permits are granted stay in the United Kingdom for only short periods.

The third group of aliens comprises those who ask to be admitted to this country not as visitors or students, nor as workers whose services are needed here, but on grounds of humanity, such as the uniting of families. Alien husbands of British wives, or alien children who have some relative or friend in this country, are examples of

[1] In Northern Ireland the Ministry of Labour and National Insurance.

[2] Applications from aliens who desire to set up in business are considered by the Home Office in consultation with Departments such as the Board of Trade or the Ministry of Food.

[3] Except in Northern Ireland, where employment is controlled by the Safeguarding of Employment Act (Northern Ireland), 1947.

those who can without difficulty usually be permitted to land and live here, but the second world war and its aftermath have created great problems in this field. During the post-war years the Home Office has administered a scheme for admitting distressed relatives of persons, whether British or alien, who are already living in this country. The broad principles were announced to Parliament, but the Home Office has inevitably had a difficult task in applying them to the varying circumstances of individual cases.

Except in the case of a national of a country with which the United Kingdom has a visa-abolition agreement an alien is not admitted unless he has a valid visa issued by a British representative abroad.

Mention may be made here of the special case of aliens who from time to time seek political asylum in this country. The so-called 'right' of political asylum is, as the textbooks make clear—and as has been frequently explained in Parliament—not the right of an individual to obtain asylum but the right of a Sovereign State to admit fugitive aliens and accord them such hospitality as in its discretion it decides to extend. It is impossible to lay down any general principles, and each application has to be considered on its own merits. But it has long been a tradition in this country not to refuse to accept an alien if to do so would mean that his life or liberty would be placed in jeopardy because of his political or religious beliefs. In dealing with individual cases the Government have to be guided by several and often conflicting considerations, which include not only our traditional practice but such matters as their obligations under international law and considerations of national safety.

Since shortly before the second world war the number of alien residents in the United Kingdom has greatly increased. In the years before the war more than 60,000 refugees from Germany and Austria were admitted. In accordance with a pledge given during the war about 120,000 members and dependants of the Polish Forces have settled in the United Kingdom. Some 24,000 former prisoners of war who were given an opportunity of staying if they were willing to undertake certain forms of work, e.g., agriculture, remained here. In the years 1946 to 1949 nearly 90,000 displaced persons were recruited for work in undermanned industries, on the understanding that, if they behaved well and observed certain conditions of employment, they would be regarded as residents. Mainly as a result of these additions, it is estimated that the number of resident aliens is almost double what it was about twenty years ago, despite the large numbers who have been naturalized in that period.[1] The United Kingdom has thus made a large contribution to relieving the distress caused by tyranny and war, and this densely-populated country cannot be expected to assimilate in the foreseeable future any large number of additional alien residents.

3. ALIENS IN THIS COUNTRY

Any alien over the age of 16 who is in the country for over three months has to register with the police of the district where he resides, giving such particulars as his name, nationality, occupation, date and place of arrival in the United Kingdom and last residence outside the United Kingdom. He must report any circumstances requiring alteration of these particulars and any change of residence. Each police district maintains a register of aliens, and these registers form the basis of the central register at the Home Office of all the aliens registered as resident in the United Kingdom.

Except for any restrictions on taking employment imposed as a condition of entry, aliens admitted to the United Kingdom enjoy practically all the rights of British subjects. They have unrestricted right of access to the courts and qualify on the same conditions as British subjects for most social service benefits. They are not, of course, entitled to vote in Parliamentary or local elections; and are debarred from Crown Service and certain professions.

4. DEPORTATION

The Aliens Order empowers the Home Secretary in certain circumstances to make deportation orders requiring aliens to leave and thereafter to remain out of the United Kingdom. When an alien has been convicted of an offence punishable by imprisonment without the option of a fine, or of any of certain other specified offences, the court may recommend that he should be deported either in addition to, or in lieu of, sentence. The Home Secretary is not bound to act on the recommendation of the court, and there are occasions when, after taking into account circumstances such as the length of the alien's residence in the United Kingdom or the risk that he would suffer political persecution on return to his own country, the Home Secretary decides not to make an order. The Home Secretary can deport an alien if he deems it to be conducive to the public good, whether or not the alien has been before a court. This general

[1] On 31st December, 1953, there were nearly 370,000 aliens over the age of 16 registered with the police, as compared with 169,000 in 1933 and 197,000 in 1938, the principal nationalities being: Poles (125,000); Germans (38,300); Italians (32,800); Russians (21,000); United States (22,000); French (12,400); Latvians (11,200); Swiss (11,200); Austrians (9,000); Yugoslavs (8,600); Dutch (8,500); Lithuanians (5,000).

power could be used to make a deportation order against an alien who persisted in ignoring the conditions on which he was given leave to land in this country. It is a generally understood convention of international behaviour that each country should re-admit any of its nationals who have been deported, but since the war the Eastern European countries have not always observed this convention, and have thus made it impossible to enforce the departure from this country of some most undesirable people.

5. THE WORK OF THE ALIENS DEPARTMENT

It is not only the consideration of questions of general policy, and of such matters as the bearing on the United Kingdom of international discussion of refugee problems, and the formulation of guidance for overseas Passport Control Offices[1] on the granting of visas, which takes place at the headquarters of the Aliens Department. Here also individual applications for permission to settle in this country or to extend a visit are dealt with.

In addition to the central register of aliens which has been already mentioned (a record, that is, of aliens who have been in the country more than three months), there is maintained at headquarters a record known as the Traffic Index, which is built up out of the cards filled up by aliens on entering or leaving the United Kingdom. The card for each alien shows the conditions on which he was allowed to land, including the period for which he was given permission to stay, and it is thus possible to check whether an alien has overstayed his time.

There is also a considerable block of work in supplying travel documents to aliens resident in the United Kingdom who are stateless or who cannot obtain passports from the authorities of their country of origin.

Under a United Nations Convention certain classes of stateless aliens are entitled to travel documents: the remainder may apply for a certificate of identity, which they can produce in substitution for a passport when they are abroad and which normally carries a guarantee that they will be readmitted to the United Kingdom if they return within a period of twelve months. Each year about 30,000 travel documents and 5,000 certificates of identity are issued or renewed.

For any necessary supervision of resident aliens reliance is placed upon the police; and the work of exercising control at the ports and investigating the circumstances of individual aliens on arrival is

[1] These are staffed by officers of the Foreign Service and the Commonweath Relations Office acting as agents of the Home Secretary.

carried out, under the general control of Her Majesty's Chief Inspector, Immigration Branch, in London, by the Immigration Officers who are stationed at those sea and air ports at which alone aliens are permitted to land. The Aliens Order provides that no alien can land without the permission of an Immigration Officer and lays down certain conditions—for example, that the alien should be able to support himself and his dependants, should not be objectionable on health grounds and should not be guilty of serious crime—which must be satisfied before leave to land is given. It will be evident that the burden of work falling upon the Immigration staff is considerable. During 1953 Immigration Officers interviewed over 1,700,000 incoming and outgoing aliens. In the course of a short interview the Immigration Officer must satisfy himself as to the *bona fides* of a traveller and decide whether to grant or refuse leave to land. The great majority of people are genuine enough, but in the present unsettled state of the world many, for worthy or unworthy motives, are anxious to seek entry to this country which could not be permitted, and some may be coming with evil intent. Stowaways and others who come in foreign ships as members of the crew with the intention to desert on their arrival in this country present just one set of the difficult problems with which the Immigration staff must cope.

CHAPTER X

Nationality and Naturalization

British nationality — British Nationality Act, 1948 — Naturalization — Registration — Renunciation and deprivation of citizenship — Nationality and Naturalization Division of the Home Office.

*

1. BRITISH NATIONALITY

BRITISH nationality is a matter of great importance to those who possess it. Apart from its sentimental value it carries with it rights to protection and many political and other rights, such as the right to vote at elections, to hold public offices and to enter and reside in the United Kingdom, as well as duties of allegiance, which are not shared by foreigners.

Questions of nationality bring the Home Office into touch with the Foreign Office, Commonwealth Relations Office and Colonial Office, and through them with the whole British Commonwealth and the varied and diverse peoples who are British subjects. Problems about the nationality of individuals or groups of persons constantly occur, and their solution often involves the Home Office in the investigation of events taking place over long periods and in distant parts of the world; and it is often necessary to study the nationality laws of other countries, both British and foreign.

The Home Secretary has a general responsibility for the law relating to nationality in the sense that it is his function to consider suggestions for its amendment and if necessary to introduce legislation for the purpose. He has also certain executive functions, the most important of which is the grant of certificates of naturalization. Before describing these duties a brief account must first be given of the development of the law relating to British nationality.

By common law, with few exceptions, all persons born in the Sovereign's dominions were British subjects and all others were aliens. If any foreign territory were annexed to the Crown its inhabitants became British subjects: if any British territory became separated from the Crown its inhabitants ceased to be British subjects. Apart from this an alien could become a British subject only if he were naturalized by an Act of Parliament (in nearly all cases by private Acts); and a British subject could not divest himself of his British nationality. Women neither acquired nor lost British nationality by marriage, and a British subject remained British even if he were naturalized in a foreign country. Aliens naturalized by Act of Parliament were not, except in rare cases, given all the rights of natural-born British subjects. They were not capable of being members of the Privy Council or of either House of Parliament, holding any public office, or acquiring any land by grant from the Crown.

The growth of British communities in foreign countries led, in the 18th century, to the passage of legislation enabling British nationality to be transmitted to the descendants born abroad of natural-born, but not of naturalized, British subjects. The British Nationality Acts, 1708 and 1730, gave British nationality to their children born abroad, and the British Nationality Act, 1772, extended this to their grandchildren in the male line.

The next change came in 1844, when an 'Act to amend the Laws relating to Aliens' made provision for the first time for the grant of certificates of naturalization to aliens by the Secretary of State. Acts of Parliament were no longer necessary, and the modern system of naturalization was thus inaugurated. No special qualifications were needed except that the alien should be resident in the United Kingdom and intended to settle therein. The certificate of naturalization gave the alien all the rights of a natural-born British subject, except the capacity of being a member of the Privy Council or of either House of Parliament and except any other rights specifically excluded by the certificate. The Act of 1844 also provided that an alien woman on marrying a British subject should be deemed to be naturalized and should have all the rights of a natural-born British subject.

The Naturalization Act, 1870, inaugurated a new policy of making it more difficult for a person to possess both British and a second nationality.[1] For the first time provision was made for loss of British nationality otherwise than by loss of territory. British subjects who were voluntarily naturalized in a foreign country and British women who married aliens were to cease to be British subjects. The Act also required that applicants for naturalization should have resided in the United Kingdom or been in Crown service for at least five years, but

[1] Since the question whether a person possesses the nationality of any given country depends on the law of that country and nationality laws differ widely, a person may easily be born with two or more nationalities: for example, a child born in England of French parents would normally be British owing to his place of birth and also French owing to his descent. Hitherto the law of this country had contained no restrictions on dual nationality.

once naturalized they were henceforward given all the rights of natural-born British subjects.

The British Nationality and Status of Aliens Act, 1914, carried the policy of discouraging dual nationality still further. It took away the power given by the British Nationality Act, 1772, to transmit British nationality to the second generation born abroad: henceforward British nationality was to cease after the first generation. As regards naturalization two important changes were made. The first was that the Governments of British possessions were given power to grant certificates of naturalization which would be effective throughout the British Empire: hitherto a certificate granted in a possession gave the grantee the rights of British subjects in that possession only. The second change was that power was given to the Secretary of State and Governments of British possessions to revoke a certificate of naturalization if it appeared that it was obtained by false representation or fraud.

The British Nationality and Status of Aliens Act, 1918, passed as a result of the war, greatly widened the power to revoke certificates of naturalization. The most important additional grounds were disloyalty or disaffection, trading or communicating with the enemy, and being sentenced to at least a year's imprisonment within five years of being naturalized. The new powers were used on a large scale for several years after the first world war. Later revocations became infrequent and there were very few after the second world war.

The British Nationality and Status of Aliens Act, 1922, made an important change as regards the transmissibility of British nationality to descendants born abroad. The provision in the Act of 1914 reducing transmissibility to the first generation had resulted in protests from British business communities and others settled in foreign countries, many of whom fought on the British side during the war; and the new Act not only abolished this provision but made British nationality transmissible from generation to generation indefinitely in the male line, subject to the condition, as regards each generation born abroad after the first, that the births of the children in question should be registered at a British consulate.

The next important change was made by the British Nationality Act, 1948, which completely changed the basis of British nationality.

2. THE BRITISH NATIONALITY ACT, 1948

Before 1948 the law of British nationality was, generally speaking, the same throughout the British Commonwealth. But the growth of self-government in the Commonwealth affected British nationality in two important ways. The Dominions' legislative independence meant that they could now enact nationality legislation independently of the Westminster Parliament: thus differences could and did appear between the law of the United Kingdom and that of some other parts of the Commonwealth, and a person might be a British subject in one country and an alien in another. Secondly, some other parts created local citizenship inside the concept of British nationality—an obvious convenience for the purpose of their international relations as well as an expression of their nationhood. At first this did not affect British nationality, since citizenship was a secondary status; but in 1946 Canada revolutionized the whole system by creating a status of Canadian citizenship and making British nationality, so far as the persons connected with Canada were concerned, dependent on the possession of that citizenship.

The Canadian Act increased the contradictions which were developing in the nationality laws of the Commonwealth; and at a meeting of Commonwealth Prime Ministers in 1946 it was decided that the common code of British nationality which had obtained throughout the Commonwealth before the development of self-government in the Dominions could no longer be maintained. In order to preserve the common status of British subjects the United Kingdom and the other self-governing countries of the Commonwealth should follow Canada's example and create local citizenships, and each country should recognize its own citizens and those of the other countries as British subjects. For this purpose the United Kingdom and the colonies should be treated as one country with a common citizenship. The details were worked out by a conference of officials in February, 1947.

These discussions provided an opportunity for dealing with the anomalous situation which had come about in Eire as regards nationality. The original constitution of the Irish Free State adopted in 1922 included a limited provision for citizenship of the Irish Free State, which did not affect British nationality; but in 1935 the Irish Nationality and Citizenship Act, passed by the Eire Parliament, made detailed provision for citizenship and at the same time repealed, so far as that country was concerned, all the existing law about British nationality. As a result, citizens of the Irish Free State were not British subjects by the law of that country, though they remained British subjects by the law of the United Kingdom. Representatives of Eire took part in the conference in 1947, and it was agreed that citizens of Eire should not as such be British subjects under the law of the United Kingdom, but should have in general the same rights and liabilities as British subjects.

These decisions were put into effect by the British Nationality Act, 1948, which came into operation on 1st January, 1949. The Act created the new status of citizen of the United Kingdom and Colonies, and provided that those citizens and also citizens of the other self-governing countries of the Commonwealth (Canada, Australia, New Zealand, the Union of South Africa, India, Pakistan, Southern Rhodesia and Ceylon) should be British subjects. The question who are citizens of any of these countries depends on the legislation of the country in question. Citizens of Eire were not made British subjects, but a special provision enabled those of them who had hitherto been British subjects (the vast majority) to remain such by giving notice to the Home Secretary of their desire to do so on any of various grounds, including association with the United Kingdom. The Act provided that citizens of Eire should not in any case be aliens, and in general it applies to them in the same way as to citizens of the self-governing countries of the Commonwealth listed above.

The same general principles which had previously governed the acquisition and loss of British nationality were preserved in the rules governing the acquisition and loss of citizenship of the United Kingdom and Colonies, but there are important differences—especially as regards married women—and the policy inaugurated by the Naturalization Act, 1870, of discouraging dual nationality has been abandoned. A person becomes a citizen of the United Kingdom and Colonies by birth in the United Kingdom or a colony (the Act applies to the Channel Islands and the Isle of Man in the same way as it does to colonies) or, subject to certain limitations more or less similar to those of the previous law, by descent from a citizen of the United Kingdom and Colonies. Otherwise the two most important methods of acquiring citizenship are naturalization and registration.

3. NATURALIZATION

As regards naturalization, the British Nationality Act follows in general the previous law, except for the modifications consequent on the sub-division of British nationality into citizenship. An adult alien possessing certain qualifications may apply to the Home Secretary[1] for a certificate of naturalization. Stated shortly, these qualifications are:

(i) that for the last twelve months before the application the applicant should have resided in the United Kingdom or

[1] Governors of colonies and other dependent territories have nearly similar powers to grant certificates of naturalization subject to the approval of the Secretary of State.

been in Crown service under Her Majesty's Government in the United Kingdom;

(ii) that during four out of the seven years before those twelve months he should have resided in the United Kingdom, in a colony or in any of certain other territories or been in Crown service as above;

(iii) that he should be of good character;

(iv) that he should have sufficient knowledge of the English language; and

(v) that he should intend, if naturalized, to reside in the United Kingdom, in a colony or in any of certain other territories, or to enter or continue in Crown service under Her Majesty's Government in the United Kingdom, or any of certain other kinds of service, e.g. the service of a firm established in the United Kingdom.

The Act leaves the grant or refusal of a certificate of naturalization to the discretion of the Home Secretary even if the applicant is qualified, and it has always been the practice to inquire into an applicant's loyalty and professional or commercial integrity as well as into his statutory qualifications. The Act also provides that the Home Secretary shall not be obliged to give reasons for his decision, and he does not do so. But at nearly all times since 1844 the policy has been to grant certificates to all applicants who can satisfy the Home Secretary that they have assimilated the British way of life. Karl Marx failed to satisfy this test because 'he has not been loyal to his own King and country.' During the two world wars grants were virtually suspended save in exceptional cases, and after the first war grants to ex-enemy aliens other than refugees were greatly restricted.

In the 1920's the numbers naturalized in the United Kingdom during a year never reached 1,400. In 1939, 2,568 were naturalized. Since the second world war the number of applicants has been greatly swollen by the refugees, displaced persons and members of allied forces who came to the United Kingdom before and after the war. In the four years 1946-9 about 45,000 certificates were granted. During 1951-53 grants were at the rate of about 4,000 a year.

Applications for naturalization are made on a form which, in addition to calling for information about the applicant's personal particulars, nationality and qualifications for naturalization, requires him to state that he is financially solvent and to give details of any proceedings of any kind taken against him in any civil or criminal court. The applicant is also asked to produce references from four British subjects who can vouch for his good character and loyalty from personal knowledge and intimate acquaintance, and to advertise his application in a newspaper, inviting persons who know of any objection to the applicant to inform the Home Office. Advertisements seldom produce objections, but a certain number of replies are received objecting on principle to the naturalization of any alien.

Applications are first checked at the Home Office to verify that conditions such as the required period of residence have been complied with. They are then referred to the police of the district where the applicant is resident, who interview him and report to the Home Office. At the same time the references supporting the applications are checked—sometimes with surprising results, as when a referee supported a Polish applicant whom he did not know because he had heard that the Pole 'played a very good game of darts and was never the worse for drink.' The information given in the application or in the police report may suggest that further inquiries should be made, and it is often necessary to consult other Departments, e.g. the service Departments on questions of Crown service.

4. REGISTRATION

The grant of citizenship by registration is a new feature of British nationality law and not to be confused with the registration at a British consulate of the births of British children born abroad. There are three classes of cases in which the Home Secretary[1] may register a person as a citizen of the United Kingdom and Colonies.

In the first place, an adult citizen of one of the self-governing countries of the Commonwealth listed above or of the Irish Republic who is ordinarily resident in the United Kingdom, and has been so resident for the previous twelve months—the Home Secretary may accept a shorter period—or is in Crown service under Her Majesty's Government in the United Kingdom, has a right to be registered as a citizen of the United Kingdom and Colonies on application.

Secondly, any woman, British or alien, who has been married to a citizen of the United Kingdom and Colonies has a similar right to be herself registered as a citizen. This provision is part of a major change of policy introduced by the British Nationality Act, 1948, as regards the nationality of married women. Under the Act a woman neither acquires nor loses citizenship of the United Kingdom and Colonies by marriage, but a woman marrying a citizen has a right to acquire citizenship by registration. The Act also restored British nationality to women who lost it under the previous law by marriage to aliens. Thus, the common law rule has been restored: married

[1] Governors of colonies and other dependent territories and High Commissioners for the United Kingdom in the self-governing countries of the Commonwealth have nearly similar powers of registration.

women have now been placed in the same position as men as regards nationality, with the additional right to registration. In this way the Act has removed a grievance about which many British women had been protesting for years.

Thirdly, the Home Secretary may, in his discretion, register as a citizen of the United Kingdom and Colonies the minor child of a citizen of the United Kingdom and Colonies or, in special circumstances, any minor. The principal test which the Home Secretary applies in exercising his discretion is whether the minor is being or will be brought up in the United Kingdom, but all kinds of special cases occur which have to be looked at on their merits.

Up to February, 1954, the Home Office has had to deal with 45,000 applications for registration. 11,000 have been on the first, 28,000 on the second, and 6,000 on the third, of the grounds mentioned above.

5. RENUNCIATION AND DEPRIVATION OF CITIZENSHIP

Under the British Nationality Act, 1948, there are only two ways in which a person may cease to be a citizen of the United Kingdom and Colonies. These are renunciation and deprivation, and they are referred to below. Once again, as under common law, naturalization in a foreign state is immaterial.

Any citizen of the United Kingdom and Colonies who is an adult or a married woman, and also possesses the citizenship of one of the self-governing countries listed above of the Commonwealth or of the Irish Republic, or the nationality of a foreign country, may make a declaration renouncing citizenship of the United Kingdom and Colonies, and on the Home Secretary's registering the declaration he or she ceases to be a citizen of the United Kingdom and Colonies. (A somewhat similar right had existed under the previous law since the Naturalization Act, 1870.) The Home Secretary is obliged to register the declaration, except that he may refuse to register a declaration made in war time if the declarant is a national of a foreign country. Declarations of renunciation are very infrequent.

The British Nationality Act, 1948, empowers the Home Secretary[1] to deprive of his citizenship a person who is a citizen of the United Kingdom and Colonies by registration or is a naturalized person—a 'naturalized person' includes a person who was originally naturalized in one of the other self-governing countries of the Commonwealth or the Irish Republic and has since become a citizen of the United

[1] Governors of colonies and other dependent territories have similar powers, subject to the approval of the Secretary of State.

Kingdom and Colonies by registration—if he is satisfied that the registration or the certificate of naturalization was obtained by fraud, false representation or the concealment of any material fact. He may also deprive a naturalized person of his citizenship if he is satisfied that that person has shown himself to be disloyal or disaffected, has in war unlawfully traded or communicated with an enemy or has within five years of being naturalized been sentenced to imprisonment for not less than a year. In addition, the fact that a naturalized person has been deprived of citizenship of one of the self-governing countries of the Commonwealth or of the Irish Republic or has been continuously resident in foreign countries for seven years, is in some circumstances a ground for deprivation of citizenship of the United Kingdom and Colonies. In all cases the Home Secretary must be satisfied that it is not conducive to the public good that the person concerned should continue to be a citizen of the United Kingdom and Colonies. Before depriving a person of his citizenship the Home Secretary must in most cases give him an opportunity of applying for his case to be referred to a committee under a chairman with judicial experience (at present the chairman is a High Court judge). If he so applies he may appear before the committee in person or by a representative and he may give and call evidence. The committee advises the Home Secretary, but the latter is not bound to follow its advice. Since the Act came into force only five naturalized persons had at the time of writing been deprived of their citizenship—in four cases after a recommendation by the committee. In the fifth case the person concerned did not exercise his right to an enquiry. So far no citizens by registration have been deprived of their citizenship.

6. NATIONALITY AND NATURALIZATION DIVISION OF THE HOME OFFICE

Other work of the Nationality and Naturalization Division includes giving advice to other Departments or the police, and sometimes to the persons concerned, about doubtful claims to British nationality. The Home Secretary has power to give a special certificate to a person about whose citizenship of the United Kingdom and Colonies a doubt exists, certifying that he is such a citizen. The passing of the British Nationality Act, 1948, has also caused a good deal of misunderstanding, especially among persons who have not read it, and the Home Secretary has often had to reassure anxious inquirers, many of them with distinguished records in India, that the Act has not turned them into foreigners.

PART THREE

The Royal Prerogative of Mercy and the Treatment of Offenders

CHAPTER XI

The Royal Prerogative of Mercy

Meaning of the Prerogative of Mercy — Death sentences — Insane and mentally abnormal prisoners: medical inquiries — Capital punishment and the law — Life imprisonment — Other uses of the Prerogative — References to the Court of Criminal Appeal — Payment of compensation — Limitations of the Prerogative — Analogous and additional powers.

*

1. THE MEANING OF THE PREROGATIVE OF MERCY

MAINTENANCE of the Queen's Peace demands careful and impartial enforcement of the law by the judiciary. But law is made for man: justice is more than codes and precedents: and there are occasions when justice and humanity demand that there shall be interference with the due course of law—that is, exercise by the Crown of the Prerogative of Mercy.

'Human institutions are fallible, and must in many respects be imperfect. No human faculties can anticipate the various temptations which may urge a man to the commission of an offence; or foresee all the shades in the circumstances of a case which may extenuate the guilt of the accused. An offence may be within the letter, but foreign to the general scope and spirit of the law . . . As, therefore, society cannot sufficiently provide for every possible transgression of its ordinances, and measure by anticipation the degree of guilt which may attach to the offender, it has entrusted the King with the power of extending mercy to him . . . The King is, in legal contemplation, injured by the commission of public offences; his peace is said to be violated thereby, and the right to pardon cannot be vested more properly than in the Sovereign.'[1]

Joseph Chitty, writing early in the nineteenth century, seems to have regarded the Prerogative of Mercy mainly as an instrument for mitigating the lot of a person properly convicted in the courts. By implication he appears to dismiss the possibility that a person may be wrongly convicted: and it is true that errors of justice in this country are rare. Nevertheless, the use of the Prerogative is not confined to mitigating unreasonable hardship; it extends also to righting wrongful convictions.

[1] *Chitty's Prerogatives of the Crown*, 1820, 88-89.

The Prerogative of Mercy is exercised in England and Wales on the advice of the Home Secretary. Shortly defined, it is the Prerogative of relieving an offender of all or some of the consequences of a conviction in, or a sentence or penalty imposed by, the criminal courts. The Prerogative may be exercised by the grant of Free Pardons, Conditional Pardons and Remissions.

A *Free Pardon* wipes out not only the sentence or penalty, but the conviction and all its consequences, and from the time it is granted leaves the person pardoned in exactly the same position as if he had never been convicted.

A *Conditional Pardon* substitutes one form of punishment for another, as for instance when a sentence of death is commuted to one of life imprisonment, or when an offender is relieved of a sentence of imprisonment on condition that he places himself under the supervision of a probation officer for a certain period.

A *Remission* reduces the amount of a sentence or penalty without changing its character, as when a sentence of imprisonment is reduced from twelve months to eight months or a fine of £6 reduced by half.

Another way in which the Prerogative is used is to postpone the carrying out of a sentence either for a fixed time or 'until further order' by issuing a *Reprieve* or *Respite.* In practice this use is restricted to cases where the Home Secretary recommends commutation of the death sentence to one of imprisonment for life.

A Free Pardon, Conditional Pardon or Remission involves the issue of a warrant signed by the Queen and countersigned by the Home Secretary. In issuing a Respite the Home Secretary signifies the Queen's Pleasure by an order under his own hand.

2. DEATH SENTENCES

In the Home Secretary's room at the Home Office, framed in plain wood, stands a card bearing particulars of persons lying under sentence of death. Engraved on the frame is a quotation from Juvenal:

Nulla unquam de morte hominis cunctatio longa est—

'You can never hesitate too long before deciding that a man must die'. The solemn reminder serves to emphasize the gravity of the most onerous and exacting of all the Home Secretary's duties, that of considering whether there are grounds for recommending the exercise by the Crown of the Royal Prerogative of Mercy when the courts pass sentence of death.

Even though a jury may recommend mercy and the Judge may concur in its recommendation, sentence of death must be passed on a person over 18 who is convicted of murder;[1] and before the law is

[1] A pregnant woman may not be sentenced to death.

allowed to take its irrevocable course, it is the long established practice for the Home Secretary to review every such case whether or not he receives any representations on the prisoner's behalf, and to consider whether there are grounds for advising the exercise of the Prerogative of Mercy. When the Home Secretary decides to advise the exercise of the Prerogative, it is the invariable practice for the sentence of death to be commuted to a sentence of imprisonment for life. The Home Secretary first issues a respite, and then submits for the Queen's signature a Conditional Pardon, which relieves the offender of the death penalty on condition that he becomes liable to serve a sentence of imprisonment for life.[1]

When the Home Secretary reviews a capital case, he has before him all the material which was before the courts, a transcript of the proceedings at the trial, police reports, all the information which can be obtained about the prisoner's antecedents, and reports on his physical and mental condition. He may think it necessary to make additional enquiries, for instance of the police, and where there is reason to believe that the prisoner is insane or mentally abnormal he orders a medical inquiry. It is always open to the Home Secretary to consult the trial Judge and, where there has been an appeal, the Judges of the Court of Criminal Appeal, and assistance is readily given by the Judges.

The Home Secretary may take account of circumstances which were not before the court or were not relevant to the issue of guilt or innocence. He is also able to consult the records of previous cases kept by the Home Office and can see what his predecessors decided in comparable cases.

The Home Secretary is always anxious to give full weight to any extenuating factors; but he must also have regard to his responsibility for the maintenance of public order and the need for avoiding capricious administration. The principles on which he decides what advice should be given to the Queen cannot be precisely defined. In some cases the decision is reasonably straightforward. The murderer may have committed a heinous and premeditated murder, and public opinion would be shocked by his reprieve; or on the other hand the prisoner may be the survivor of a genuine suicide pact, or may be a devoted mother who killed her imbecile child to save it from a life of misery, and public opinion would be equally shocked if the law were allowed to take its course. Occasionally the Home Secretary feels that some slight doubt remains as to the prisoner's guilt, and although the doubt is not strong enough to warrant a reversal of the

[1] The effect of such a sentence is described on page 118.

conviction, it is enough to warrant a decision not to carry out the irrevocable sentence of death. But there are a good many cases in which the decision can be reached only after the most careful review of the circumstances of the particular case, and even what appear to be comparatively straightforward cases are meticulously examined. The explanation which Mr. Herbert Gladstone gave in the House of Commons on 11th April, 1907, is still valid: 'Numerous considerations—the motive, the degree of premeditation or deliberation, the amount of provocation, the state of mind of the prisoner, his physical condition, his character and antecedents, the recommendation or absence of recommendation from the jury, and many others—have to be taken into account in every case; and the decision depends on a full review of a complex combination of circumstances and often on the careful balancing of conflicting considerations.'

On average, over the past fifty years nearly half of those sentenced to death have had their sentences commuted to imprisonment for life, although the proportion in any particular year may vary widely. Some indication of the number of murder cases coming before the courts is given by some figures for 1952. Of the persons charged with murder during that year 15 were found insane on arraignment and unfit to plead, and 17 were found guilty but insane. 33 were sentenced to death, of whom one was certified insane after conviction and removed to Broadmoor, 15 had their sentences commuted to life imprisonment, and 17 were executed.

3. INSANE AND MENTALLY ABNORMAL PRISONERS: MEDICAL ENQUIRIES

Problems of especial difficulty arise when there is doubt as to the mental condition of a person convicted of a capital offence. As the figures given in the preceding paragraph indicate, a considerable proportion of the persons charged with murder are found by the jury to be insane on arraignment and unfit to plead, and others are found by the jury to be guilty but insane at the time they committed the act; the court orders the detention of such persons during Her Majesty's Pleasure and they become Broadmoor patients. But when the jury is considering whether a person was insane at the time he committed the offence, it is concerned with the question, not whether he was insane within any current medical definition of insanity, but whether his mental condition was such as to relieve him of criminal responsibility, and for this purpose it must have regard to the test laid down by the Judges in 1843 in the case of McNaughton, namely, whether at the time of committing the act he was labouring under such a defect of reason, from disease of the mind, as not to know the nature and quality of the act, or if he did know, that he did not know that it was wrong.

There are many cases in which the jury, applying this test, does not find the prisoner insane, but in which it is necessary for the Home Secretary to consider whether the prisoner, apart from his condition at the time of the offence, is now certifiably insane or mentally abnormal. When the Home Secretary has reason to believe the prisoner to be insane he is under a statutory obligation, under the Criminal Lunatics Act, 1884, to hold a medical enquiry. Under the common law an insane person may not be executed, and if the doctors holding such an enquiry certify the prisoner as insane the death sentence is not carried out and he becomes a Broadmoor patient. These statutory enquiries are normally held by three experienced doctors. It is also the Home Secretary's practice to have a non-statutory inquiry on similar lines where there is information to suggest that the prisoner may be mentally abnormal, although not certifiably insane, or where the defence of insanity has been raised at the trial but has not been accepted by the jury as coming within the McNaughton rules. In such cases, the doctors' report may provide information as to the prisoner's mental condition which is relevant to the question whether the sentence of death should be carried out.

4. CAPITAL PUNISHMENT AND THE LAW

Courts may pass sentence of death for murder, treason, piracy with violence and setting fire to ships of war; but during this century the capital sentence has been executed only for murder, except in one case of treason during the period of the first world war and in two cases of treason and 15 cases under the Treachery Act, 1940, during the period of the second world war. The law now restricts the scope of capital punishment in that a person under 18 at the time of the offence may not be sentenced to death, a pregnant woman may not be sentenced to death, and a mother convicted of causing the death of her child under the age of twelve months may in certain circumstances be convicted of infanticide and punished for manslaughter, not murder.

There have been various proposals further to restrict the scope of capital punishment. For example, it has been urged that it is wrong that nearly half of those who suffer the anguish of being with all solemnity sentenced to death are in the end reprieved, when it has often been clear to all, except perhaps the prisoner, that there was small prospect of the sentence being carried out. It has also been urged that the law relating to insanity and criminal responsibility should be brought into closer conformity with modern views of mental disease. Many people would go further and abolish capital punishment for murder altogether. In 1948, on a free vote, the House of Commons added a clause to the Criminal Justice Bill providing for the suspension of the death penalty for an experimental period. The clause was deleted by the House of Lords, but as the debates in both Houses had disclosed considerable support for some change in the existing law, the Home Secretary proposed a new clause drawn on the basis that life imprisonment should be the normal penalty for murder, but that the death penalty should be retained for certain heinous types of murder which the clause attempted to define. The clause was however rejected by the House of Lords and the Criminal Justice Bill was passed into law without any provision being included on this question.

The Government subsequently decided to set up a Royal Commission with the task of considering whether liability under the criminal law in Great Britain to suffer capital punishment for murder should be limited or modified, and for how long and under what conditions persons who would otherwise have been liable to suffer capital punishment should be detained.[1]

5. LIFE IMPRISONMENT

It has been explained that where a capital sentence is commuted it is commuted to imprisonment for life. There is however no case on record in which it has been decided that a person shall be kept in prison until he dies, and it is for the Home Secretary to decide in each particular case what the period of detention should be. He has a statutory power to release on licence at any time a person who is serving a life sentence, and in considering such cases he takes into account the questions whether the prisoner will be less likely to commit another crime of violence if he is detained for a longer period, and whether he can be released without weakening the deterrent effect of the criminal law in relation to such crimes. He has regard to the progress made by the prisoner during his sentence and the impressions which the Governor, Chaplain and Medical Officer have formed of him, and also to the length of sentences imposed by the courts for other offences, particularly offences of violence.

During the past hundred years there have been wide variations of practice in fixing the period of detention of life-sentence prisoners, but it has now come to be accepted that detention for more than ten

[1] The Report of the Royal Commission was published in September, 1953 (Cmd. 8932).

or twelve years makes it increasingly difficult for the prisoner to re-establish himself in outside life and adds to the risk of physical or mental deterioration. A longer period may be fixed in a particular case (in eleven cases since 1907 it has been as high as twenty years), but on the other hand the Home Secretary may decide that a much shorter period of detention is adequate—for instance a mother who killed her own young child in pathetic circumstances has been detained for less than a year. Since the war the 'average' period of detention has tended to lengthen, and there would have to be some unusual feature about the case to warrant release before the completion of about nine years' detention.

A person serving a sentence of life imprisonment is always released on licence, but the terms of the licence are not onerous, and it does not often happen that a licence holder is recalled to prison for a breach of conditions of the licence. Only a comparatively small number of murderers, after release on licence, commit serious criminal offences. A survey in 1948 showed that five out of a total of 112 released during the previous 20 years had been again convicted of serious offences, and there is only one case recorded of a person convicted of murder and reprieved being convicted of a second murder after his release.

It was stated above that a person under 18 who is convicted of murder may not be sentenced to death; instead, the court has power to order him to be detained during Her Majesty's Pleasure, and the Home Secretary is then responsible for deciding the type of detention and for fixing its term. Similarly a person sentenced by a court to a term of life imprisonment—a penalty which can be imposed for example for manslaughter—is released from that sentence after a period of detention fixed by the Home Secretary.

6. OTHER USES OF THE PREROGATIVE

The use of the Prerogative of Mercy is by no means confined to capital cases, although these naturally attract the greatest attention. The Home Office receives many representations by or on behalf of persons convicted of offences of all kinds, for the Home Secretary represents the final chance of redress against what they may, rightly or wrongly, regard as the harsh rigours of the law. Prisoners may petition from prison about their conviction or sentence, or their relations or legal advisers may write on their behalf; or representations may be made by or on behalf of persons who have been fined. Every such representation is carefully examined, and enquiries are often made, and although in the end the answer must usually be that no grounds have been disclosed for action on the part of the Home

Secretary, nevertheless it is found from time to time that an error of justice has been made which ought to be corrected or that on grounds of clemency the sentence of the court should be mitigated.

In considering petitions for the exercise of the Prerogative of Mercy the Home Secretary is not acting as a Court of Appeal. He must always bear in mind that it is not the function of the Home Office to re-try a case, that persons sitting in the Home Office and reading documents containing information about the case are in a less favourable position for arriving at a true view than a court which has seen all the witnesses and has heard all the evidence under examination and cross-examination, and that since in law the court has the primary responsibility for determining what sentences are appropriate it is not right that the Home Secretary should recommend a modification of the court's sentence merely on the ground that if he himself had been presiding in the court he would have imposed a different sentence. Before he advises interference with a conviction or sentence he must have stronger and more specific grounds than that.

Such grounds for interference may arise in a variety of ways. Enquiries made by the Home Secretary after conviction, following representations made to him, may bring to light new facts which show beyond dispute that a person was wrongly convicted and that a miscarriage of justice has occurred which should be remedied by the grant of a Free Pardon. The view is sometimes expressed that a Free Pardon, which seems to imply forgiveness for a crime committed, is not really an appropriate instrument in cases where it is shown that the person concerned did not commit the offence of which he was convicted, but the effect of a Free Pardon is in general well understood.

Sometimes enquiries may show that although the person would not have been convicted if all the facts had been before the court, he was himself to blame for the court being inadequately informed. It occasionally happens, too, that a person may be morally guilty in that, so far as he was aware, he was committing an offence. For example the law provides that a motorist must not exceed 30 miles an hour when driving along a road where the lamp posts are not more than 200 yards apart. A motorist stopped by the police for driving at 50 m.p.h. may well regard himself as fairly caught and properly convicted—and be agreeably surprised, later, to learn that the distance between the lamp posts on that particular stretch of road exceeded 200 yards and that he was technically innocent. In such cases, it would be right that, at least, the penalty should be remitted.

Cases in which it comes to light, after the conviction and after appeal rights have been exhausted, that there has been a miscarriage of justice are infrequent. The Home Secretary, before recommending a Free Pardon or Remission in such circumstances, always consults the Judge or magistrates who tried the case or heard the appeal.

There are more frequent cases in which there is no dispute about the fact or degree of guilt, but in which there may nevertheless be considerations which move the Home Secretary to recommend some reduction of the sentence as an act of clemency. A prisoner who comes to the assistance of a prison officer attacked by other prisoners may be rewarded by some reduction of his sentence; a man who is nearing the end of a long sentence may be released a few weeks before his normal date in order to be with his dying wife; or a bench of magistrates may find that they were inadequately informed about a defendant's means when they imposed a fine and ask the Home Secretary to invoke the Prerogative to reduce the fine to the amount which they now think appropriate. The Home Secretary is always ready to consult the court which passed the original sentence, but in many of these cases the considerations which governed the original decision of the judicial authority have little relevance to the questions which the Home Secretary has to consider in advising on the exercise of the Prerogative of Mercy.

Particulars of the numbers of cases in which the Prerogative of Mercy is exercised are given in the annual Criminal Statistics. In 1952, 15 Free Pardons were given, and remission of fines or of sentences of imprisonment or corrective training was granted in 78 cases. Conditional Pardons in other than capital cases are infrequent, and in 1952 there were none. These figures are the result of scrutiny of several thousands of applications made to the Home Secretary for the exercise of the Prerogative of Mercy, and the officers who scrutinize these numerous applications must always remember that any one of them may prove to be a case in which it is the Home Secretary's duty to right a wrong or mitigate a hardship.

7. REFERENCES TO THE COURT OF CRIMINAL APPEAL

It has been explained that the Home Secretary frequently consults the Judge or magistrates concerned before recommending the exercise of the Prerogative, but there are some cases where consultation is not enough, and where the point at issue should be settled by the courts, particularly when the decision whether the original finding of the courts should be varied depends on evaluating some new evidence which has come to light.

The Criminal Appeal Act, 1907, took account of this difficulty. Whilst providing that nothing in the Act was to affect the Prerogative of Mercy, it gave power to the Home Secretary to refer a case to the Court of Criminal Appeal with a view to its being heard and determined by the court as in the case of an appeal by a convicted person, and also power to refer to the court any point on which the Home Secretary desired its assistance with a view to determining a petition that had been submitted to him. The Home Secretary can exercise these powers even if the person concerned has previously appealed to the Court of Criminal Appeal. During the four years 1950-1953 nine cases were referred to the Court of Criminal Appeal under the first of these powers. In three of the cases the conviction was affirmed without variation of the sentence; in two cases the conviction was quashed; and in the remaining four cases the conviction was affirmed but the sentence varied.

8. PAYMENT OF COMPENSATION

When a Free Pardon is granted, or when a conviction is quashed on a reference by the Home Secretary to the Court of Criminal Appeal, the question arises whether any *ex gratia* payment should be made to the person concerned. Not every case justifies the payment of compensation out of public funds, but in some cases, particularly where the person concerned has served a sentence of imprisonment, a sum of money may be paid as compensation. It is not supposed that a sum of money can make full reparation for the hardship caused by a miscarriage of justice, but the principle underlying such a payment is that the State should show its willingness to make reasonable reparation and so far as possible to square its account with the person wronged.

9. LIMITATIONS OF THE PREROGATIVE

The power of the Queen to pardon extends only to crimes, not to civil cases, so that for example the Prerogative is not regarded as applying to a committal to prison for an indefinite term for contempt of court or to imprisonment for non-payment of rates or arrears due under a wife maintenance or affiliation order. Nor is the Prerogative held to apply to an order of court such as a disqualification for holding a driving licence, although if the conviction itself is expunged by the grant of a Free Pardon the disqualification is thereby also expunged.

10. ANALOGOUS AND ADDITIONAL POWERS

The Home Secretary has certain statutory powers somewhat akin to his responsibilities for the exercise of the Prerogative. He may for instance require the Prison Commissioners to release on licence at any time a person serving a sentence of corrective training or preventive detention. He can direct the release at any time of a person undergoing Borstal training: and the effect of the Prison Rules is that only the Home Secretary (and not the visiting committee or the board of visitors) can restore to a prisoner remission of his sentence which he has lost for a disciplinary offence in prison.

An activity of the Home Office which is sometimes confused by the public with the exercise of the Prerogative is that of enquiry into cases where it appears that a person may be detained in custody without proper authority. A prison Governor may submit to the Home Office for examination a warrant or order of court which he thinks may be of doubtful validity, or a court may discover after the trial that it acted in excess of jurisdiction. If the Home Secretary is satisfied, usually after consultation with the court concerned, that a warrant or order does not provide good authority for a person's detention, he will order the person's discharge from custody. This action is taken irrespective of whether on the merits of the case the person deserves his punishment or not.

CHAPTER XII

The Administration of Justice

General scope of the Home Secretary's responsibilities — The criminal law — The criminal courts — Powers in individual cases — Broadmoor patients and mental defectives — Extradition, fugitive offenders and letters of request — Prosecutions — Coroners — Criminal statistics — Research — Home Office not a Ministry of Justice.

*

1. GENERAL SCOPE OF THE HOME SECRETARY'S RESPONSIBILITIES

THE Home Office acquires, in the course of its day-to-day examinations of cases in which application is made for the exercise of the Prerogative of Mercy or in which advice is sought by a court, a good deal of information about the procedure in criminal courts and the working of the criminal law; and it becomes aware of defects that can be removed only by legislation. The Home Secretary, moreover, has statutory powers to deal with certain types of individual cases that come to his attention (some of these have been described in the preceding chapter, and others are described below); and he is the Minister primarily concerned with the treatment of offenders after they have been found guilty by the courts. He has available to him a good deal of expert advice, apart from that which he receives from his own officials. He keeps in close touch with the courts—the Chief Magistrate at Bow Street is traditionally an adviser of the Home Office on matters of summary jurisdiction, and, especially in recent years, the Home Secretary often consults, and receives much assistance from, the Lord Chief Justice and other Judges. Since 1944 he has had the advice of the Advisory Council on the Treatment of Offenders, a body which, under the Chairmanship of a Judge or a Chairman of Quarter Sessions, includes members bringing practical experience from many fields, and both tenders advice on questions referred to it by the Home Secretary (some of which may impinge on aspects of Home Office administration referred to in other chapters) and also makes proposals on its own initiative.

The Home Office is thus brought into touch with many aspects of the administration of justice, itself accumulates knowledge, and constantly verifies and supplements this by seeking counsel of those intimately concerned with its day-to-day working; and it falls to the Home Secretary to promote new legislation affecting the form and content of the criminal law, and legislation affecting the functioning and procedure of the criminal courts themselves. These subjects overlap to some extent, but an attempt will be made to give some indication, first, of the nature of the Home Secretary's responsibilities in relation to the criminal law, secondly, of his responsibilities in relation to the criminal courts, and thirdly, of some of his statutory powers in dealing with particular offenders. Other duties of the Home Secretary which touch upon the administration of justice, but which are not particularly relevant to these three main heads, are described later in the chapter.

2. THE CRIMINAL LAW

The Home Secretary has a general concern for the form and content of the criminal law. It is for him to consider its adequacy in relation to the incidence of crime generally, and of particular offences. From time to time he has also to consider the suitability of penalties for offences which may arise either from legislation with which he himself is concerned, or for which other Ministers take prime responsibility. (He was, for example, responsible for the Bill passed in 1948 to increase the penalty for the offence of attempted rape.) He was also responsible for the provisions in the Criminal Justice Act, 1948, which widened and made more flexible the powers of the courts in dealing with offenders by making better provision for the courts to have information about the persons appearing before them, and by giving them new methods of dealing with offenders.

It is part of the Home Secretary's general duty to watch that the penalty provisions included in legislation promoted by other Departments are not out of keeping with those in existing statutes, and that they are reasonable in themselves. The creation of new criminal offences and penalties may sometimes have unexpected consequences, and the Home Office is constantly on its guard to foresee and prevent them. The experience of a senior official of the Home Office illustrates the need for such caution. He was, he records, 'surprised to find a coster in prison, whose committal warrant showed that he "contrary to the peace of our Lord the King, his laws and ordinances had from a barrow containing old clothes, disposed of a toy, to wit a ballon"'. He goes on:

> 'I was interested to discover which of His Majesty's laws and ordinances the man had broken. It proved to be a provision in the Public

Health Act of 1925 that a dealer in rags must not have rags and toys on the same barrow. The provision has since been repealed, but no doubt the object was to prevent infection spreading to children. I could not help wondering whether those who were responsible for that provision in the Public Health Act had ever thought that it might one day lead to someone being put in prison.'

The Home Office is concerned in such matters, not only because individuals may suffer unreasonably, but because punishments for acts which are not clearly defined and are not condemned by public opinion discredit the law and in so doing may adversely affect the maintenance of law and order in this country. The question must often be asked, whether the practical benefits achieved by prohibition will be valuable enough to justify the penalties imposed by that prohibition.

The provisions of the Criminal Justice Act referred to above bring out clearly the close relation between the Home Secretary's responsibilities in relation to the criminal law and his cognate responsibilities in relation to the procedure in the criminal courts, and incidentally underline the difficulty of attempting to distinguish between the two. For the law can be administered well only if the machinery for its administration works effectively; so that when (for example) the Act authorized new types of sentence for persistent offenders[1] it introduced at the same time new procedures to give the courts better opportunities for considering the suitability of an offender for a particular type of sentence.

3. THE CRIMINAL COURTS

Other provisions in the Criminal Justice Act, 1948, for which the Home Secretary was responsible removed a whole variety of anomalies and difficulties which had been met with in court procedure. Three examples out of a considerable number of such changes are that the Act abolished the privilege of the peers to be tried for their felonies by their own order in Parliament or by the court of the Lord High Steward; enabled Quarter Sessions to extend the limit of fourteen days for making an appeal against the decision of a magistrates' court; and gave power to the superior courts to impose a fine on a person convicted of felony.

Another example of the Home Secretary's responsibilities in this field occurred during the last war, when he was the Minister primarily concerned with the code of Defence Regulations which made

[1] The nature of these sentences, corrective training and preventive detention, is described in Chapter XIV.

provision for the 'war zone courts' which were to function in an emergency in which ordinary communications were not possible. At that time too he was much concerned with the legislation affecting the jurisdiction which our Allies exercised over their forces in this country[1] and enabling the exiled Governments to set up maritime courts here to deal with offences by members of their merchant navies.[2]

But it is with magistrates' courts that the Home Secretary is in practice principally concerned. During 1952 the Home Office was primarily responsible for the work on a Bill[3] consolidating the various enactments relating to their functioning. It is for the Lord Chancellor to make Rules dealing with certain aspects of procedure, but the Home Office takes an active part in the preparation of these Rules and is represented on the Rule Committee which advises the Lord Chancellor.

The Justices of the Peace Act, 1949, made important changes in the functioning of magistrates' courts; it not only confirmed certain powers previously exercised by the Home Secretary (such as that of confirming the appointment of a clerk to the justices) but added very considerably to his duties.[4]

The Act makes provision for the setting up of Magistrates' Courts Committees in each county and county borough and in certain non-county boroughs, or in areas combining different counties or boroughs, and gives to these Committees responsibility for justices' clerks in their area, for the division of counties into petty sessional divisions, for the instruction of Justices, and for other administrative duties which the Home Secretary may authorize them to undertake. Any proposals for the alteration of county petty sessional divisions

[1] The Home Secretary was the Minister responsible for introducing into Parliament the Visiting Forces Act, 1952, which repeals earlier legislation relating to visiting forces in this country, and extends to visiting forces from the Commonwealth and all other countries to which the Act is applied.

[2] The Allied Powers (Maritime Courts) Act, 1941.

[3] The Magistrates' Courts Act, 1952.

[4] The Act also transferred to the Lord Chancellor some responsibilities previously exercised by the Home Secretary, notably the appointment of Recorders and Stipendiary Magistrates (although the Home Secretary was left with certain responsibilities for Stipendiaries, for example the fixing of their salaries); and the responsibility which it put on the Lord Chancellor of making Rules regulating the procedure and practice to be followed in magistrates' courts and by justices' clerks, ended the somewhat anomalous situation whereby the Lord Chancellor formerly made most of the Summary Jurisdiction Rules but the Home Secretary had certain related powers, for example that of prescribing the forms to be used in affiliation proceedings.

require the approval of the Home Secretary and he can himself direct a Magistrates' Courts Committee to undertake a review of the divisions. His approval is also required for the appointment of any clerk to justices or for any change in the number of justices' clerks in a petty sessions area. If there is a dispute between the Magistrates' Courts Committee and the county or borough council as to the salary of a clerk to justices, that dispute may be determined by the Home Secretary on appeal.

The Magistrates' Courts Committees have only recently been set up, and it is too early to say what effect they are likely to have on the administration of the courts. It is clear from what has been said, however, that the Home Secretary will be the Minister primarily concerned with their activities.

The Act also makes a fundamental change in the financial arrangements for maintaining magistrates' courts. Hitherto, the fines and fees received by magistrates' courts have been appropriated by statute in a variety of ways. It is only those fines not otherwise appropriated (together with the court fees) which have gone to the local authorities, but they have been entirely responsible for maintaining the courts and paying the staff, without any direct subvention from the Exchequer. The books of the courts have been subject to examination by representatives of the Home Office so far as fines payable to the Exchequer are concerned. Under the provisions of the new Act, however, the fees and almost all the fines (excepting the sums which were already payable into the Exchequer, such as fines for road traffic offences) are paid into a central pool, and this pool is shared by the Home Secretary between the authorities who maintain the courts and pay the clerks. If the amount for distribution is less than the cost which these authorities have incurred, as it is likely to be, the Home Secretary may, with Treasury agreement, pay up to two-thirds of the deficiency. This pooling of most of the receipts, and the provision of some form of Exchequer grant, for the first time implies some central responsibility for magistrates' courts. The Home Secretary will obviously be careful not to use these new powers to interfere with the exercise by individual courts of their judicial functions. It remains to be seen how far they will come to be used by him in exercising control over the administration of the courts, for example by urging a particular authority to replace an unsuitable court building.

The Home Secretary is also primarily responsible for legislation affecting the civil functions of the magistrates' courts, such as proceedings in relation to wife maintenance and affiliation.

As a natural consequence of the Home Secretary's responsibilities in relation to the criminal courts it has for long been the practice for him to issue circular letters, particularly to magistrates' courts, supplying them with information about their work, for instance about new legislation.[1]

4. POWERS IN INDIVIDUAL CASES

The foregoing discussion of the Home Secretary's concern with the administration of justice has been limited to outlining his responsibilities in relation to the criminal law and the functioning of the courts. In these matters the Home Secretary does not deal with the men and women who come before the courts, nor with the dispensation of justice in particular cases: it is with the machinery of its dispensation that he is principally concerned, and he is careful not to interfere with a case that is *sub judice.*

It was explained in Chapter XI, however, that the Home Office is concerned with particular offenders every time it receives a petition for the exercise of the Prerogative of Mercy, and that patient and protracted enquiries are often made into the merits of such cases. There are in addition other classes of individual case that engage the attention of the Home Office—not because the offenders concerned apply for exercise of the Prerogative of Mercy on their behalf, but because Parliament has conferred on the Home Secretary certain statutory powers for dealing with them. Two such classes were mentioned in the preceding chapter—involving cases arising

[1] These responsibilities cover a wide field, and the examples given in the text are no more than illustrations. Other examples are that grants of separate courts of quarter sessions to boroughs are made by Order in Council on the Home Secretary's advice. He is responsible for making regulations under the Costs in Criminal Cases Act, 1952, and under similar powers made the Witnesses' Allowance Regulations, 1948, prescribing the allowances which may be made to witnesses in indictable cases. He is responsible for making regulations under the Criminal Appeal Act, 1907, about the rates and scales of payment of appellants' legal advisers and to witnesses. He and the Lord Chancellor approve the Rules made by the Attorney General about legal aid to poor persons in criminal cases. The Legal Aid and Advice Act, 1949 (in sections not yet in operation) contemplates arrangements under which the Home Secretary will refund to local authorities the costs of legal aid in criminal cases. The Juries Act, 1949, gave power to the Home Secretary to make regulations for the payment to jurors of travelling and subsistence allowances and compensation for loss of earnings. Under the Maintenance Orders (Facilities for Enforcement) Act, 1920, the Home Secretary is the central authority for transmitting documents between the English and the oversea courts for the purpose of making and enforcing wife maintenance orders in cases where one spouse is in this country and the other is in a different part of the Commonwealth.

out of the Home Secretary's statutory powers to release on licence persons serving sentences of life imprisonment, and his powers to release certain prisoners and Borstal inmates on licence and to restore lost remission. Another class comprises a variety of cases arising out of the Home Secretary's powers under the Prison Act, 1952,[1] in particular to commute to imprisonment the unexpired part of a Borstal sentence if the inmate is reported by the Board of Visitors of his institution to be incorrigible or to be exercising a bad influence on other inmates; to authorize (after consultation with the court concerned) the transfer to Borstal of a person under 21 sentenced to imprisonment; or to transfer a prisoner or Borstal inmate to a prison or Borstal in Scotland. Every such case is considered carefully on its merits. Another large class comprises the irresponsible offenders, insane or mentally defective, who drift through the courts and whose subsequent disposal sometimes presents grave problems to the Home Office; and the Home Office deals with yet another class of individual case arising out of its concern with extradition proceedings. Some of the problems concerning these last two classes are discussed in the following paragraphs.

5. BROADMOOR PATIENTS AND MENTAL DEFECTIVES

Reference has already been made in Chapter XI to persons charged with murder who are found by the jury to be insane on arraignment and unfit to plead, or guilty but insane. In both classes of case (whether or not the charge is a capital one) the court orders the individual's detention during Her Majesty's Pleasure. Such persons were formerly known as criminal lunatics, but the Criminal Justice Act, 1948, changed their name to 'Broadmoor patients'.

Those who are certified as insane after being sentenced to death also become Broadmoor patients. Like the two classes of 'Queen's Pleasure' patients referred to in the last paragraph, they are liable to detention for an indefinite period.

Another class of Broadmoor patients consists of the prisoners, or Borstal inmates, who are certified insane during the currency of their sentences. The Home Secretary is empowered to order their removal to a mental hospital. Their liability to be detained there as Broadmoor patients remains until the sentence expires.

Broadmoor patients who are dangerous or violent, or have been charged with serious crimes, are normally moved by the Home Secretary's order to Broadmoor Institution at Crowthorne, Berk-

[1] These powers were formerly exercised under the Criminal Justice Act, 1948.

shire. He orders the removal of the others to the appropriate local mental hospital.

A prisoner or Borstal inmate who has become a Broadmoor patient can be returned to prison or Borstal to complete his sentence if he is certified as sane. More difficult questions arise over the discharge of Broadmoor patients liable to detention for an indefinite period. Broadmoor Institution is administered by the Board of Control, and other mental hospitals are administered by Hospital Management Committees under the Regional Hospital Boards, but the decision whether a Broadmoor patient may properly be discharged is the responsibility of the Home Secretary.

This is a weighty responsibility. Discharge in the case of those concerned in the more serious offences is normally conditional in the first instance, and is to the care of a friend or relative who undertakes responsibility for the patient. The Home Secretary will authorize discharge in such cases only if, after taking medical advice and making enquiries into home surroundings, he considers that there is a reasonable likelihood of the patient's settling down in conditions in the outside world without serious risk of a further breakdown. The period for which those who are discharged have been detained must inevitably vary widely. Where a Broadmoor patient was before the courts on a very serious charge, the Home Secretary will not normally feel that he can authorize discharge until there has been a substantial period of observation. Some patients unfortunately can never be regarded as fit for discharge, but every case is periodically examined to see whether discharge, or transfer to another hospital, can properly be considered.

The number of cases involved may be illustrated by the figures for 1952. During that year, 63 persons were received at Broadmoor Institution and 121 Broadmoor patients (most of whom had been certified after conviction) were received at local mental hospitals. At the end of 1952, 1,013 Broadmoor patients were detained, 897 of them at Broadmoor Institution. Of this total of 1,013, 597 had been detained over five years, including 224 who had been detained for over 20 years.

Some prisoners and Borstal inmates may be found, after conviction, to be certifiable as mental defectives and may be removed by order of the Home Secretary to an institution for mental defectives. The arrangements are made in consultation with the Board of Control. A person who has been removed by the Home Secretary's order to an institution for mental defectives cannot without the Home Secretary's consent be discharged during the time for which he would have been liable to be detained in prison or Borstal. If for instance a murderer serving a life sentence is removed to the State Hospital for mental defectives at Rampton, he cannot be discharged from Rampton without the Home Secretary's agreement.

6. EXTRADITION, FUGITIVE OFFENDERS, AND LETTERS OF REQUEST

The Home Secretary is concerned in all extradition proceedings, whether for the surrender to a foreign country of a criminal who has sought refuge in this country or for the recovery of a criminal who has escaped to another country from the jurisdiction of the British courts, and he is much concerned with the negotiation of any new extradition treaty with a foreign Power.

If the Government of a foreign Power with which we have an extradition treaty desires the surrender of a criminal for an offence covered by the treaty, one of two courses may be followed. A diplomatic request for extradition may be made to the Foreign Office, accompanied by the evidence on which the criminal charge is based. These documents are forwarded to the Home Secretary. If the documents appear to be adequate and correct, he sends an order to the Chief Magistrate at Bow Street to issue a warrant, if satisfied that the conditions of the Extradition Acts are complied with, for the arrest of the fugitive. Alternatively, if the case is urgent, the preliminary proceedings for the issue of a warrant by the Chief Magistrate may be taken on sworn information supplied to him by the police or judicial authorities of the foreign country, but further progress must await the Home Secretary's order to proceed when the diplomatic application and the evidence are received.

The Chief Magistrate hears the case against the offender in the same way as that of a person charged with an indictable offence committed in England, except that written evidence is accepted. If he is satisfied that there is a *prima facie* case he commits the accused to custody to await his surrender, and after fifteen days, or after the result of any application made to the High Court for a writ of *habeas corpus*, the Home Secretary may issue a warrant of surrender.

The Extradition Acts provide that a criminal is not to be surrendered for a political offence, and this point is always carefully watched by the courts and the Home Secretary.

Any application for the arrest and return of a fugitive wanted for an offence here who has escaped to a foreign country must be made through the Home Office. An application for surrender can be made only if there is an extradition treaty with the country concerned and the offence is one covered by the treaty. If the case is urgent, the Home Office prepare instructions which the Foreign Office cable to the British representative in the country in question to obtain provisional arrest. Whether or not there is an application for provisional arrest, the evidence in support of the request for extradition must be submitted to the Home Office, and when the Home Secretary is satisfied that it is in proper order he asks the Foreign Secretary to make a formal application for surrender. It is not always easy to ensure that adequate evidence is supplied and drawn up in a form which meets the requirements of foreign law.

The Fugitive Offenders Act, 1881, provides a rather simpler procedure for the surrender of fugitive criminals from this country who may be in one of the Commonwealth countries or in the Colonies, or for the arrest and return of a fugitive offender from one of those countries who may be in Great Britain.

The Extradition Act, 1873, includes provision for taking evidence in this country for the purposes of criminal proceedings in other countries. If a criminal court in France for instance wishes to have evidence from a person living in this country, a letter of request may be forwarded through diplomatic channels and (provided that the case is not of a political character) the Home Secretary sends this letter to the appropriate magistrates' court with an order for the taking of evidence by the magistrates. This evidence, when duly certified, is acceptable in the French court. This power is frequently exercised. No reciprocal arrangements are in force, since written evidence taken abroad in such circumstances is not acceptable in our courts.

7. PROSECUTIONS

Closely though the Home Secretary is concerned with the administration of justice, the treatment of offenders convicted by the courts, and the merits of individual cases brought to his notice, he has no significant concern with prosecutions. This has not always been so. In the past he had certain powers of directing prosecutions and some traces of these powers are still left on the statute book. For instance, the Indictable Offences Act, 1848,[1] provides that a person charged with treason may not be admitted to bail except by order of a Judge of the High Court or the Home Secretary, which is presumably a survival from the days when the Home Secretary could order arrest and committal to prison for treason; and under the Territorial Waters Jurisdiction Act, 1878, the prosecution of an alien for an offence committed on a foreign ship cannot be instituted except under the Home Secretary's

[1] Now repealed and re-enacted in the Magistrates' Courts Act, 1952.

authority. But now, although there is close liaison between the Director of Public Prosecutions and the Home Office on criminal matters, the Home Secretary is not responsible for the work of, and does not give instructions to, the Director.

The Home Secretary is responsible for appointing the Director of Public Prosecutions and the Assistant Directors, and the Director makes an annual return of his prosecutions to the Home Secretary for submission to Parliament; but the Director acts in his day-to-day work under the general superintendence and direction of the Attorney General, and it is the Attorney General who makes regulations (which have to be approved by the Home Secretary and the Lord Chancellor) regulating his duties. It is in the changing content of these regulations that the significant alteration in the relation between the Home Secretary and the Director, mentioned in the last paragraph, is to be found. The regulations which were made in 1886 under the Prosecution of Offences Acts provided that among the cases in which it was to be the duty of the Director of Public Prosecutions to prosecute were cases 'where an order in that behalf is given to the Director by the Secretary of State. . . .' When the regulations were repealed and replaced by a new set of regulations in 1946, this particular provision was not repeated. Nowadays it is well recognized and has frequently been stated in Parliament that the Home Office is not a prosecuting authority.

8. CORONERS

Coroners are independent judicial officers, but the Home Secretary has some responsibility for certain aspects of their work, and he is the Minister primarily responsible for any legislation affecting them.

Coroners are appointed by county and certain borough councils and no confirmation of their appointment is needed from any Minister, although notice that the appointment has been made must be given to the Home Secretary. The Lord Chancellor (or in the County of Lancaster the Chancellor of the Duchy) has power to remove any coroner from his office for inability or misbehaviour in the discharge of his duty, and if circumstances should arise requiring him to consider whether to exercise this power, those circumstances would ordinarily be brought to his notice by the Home Office. The Lord Chancellor has power to make rules regulating the procedure at inquests and post-mortem examinations, but such rules require the concurrence of the Home Secretary. The Home Secretary is responsible for fixing the salaries of coroners in case of disagreement between a coroner and the local authority.

Coroners are required to make to him statistical returns of their inquests and verdicts. Alterations in county coroners' districts require his approval and he can direct that the number of county coroners shall be increased if changes in the districts seem to him to call for an increase. An inquest can be held only by direction of the Home Secretary in those cases where a body has been destroyed or for some other reason no body can be found.

It has long been accepted that it is for the Home Secretary to issue general guidance or information to coroners by means of circular letters, for example about the effect of new legislation, and coroners often ask the Home Office for advice on questions of law or procedure.

9. CRIMINAL STATISTICS

The Home Secretary lays before Parliament each year a volume giving the criminal statistics for England and Wales. The statistics include a return of offences furnished by the police, detailed particulars of the proceedings before the various criminal courts, the return submitted to the Home Secretary by the Director of Public Prosecutions, and statistics of extradition cases, Broadmoor patients, cases in which the Prerogative of Mercy has been exercised, and cases in which legal aid has been given.

10. RESEARCH

The Criminal Justice Act, 1948, gave power to the Home Secretary to meet the cost of research into the causes of delinquency and the treatment of offenders. In present financial difficulties, it has so far been possible to make only a very modest use of these powers, but a few useful enquiries have already been initiated and in addition certain facilities have been provided for research financed from sources other than public funds. Much remains unknown about delinquents and delinquency; and this provision in the Criminal Justice Act at any rate indicates that it is recognized that research, as well as day-to-day practical experience, may throw light on the causes of crime and the best ways of dealing with offenders.

11. THE HOME OFFICE NOT A MINISTRY OF JUSTICE

It will be seen from the foregoing that the functions of the Home Secretary fall far short of those of a 'Minister of Justice'. This chapter has outlined the more important of the Home Secretary's various and extensive responsibilities for the administration of justice, but it would be as well, in conclusion, to recapitulate some of the things which he cannot or should not do. The Home Secretary has no significant responsibility for prosecutions in individual cases. He does not now appoint, or dismiss, any of those who hold judicial office. He would never attempt to interfere in a case which was *sub judice*. He would forfeit the confidence of the judiciary, and ultimately the public, if he exercised his functions in regard to the Prerogative of Mercy in an arbitrary or capricious way and without adequate consultation with the courts. He is often asked to urge magistrates to impose heavier penalties for some particular type of offence which happens to have attracted public attention; but he declines to act on such requests, since in matters in which the courts exercise an independent judicial discretion they should not be called upon to accept the views of a Minister as to what kind of offences are specially culpable.

CHAPTER XIII

The Probation Service

Purpose and use of probation — Home Office as central authority — Local organization — Probation officers and probation training — Probation officers' other duties.

*

1. THE PURPOSE AND USE OF PROBATION

INSTITUTIONAL forms of penal treatment work on the principle that to rehabilitate an offender it is first necessary to isolate him from his normal community. The probation system seeks to effect rehabilitation of an offender while he remains in the community at his normal work or at school.

A probation order requires the probationer to be under the supervision of a probation officer whose duty, in the words first used in the Probation of Offenders Act, 1907, is to 'advise, assist and befriend him'. The period of probation lasts for from one to three years as may be specified by the court order. The court usually inserts one or more additional requirements of a general nature intended to help the probationer; in particular it is usual to require him to receive visits from the probation officer at home and to call at the probation office from time to time as the probation officer may direct. Sometimes, too, there are special requirements to meet special circumstances; for instance that the probationer should reside in a place named by the court, or receive special treatment for his mental condition.

To succeed, the system requires the offender's co-operation, for unless a good personal relationship can be established between the probationer and the probation officer, effective supervision never becomes possible and the probationer cannot be helped to help himself. The law recognizes this in providing that a probation order cannot be made in respect of an offender who has reached the age of fourteen unless he expresses his willingness to comply with all the requirements of the order.

Some form of sanction is required against probationers who fail to comply with the terms of a probation order. Such a person may be brought before a court and either fined not more than £10 or, if between the ages of twelve and twenty-one years, be required to attend at an attendance centre (if one is available), the probation order continuing in force; or he may be dealt with for the offence for which he was placed on probation as though he had just been found guilty of it, in which case the order is terminated. A probationer who commits a further offence during the currency of the order may then be dealt with for the original offence at the same time.

The object of including in a probation order a requirement that a probationer must reside in a place named by the court is to enable the court to remove him from the influence of an unsuitable home or undesirable companions by placing him, for example, with relatives or in lodgings where he will receive friendship and guidance within a family. Sometimes too, where the offender has lost or never acquired the habit of steady work, it is useful to give him a short period of training and discipline in an institution. Accordingly the Home Secretary has power to approve hostels from which the residents go out to work daily, and homes in which training is given on the premises. Thirty-one hostels and eleven homes are approved for boys and girls who have reached school leaving age and are under the age of twenty-one. They are run by voluntary bodies, and, since 1949, have been financed mainly out of public funds.

At the end of 1952 there were 47,746 persons on probation, of whom 28,166 were under the age of seventeen. It is sometimes said that courts use probation too freely, especially for children and young persons: on the other hand, there is little doubt that some older offenders who are now sent to prison might well be placed on probation, and that some of those who are discharged conditionally (that is, subject to the condition that they commit no offence during a period not exceeding twelve months) could benefit, both in observing this condition and in their adjustment to society, by being under the supervision of a probation officer. The marked variation in the use made of probation by different courts indicates that there may well be room for a greater use of probation throughout the country, and for a more discriminating use.

2. THE HOME OFFICE AS CENTRAL AUTHORITY

The cost of the probation service, like that of the police, and the child care service of local authorities under the Children Act and of approved schools and remand homes, is shared equally by the local authorities and the Exchequer; and it follows that the Home Secretary, as the Minister responsible for the administration of the law relating to the probation of offenders, is responsible also for the efficient working of the service. To this end he appoints inspectors to help with the training of probation officers, to examine their work and advise them, and to review and report upon the efficiency of the local services. Like the Inspectors of Constabulary, the Fire Service Inspectorate and the Children's Department Inspectors, they provide a two-way channel of information between the Home Office and the local service, on the one hand guiding probation officers and the local probation authorities in the performance of their duties, and on the other advising the Home Office of defects in the system which local experience may have brought to light.

The Home Secretary makes rules under the Criminal Justice Act, 1948, regulating the constitution, duties and expenditure of local probation authorities, and prescribing the duties and conditions of service of probation officers. Until 1950, conditions of service were settled by the Home Office; in that year a Joint Negotiating Committee was set up, composed of representatives of the local authorities associations, the Magistrates' Association and the Home Secretary (as probation authority for the Metropolitan Magistrates' Courts area) on the employers' side, and the National Association of Probation Officers on the staff side, to consider questions relating to pay and conditions of service.

The Home Secretary's Advisory Council on the Treatment of Offenders was mentioned in the last chapter. Its work is supplemented, in the special field of probation, by the Probation Advisory and Training Board. This was set up by the Home Secretary in 1949 to replace the Probation Advisory Committee and the Probation Training Board, which were first appointed in 1922 and 1937 respectively. As its name implies, the Board has two functions: to advise on questions relating to the administration of the probation service and on training facilities, including the selection of men and women for training. The Board includes among its members justices, clerks of the courts, probation officers, representatives of the universities, and officers of the Home Office.

The potential value of research in throwing light on the causes of crime and on the best way of dealing with offenders has already been stressed; and it has been recognized for some time that more information is needed about the way in which those who have been on probation fare afterwards. As a pilot project, special records were kept, for the three years following termination of probation, of the progress of persons in the counties of London and Middlesex whose orders came to an end in the years 1948, 1949 and 1950. At the time of writing these records were being analyzed by the Cambridge University Department of Criminal Science.

People abroad are keenly interested in the probation system as developed in this country; this results in a steady demand for information and advice in planning similar services, not only from the Commonwealth and the Colonies, but also from foreign countries. Probation Inspectors have visited Germany since the war, and the Home Office has arranged programmes for German judges, administrators and social workers to enable them to study the working of the probation service in this country with a view to planning a service in Germany. Programmes are arranged to suit the particular needs of many other persons from abroad. In 1951, the New Zealand Government appointed one of the Home Office probation inspectors to organize their probation service.

In October, 1952, the United Kingdom Government, at the request of the United Nations, was host to a European seminar on probation held in London. This seminar, the first in Great Britain to be sponsored by the United Nations, made a special study of the probation system as it has been developed in this country during the past forty years and considered its application to European continental countries.

3. LOCAL ORGANIZATION

The statutory unit of the probation service is the petty sessional division, of which there are about 1,000 in England and Wales. The Criminal Justice Act, 1925 (now superseded by the Criminal Justice Act, 1948) empowered the Home Secretary to combine any two or more petty sessional divisions to form one probation area; this power was used extensively, and it is generally recognized that, outside the county boroughs, the successful development of the service is due in large measure to the formation of combined probation areas of suitable size, consisting for the most part of administrative counties and in some instances of county boroughs as well. At the end of 1953 there were 121 probation areas in England and Wales.

The local probation authority is a probation committee appointed from among their number by the justices in the probation area. The committee is responsible for the administration of the service, including the appointment and general supervision of the work of the probation officers. In a petty sessional division which is a self-contained probation area, the probation committee acts also as a case committee to supervise the work of the officers. In combined areas, the justices for each petty sessional division appoint a case committee from among their number. In forty-two of the larger areas, there are principal probation officers responsible for the general organization and supervision of the service and for advising on technical matters. In the Metropolitan Magistrates' Courts area the probation authority is the Home Secretary, who appoints an advisory committee of Metropolitan Magistrates and London Juvenile Court Justices.

4. PROBATION OFFICERS AND PROBATION TRAINING

Now a public service staffed by salaried officers, probation began, like so many other social services in this country, by voluntary effort. The forerunners of the probation officers (the first of whom were appointed under the Probation of Offenders Act, 1907) were the police court missionaries who made a place for themselves in the courts as agents of voluntary societies and, without official status, showed what could be achieved by personal influence exercised over offenders at large in the community.

Every probation committee is now required to appoint a sufficient number of officers, and to make at least one man and one woman officer available at each court, including any superior court, in its area. In practice several officers work at each court in the large centres of population, while in the rural areas an officer often serves two or more courts. The extent of the recent development of the probation service in England and Wales can best be measured by the fact that in 1938 there were about 400 whole-time and 600 part-time probation officers; in 1954 the numbers had changed to 1,191 whole-time and 75 part-time officers. 144 of the whole-time officers work in the Metropolitan Magistrates' Courts area, serving the Central Criminal Court and London Sessions as well as the magistrates' courts. About one-third of the officers are women.

The probation service requires men and women with a sound education, good intelligence, a genuine interest in personal case work, and the character and personality to exercise the right influence on probationers and others they are called upon to help, and to withstand the difficulties and disappointments inevitable in this form of social work. In addition, careful training for probation work is necessary. The need for the careful selection and training of recruits was first met by a training scheme, started in a small way in 1930. Now the Home Office training scheme, administered by the Probation Division with the advice and help of the Probation Advisory and Training Board, offers the normal method of entry to the service; and about seventy students complete their training each year, providing trained men and women to fill most of the vacancies. Students receive training free of cost, and are paid to enable them to keep themselves during training. Those under thirty years of age commonly follow a whole-time course of study at a university for a diploma in social science, and then do practical work under experienced probation officers. For older students, a course of practical training is arranged. All students attend a course of specialized lectures at a residential centre provided and managed by the London Police Court Mission. Colonial and foreign students are admitted to the training course, and prove a stimulating and helpful element. Refresher courses and courses on special subjects for serving officers are also provided.

5. PROBATION OFFICERS' OTHER DUTIES

The supervision of offenders is the probation officer's primary duty but is not his only function.

A boy or girl under seventeen who is found by a court to be in need of care or protection or beyond control, or a school child who fails to attend school regularly, may be placed under the supervision of a probation officer by means of a supervision order. The conditions and methods of supervision are similar to those under a probation order. At the end of 1952, 3,792 boys and girls were subject to supervision orders.

A great deal of time is occupied in making inquiries into the circumstances and home surroundings of people to help the court to decide how best to deal with them. A probation officer has also a duty to undertake the after-care supervision of boys and girls released from approved schools, if he is asked to do so by the school managers; and a duty to supervise young people released from Borstal institutions and detention centres and certain classes of persons who have been in prison. On the direction of the court, he supervises offenders, particularly those under the age of twenty-one, who have been ordered to pay fines; this arrangement is intended to encourage regular payments and so to avoid the risk of imprisonment for those who fail to pay.

The probation officer's duties range over all the social services of the magistrates' courts. He acts as a conciliator between husbands and wives who bring their matrimonial difficulties to the court. In proceedings involving maintenance payments he investigates the means of the parties to enable the court to fix equitable amounts, and he makes enquiries to help the court in deciding such grave matters as the custody and sometimes the adoption of children.

In 1950, the Home Office, at the request of the Lord Chancellor's Office, arranged for a probation officer, when so required by the High Court, to inquire into the circumstances and home surroundings of children who were the subject of applications for custody or access.

CHAPTER XIV

The Prison Commission

The Prison Commissioners — Functions of a prison — Imprisonment as a legal punishment — Prison development before the Criminal Justice Act, 1948 — Imprisonment today — Persistent offenders — Treatment of young offenders — Administration and staff — Visiting committees and boards of visitors.

*

1. THE PRISON COMMISSIONERS

THE responsibility of the Home Secretary in the field of prevention of crime and treatment of offenders extends, under various statutory powers, to the prison system and to Borstals and certain other institutions designed to replace the prison in the treatment of young offenders. The administration of prisons and related institutions is vested by statute in the Home Secretary, who exercises this responsibility through Prison Commissioners. The Prison Commission forms a separate department of the Home Office.

The organization of this department and the way it carries out its work will be described when the nature of the work has been explained, but it will be convenient to say briefly at the outset how it fits into the general framework of Home Office and Civil Service organization.

The Prison Commissioners are responsible to the Home Secretary through their Chairman for the formulation and application of policy relating to the establishments under their control, and for their inspection and administration. They work in close co-operation with other departments of the Home Office whose interests lie in the same field, e.g. the Children's Department, the Probation Division, and the Criminal Division, and they rely on the Legal and Statistical Advisers, the Chief Medical Officer and the Public Relations Officer, of the Home Office, and on the Senior Chief Inspector of the Ministry of Education, for advice and help where necessary. With the Treasury and other Government Departments they conduct their business direct and the Chairman as Accounting Officer answers to the Public Accounts Committee for the Prisons Vote, which is distinct from the Home Office Vote.

The Home Secretary may also consult the Advisory Council on the Treatment of Offenders on matters within the field of the Commissioners.

In 1953, the Prison Commissioners were responsible for 47 prisons, 21 Borstal Institutions, and one institution for young offenders of a new type known as detention centres.

2. THE FUNCTIONS OF A PRISON

A prison today serves three purposes, which may be described as custodial, coercive and correctional. Though the last of these, which concerns the use of imprisonment as a form of legal punishment, now takes the primary place, it is in historical perspective a comparatively new conception, not all the implications of which have yet been worked out. In its origins the prison served only the custodial function: it was a place in which an alleged offender could be kept in lawful custody until he could be tried and, if found guilty, punished. The judges went out to 'deliver the gaols'—to clear them, not to fill them. The punishments for treasons and felonies were banishment or death; for misdemeanours, public shame, physical punishments, or fines. It is less than a hundred years since the use of imprisonment as a primary punishment for crime began to receive serious consideration.

This first or custodial function of the prison has not lost its importance: in 1951 over 19 per cent of the total receptions into prisons were of persons committed on remand or for trial who did not return again on conviction, that is to say they were either found not guilty or dealt with otherwise than by imprisonment. It is also applicable to aliens awaiting the execution of deportation orders, and to various categories of offenders awaiting removal to other types of institution to which they have been committed by the courts.

The coercive function means that imprisonment may be used to persuade a person to comply with an order made by a court of law, whether civil or criminal; if he complies, he is released. The first use of the prison in this way was against convicted offenders who had been ordered to forfeit property, or to pay fines, and had failed to do so. Prisons are still so used: in 1951 some 13 per cent of the total receptions of men on conviction, and some 22 per cent of women, were for non-payment of fines. All these persons could at any time obtain release by paying. The courts, civil or criminal, may also use imprisonment to persuade persons before them to comply with orders to do or refrain from doing certain things: persons deemed to be 'in contempt of court' through failure to comply with such a direction of the court may be committed to prison until they 'purge their contempt.' Such persons are received from time to time. Here the function of the prison lies somewhat outside the field of crime, as does another use of its coercive function. Imprisonment has long been used in England to enforce the payment of moneys ordered by a court to be paid under civil process—not only the payment of rates and taxes due to public authorities, and of sums due under wife maintenance and affiliation orders, but of private debts recoverable in the county courts. In 1951 over 5,600 persons were received into prison in default of payments of this nature.

Finally, imprisonment takes its place as one of the punishments which a court may impose on those convicted of offences against the criminal law. In dealing with persons over the age of 17 convicted of indictable offences, the courts in 1947 used fines for 39 per cent, probation for 11 per cent, and imprisonment for 29 per cent. Of all offences indictable and non-indictable dealt with in that year, imprisonment was used for only 4·7 per cent. Thus it appears that the majority of persons convicted of crime are not nowadays sent to prison: nor is the correctional concern of the prison only with those who have committed the more serious offences, since only 71 per cent of the men received on conviction in 1951, and only 58 per cent of the women, had been convicted of indictable offences.

This statement of the functions of our prisons shows that their effort must be spent in various ways, all necessary for the support of the law, but by no means directed to their central function, which concerns those sent to prison as a punishment for crime.

3. IMPRISONMENT AS A LEGAL PUNISHMENT

Discussion of the principles of imprisonment as a form of legal punishment must start from the consideration that a sentence of imprisonment in itself is no more than an order that the offender be deprived of his liberty in a lawful prison. The problem of the correctional function of the prison is concerned with the question—how can the treatment of the convicted offender thus confined in prison best be made to serve the purpose of legal punishment, which is the prevention of crime. The view which in the early nineteenth century still prevailed in Parliament and on the Bench was that crime could be prevented only by the deterrent effect of uniform maximum severity, hitherto achieved by cutting the offender out of the community by banishment or death. There had been other views, notably those of John Howard and Elizabeth Fry, suggesting that in so far as the prison played a part in this purpose it would be better to use it to attempt to improve the offender, so that he would be less likely to revert to crime on release, rather than 'by the greatest possible degree of misery, producing the greatest possible degree of wickedness . . . receiving [the prisoner] because he is too bad for society, you return him to the world impaired in health, debased in intellect, and corrupted in principles'.[1] These views did not however prevail in 1863, when a Committee of the House of Lords, set up to decide on the principles and practice of imprisonment and penal servitude, pronounced in favour of deterrence by severity as the object of imprisonment, with the reform of the prisoner as a subsidiary object which need not be sought and was scarcely to be expected.

This principle, to which statutory effect was given by the Prisons Act, 1865, held good to the end of the century. It was then assailed on both moral and practical grounds, and in 1895 a Departmental Committee under the Chairmanship of Lord Gladstone (then Mr. Herbert Gladstone) reconsidered the principles of 1865, and made a report on which the principles of the contemporary system still largely rest. They found that the system of 1865 had indeed, by creating 'the greatest possible amount of misery,' produced 'the greatest possible degree of wickedness,' and that in its primary purpose of preventing crime it had demonstrably failed. The prisoners had been 'treated too much as a hopeless or worthless element of the community,' and it would be better for the system to be designed 'to turn them out of prison better men and women physically and morally than when they came in . . . prison treatment should have as its primary and concurrent objects deterrence and reformation.' The Prisons Act, 1898, laid the statutory foundations of the new system.[2]

During the next phase of development, up to the first world war, these more humane ideas spread throughout the penal system. Legislation was primarily concerned with the abatement of imprisonment by providing alternative forms of treatment, as in the Probation of Offenders Act, 1907, or in the Borstal system for young offenders provided by the Prevention of Crime Act, 1908; by ensuring the removal of the mentally defective from prison in the Mental Deficiency Act, 1913; and by reducing the numbers committed for non-payment of fines in the Criminal Justice Administration Act, 1914. The Act of 1908 further sought to remove habitual criminals, who were neither deterred nor reformed by prison

[1] Sir T. Fowell Buxton, *Inquiry into Prison Discipline*, 1816.

[2] The various statutory provisions relating to prisons and prisoners to which reference is made in this chapter, including those in the Criminal Justice Act, 1948, have now been consolidated in the Prison Act, 1952.

sentences, out of the normal prison system into a form of prolonged internment known as preventive detention. Thus the courts were furnished with a variety of forms of punishment which enabled them to adapt the treatment of the offender to his character and needs as well as to the nature of his offence.

After the first world war, the prison system itself moved far in this direction of individualization of treatment, and also in a revaluation of its 'primary and concurrent objects,' deterrence and reform. Experience had shown that the difficult task of reconciling punitive deterrence and reform within one method of treatment would not succeed so long as the regime was based on a careful balance of 'deterrent' and 'reformative' elements. 'Better men and women' could not be made by methods which sought at the same time to hurt and humiliate them. If this end was sincerely sought, the deterrent effect of prison must be deemed to lie in the *fact* of imprisonment, with all that this inevitably implies—complete loss of personal liberty; separation from home and friends; subjection to forced labour and disciplinary control; and deprivation of most of the amenities and intercourse of ordinary life. Further, it is not enough to seek the 'reform' of the offender: that can only come from within, through the exercise of the right personal influences. The treatment should seek positively to fit him to lead a good and useful life after release: it is a grave danger of imprisonment, especially of prolonged imprisonment, that it may cause deterioration both of body and of mind, and the prevention of crime is not served if the offender returns to society unfitted rather than fitted to adapt himself to its life.

The system based on this re-interpretation of the Gladstone principles was evolved in administrative practice, not as the result of any further legislation or official inquiry. It is the system which led, in the Criminal Justice Act, 1948, to the provision that rules should be made for, *inter alia,* the 'training' of prisoners, and to Rule 6 of the Prison Rules, 1949, which reads:

> 'The purposes of training and treatment of convicted prisoners shall be to establish in them the will to lead a good and useful life on discharge, and to fit them to do so.'

4. PRISON DEVELOPMENT BEFORE THE CRIMINAL JUSTICE ACT, 1948

The county gaols were the responsibility of the local justices, and though Howard and his friends had successfully promoted legislation for their reform the Government had no power to enforce it against unwilling or apathetic local authorities. But to complete the radical reforms of the police and penal systems carried through when Peel was Home Secretary, it was essential that the prisons should become an effective instrument of legal punishment, and his Gaol Act of 1823 took the first steps to making them so. This Act was mandatory, and laid on the justices the duty to organize their prisons in accordance with a code of rules annexed to the Act, to inspect them regularly, and to report to the Home Secretary on their administration. This laid the foundation of Home Office control, but the Home Secretary had still no power to do anything but receive the reports, nor any staff to act on them had he the power. The next steps followed in 1835 and 1844 when he was empowered to appoint first Inspectors of Prisons, and then a Surveyor-General to advise both the Home Office and the local justices on prison construction. This last appointment, which fell to Colonel J. Jebb, R.E., later Sir Joshua Jebb, was to have effects of monumental duration, for to his advice and activity we owe the great majority of the prisons which must still serve the purposes of the Criminal Justice Act, 1948.

Meantime new impulses came from America, where the use of imprisonment to replace capital punishment had developed rival systems, both including the conception of reform as an object of imprisonment. The Quakers of Pennsylvania thought this might come through contemplation of the wages of sin in monastic solitude and silence; their new prisons therefore provided not only separate cells for sleeping, as Howard had long advocated, but complete separation for all purposes at all times. The other system derived from the new prison at Auburn, N.Y., where cells were used for sleeping, but work and other activities took place in association under a rigid rule of silence. Both systems, separate and silent, aroused great interest in Europe, and both were followed at different times and places by their partisans.

The new Inspectors exercised their influence in favour of the separate system, of which a structural pattern was set by Jebb's penitentiary at Pentonville (1842), built to supplement the hulks and the Millbank penitentiary of 1821 as a prison for convicts awaiting transportation. In the next few years over 50 local prisons were rebuilt on the Pentonville model, and more cellular prisons had to be built by the Government for convicts who could no longer be transported.[1] With the hulks, the penitentiaries, and its new convict prisons the Home Office had now so considerable a system of its own that in 1850 it took statutory powers to appoint Directors

[1] The Australian colonies finally refused to receive any more convicts in 1846.

of Convict Prisons to manage it: their first chairman was Sir Joshua Jebb.

The Home Secretary was now responsible directly for the convict prisons for prisoners sentenced to penal servitude[1] (3 years and upwards) and indirectly through his inspectors and statutory powers for the local prisons for those sentenced to imprisonment (up to 2 years). But uniform and effective implementation of the principles of 1865 in the local prisons could not be secured by indirect control, and by the Prisons Act, 1877, their ownership and control, with all the powers and duties of the justices in relation to them, were vested in the Secretary of State. Subject to his control, their superintendence was vested in a Board of Prison Commissioners, assisted by inspectors and their own staff. The first Chairman of the new Board was Sir Edmund du Cane, K.C.B., R.E., who had succeeded Sir J. Jebb as Surveyor-General and Chairman of Directors.

The two Boards, separate in law, became in practice one, and their members remained Directors of Convict Prisons as well as Commissioners of Prisons until penal servitude was abolished by the Act of 1948. Under Sir E. du Cane's management the principles of 1865 were rigidly and uniformly enforced, and the prisons throughout the country were brought under an economical and efficient central control on a pattern which still endures. To his successor, Sir E. Ruggles-Brise, K.C.B., there fell in 1895 the tasks of reconstructing the system in the light of the Gladstone Report and the Prison Act, 1898, and later of starting the Borstal system for young offenders and the preventive detention system for habitual offenders. In the development of the correctional function of the prison this was a transitional period. Its main contribution was the substitution of useful work in association under the 'rule of silence' for useless labour on the treadmill—in effect, a return from the separate to the silent system. The time had not yet come when 'reform' could take more than a nominal place alongside 'deterrence'. Sentences of imprisonment might still be, and commonly were, passed 'with hard labour' to emphasize the deterrent nature of the sentence, and effect was given to them *inter alia* by a preliminary period of 28 days separate confinement. After the first world war this preliminary separate confinement ceased, and for many years before the abolition of the hard labour sentence by the Act of 1948 it had become a form of words with no significant effect.

The Act of 1898 made two other contributions which were both valuable and durable. First, it enabled ordinary prisoners to earn earlier release by good conduct and industry, a facility which had

[1] This form of sentence was established in 1853 in place of transportation.

hitherto been reserved for prisoners undergoing penal servitude. This remission of sentence remains one of the bases of prison discipline. The amount under the Prison Rules, 1949, is one-third of the sentence: when the prisoner is discharged on remission his sentence is deemed to have expired.

Second, it repealed the statutory code of 1865 and gave the Secretary of State power to make Statutory Rules for the government of prisons, subject to their being laid before Parliament. Under this more elastic procedure the prison system developed without further legislation for the next fifty years.

The contemporary 'training' system, as now established by the Act of 1948, was first developed under the leadership of Sir Maurice L. Waller, C.B., who succeeded Sir E. Ruggles-Brise as Chairman in 1921, and Sir Alexander Paterson, who became a Commissioner in 1922.

5. IMPRISONMENT TODAY

A sentence of imprisonment[1] today, in the terms of the Criminal Justice Act, 1948, and the Prison Rules, 1949, is an undifferentiated sentence to confinement in a prison for the period stated, which may be from 5 days to life. Its primary purpose is set out in Rule 6 (p. 147) and the manner in which the prisoner is to be treated to this end is determined by the prison administration in accordance with the Prison Rules.

The basic principles of the system have been set out as follows:

'First, that for all prisoners with sentences of suitable length, the prison regime should be one of constructive training, moral, mental, and vocational; second, that such training can be fully carried out only in homogeneous establishments set aside for the purpose, though the principle should apply, so far as practicable in the limitations of an ordinary prison, to all prisons alike; third, that the special training prisons need not, for all prisoners, provide the security of normal prison buildings, since men can only acquire a sense of responsibility by exercising it, and experience has shown that a high proportion of prisoners can be trusted to exercise it in open conditions; fourth, that the services of the community outside the prison should be enlisted to help in the training at every practicable point, so as to break down the tradition that the prisoner is a person cut out of society; and fifth, that this continuing responsibility of society should be maintained after his discharge by effective aid towards social rehabilitation.'[2]

The first principle emphasizes that for effective training the

[1] There are other forms of sentence for persistent offenders, to be described in the following section.

[2] *Prisons and Borstals*, H.M. Stationery Office, 1950.

sentence must be of suitable length, and this means in practice a sentence of over 6 months. Yet of the prisoners received in 1951 no less than 70·5 per cent of men and 85·6 per cent of women had sentences of six months or under, and 24·9 and 41·4 per cent not more than one month. The prevalence of very short sentences remains a major difficulty of prison administration.

The methods of training those whose sentences are long enough for it to be effective vary according to the history, character and length of sentence of the offender and are carried out in different types of prison. Every prisoner is received first in one of 24 local prisons, where the convicted are seen by a Reception Board for classification and fixing of training programmes. Those who have not been in prison before, with others suitable to mix with them, are placed in the Star Class, others in the Ordinary Class. Male Stars are removed to separate prisons: if the sentence is over 3 years this will be to one of the two central prisons for long-term Star prisoners; if 12 months but not more than 3 years, to one of the six regional training prisons which are the 'homogeneous establishments set aside for the purpose'; if under 12 months to a special local prison set aside for Stars and civil prisoners. Ordinaries with sentences of over 4 years[1] go to the central prison for long-term Ordinary Class prisoners: others may be selected, if by record and character they seem suitable, to go to a regional training prison for their last year, but normally serve their sentences in the local prison. The small numbers of women preclude special local prisons for Stars. For Stars with sentences of 3 years or more there is a separate central prison: long-term Ordinaries are accommodated in a part of Holloway Prison, London. There are two regional training prisons for women.

So in the 24 ordinary local prisons we find an *omnium gatherum* of untried and civil prisoners, convicted prisoners of both classes serving short sentences, prisoners of the Ordinary Class serving longer sentences, and prisoners of all kinds awaiting transfer. These are the prisons built 100 years ago for separate confinement and treadmill hard labour, and all practicable reconstruction and extension has failed to fit them for the purposes of today. Moreover, the prison and Borstal population in the last 10 years has mounted to more than double its pre-war size, and reached during 1952 a total[2] of approximately 24,000—the highest recorded for some 70 years. There is therefore a serious shortage of accommodation, which in

[1] In principle 3 years, but now raised to 4 owing to shortage of central prison accommodation.
[2] Including some 3,400 in Borstal Institutions.

present economic conditions cannot be remedied, and much overcrowding of the local prisons. It has also been necessary to limit the staffs of the local prisons and central prisons for Ordinaries to a 'one-shift' system, which limits the prisoners' working hours to four to five hours a day.

In these conditions constructive training cannot be made effective: it is therefore concentrated in the regional prisons and the central prisons for Stars, where the whole effort can be devoted to the one task in a system based on self-discipline and trust. The methods used are set out in the Prison Rules as follows:

(i) The provision of work which will so far as practicable help to fit [prisoners] to earn their living after release, with technical training in skilled trades for suitable prisoners.
(ii) Special attention to education.
(iii) The exercise of personal influence on the character and training of individuals by members of the prison staff.
(iv) The provision of every opportunity for the development of a sense of personal responsibility, including for suitable prisoners training in open conditions.

These methods are in principle equally applicable in other prisons, and with those whose sentences are long enough they are taken as far as the conditions allow.

This system reaches its fullest effect in the open prisons. Here there are no physical barriers to escape and safe-custody and good order rest on the high morale and interested co-operation which a skilled staff can secure, in this more relaxed and human atmosphere, with well-selected prisoners. But careful selection of the prisoners is the essential basis of success. One central prison for Stars and four regional prisons (two for women) are open, and one regional prison is of medium security. Two other regional prisons and two local prisons have attached camps for selected prisoners, and there are four open local prisons and one of medium security for Stars (up to 12 months) and civil prisoners.

The fourth of the basic principles is applied in many ways. Good relations of prisoners with their families are encouraged, and they are kept in touch with the outside world through newspapers, the wireless, lectures and the like. Education is provided by the local education authorities, and library service by the local Public Library. All prisoners participate in the benefits of the National Health Service, and their position under the National Insurance scheme is preserved so far as the conditions of imprisonment permit. Ministry of Labour officers visit the prisons to advise and help those about to be released who need work. And the generalized good-will of the community is represented by Prison Visitors, who as a form of voluntary social service come in to pay friendly evening visits to prisoners in their cells.

Finally, the transition from confinement to freedom, with its anxious economic and psychological problems, is helped by a nationally organized system of aid-on-discharge and after-care. Those released from local prisons are cared for by Discharged Prisoners' Aid Societies—voluntary bodies dependent primarily on private benevolence, but approved by the Home Secretary and assisted by grants from public funds. The National Association of D.P.A.S. co-ordinates their work, and makes arrangements for prisoners discharged from regional and special local prisons. For those discharged from central prisons, and for the various categories released on conditional licence under statutory supervision,[1] the Central After-care Association makes the necessary arrangements; its agents in the field are normally the Probation Officers, on whom now falls the duty, under the Probation Rules, of supervising and befriending specified categories of persons discharged from custody.

6. PERSISTENT OFFENDERS

Of those who come to prison for the first time some three out of four will not return. But of those who do return a proportion, either choosing to live by crime or too socially defective to refrain from it, return again and again. The Prevention of Crime Act, 1908, provided that, for the protection of society, offenders who were proved to be habitual criminals might be detained for prolonged periods in a form of 'non-punitive' confinement called preventive detention. This measure failed of its intended effect, through technical difficulties which were removed by the Criminal Justice Act, 1948: by section 21 of this Act a person of 30 or more years of age who fulfils the qualifications of the section may be sentenced to preventive detention for not less than five nor more than 14 years, and by the end of 1953, 1,180 men and 33 women had been sentenced to preventive detention.

Preventive detention is in principle custodial, but it is difficult to devise a regime for this large number of difficult and often dangerous men which is essentially different from long-term imprisonment: safe-custody and good order must be preserved. Again, although they have received this sentence because they have seemed to be beyond hope of change through normal methods, the administration cannot treat them as hopeless. The system adopted under the

[1] See following sections on persistent offenders and young offenders.

Prison Rules, 1949, attempts to reconcile these difficulties. After a 'first stage' in a local prison[1] the second stage of the sentence is served in a central prison, where there is good industrial or agricultural work, full association for meals and recreation, evening education and certain privileges and amenities—including higher pay—beyond those available to a long-term prisoner.

Prisoners who remain in the second stage may earn release on a conditional licence after serving five-sixths of the sentence, thus keeping hope of improving their lot by good conduct. They pass to the supervision of the Central After-care Association, and may be recalled if they do not comply with the conditions.

There is however provision for prisoners who have responded really well, and look like maintaining their effort with some success after release, to earn that release after two-thirds of the sentence if they are selected for the third stage. This stage seeks to help re-adaptation to normal life by special vocational and social training, and a gradual tapering off of control: towards the end of the stage those who do well may be allowed to live in hostel conditions and take up ordinary outside work. Selection is made by an Advisory Board presided over by a Metropolitan Magistrate.

Section 21 also seeks to reduce the numbers of persistent offenders by taking them in good time and, instead of punishing them solely in relation to the particular offence, giving them training calculated to divert them from a life of habitual crime. To this end the courts may pass on offenders of 21 years or more who fulfil the statutory qualifications sentences of not less than 2 nor more than 4 years 'corrective training'.

Corrective training as a method of treatment does not differ from the training system already described, and is carried out in the regional training prisons for those who are found suitable for that regime. Others are trained on the same principles in separate corrective training prisons, where control and supervision are closer. The type of prison in which the sentence will be served is determined after observation in an allocation centre. Of about 1,300 men and 50 women serving sentences of corrective training in March, 1954, over 200 men and 3 women were in regional prisons, open or closed. Release on conditional licence to the care of the Central After-care Association, subject to recall on failure to comply with the conditions, may be earned when two-thirds of the sentence have been served.

[1] This may last not less than one nor more than two years, dependent on conduct.

7. THE TREATMENT OF YOUNG OFFENDERS

Before the mid-nineteenth century the penal system mitigated no horror for offenders of tender years. Certainly in 1838 the government had opened Parkhurst prison as a Government reformatory for offenders under 18 sentenced to transportation—with a junior class for those under ten years old: but the inmates would eventually be transported, unless they had been pardoned on condition of entering one of the reformatories established by private benevolence. It was not until 1854 that the courts were enabled to commit offenders under 16 to a reformatory, and then (until 1899) after not less than 14 days imprisonment.

The Prisons Act, 1865, required 'juveniles' under 16 to be kept separate and given special treatment, and by the time of the Gladstone Committee there were (on 31st March, 1894) some hundred 'juveniles' in prison and 2,226 between the ages of 16 and 20. The Committee did not approve the suggestion made to it that the imprisonment of juveniles should be prohibited, though they recommended that the age should be raised to 17, and that 'the fact of imprisonment should be the main deterrent . . . treatment should be altogether of a reformatory character'.

For the age group 16-21, however, their views resulted in the setting up of the present Borstal system. Satisfied that between these ages 'the majority of habitual criminals are made' they advised the establishment of a 'penal reformatory under Government management . . . to prevent them by strong restraint and rational treatment from recruiting the habitual class'. In 1897 Sir E. Ruggles-Brise obtained authority to establish a special prison for 'juvenile-adults', on reformatory lines, in the disused convict prison at Borstal, Kent. This experiment was however still within the prison system, and it was not until 1908 that the Home Secretary was empowered to establish 'Borstal Institutions', and the courts to commit to them direct offenders aged 16-21 under a sentence of 'Borstal detention' for 2 or 3 years.

The Criminal Justice Act, 1948, took still further the measures instituted by the Children Act, 1908, and the Children and Young Persons Act, 1933, for keeping young people out of prison. The age for complete prohibition of imprisonment was raised to 15, and for imprisonment by courts of summary jurisdiction to 17. For those over 17, the Home Secretary has power to extend the age of prohibition up to 21, by Order in Council, when satisfied that adequate methods of treatment other than imprisonment are available. The other methods provided by the Act with which the Prison Commissioners are concerned are two.

Remand centres are intended to provide an alternative to prison for the 17-21 age group on remand or committed for trial, and for the unruly under 17 who cannot be kept in remand homes.[1] The need for them is great: in 1951 no less than 3,275 such persons were received in prison before conviction who were subsequently discharged or dealt with otherwise than by Borstal training or imprisonment. But the new buildings which these centres will need cannot be provided in the present economic circumstances of the country.

Detention centres are intended to provide a more effective instrument than detention in a remand home as an alternative to short sentences of imprisonment for young offenders who, though they do not yet require prolonged residential training in a school or Borstal, do require a sharp lesson. The normal sentence provided by the Act is three months. It is intended to be primarily a deterrent rather than a reformative experience, but it may be hoped that formative influences can be brought to bear which will have some positive effect for good. Again, the need is shown by the figures—in 1951 the number of young offenders received with sentences of imprisonment was 1,243, of which 701 were for not more than three months: and again it has been impossible hitherto to meet the need. Plans have been prepared to open two detention centres as a pilot scheme in adapted buildings, which will serve a substantial portion of the south of England. The first of these, in Oxfordshire, was opened in August, 1952.

For those who must still come to prison, there is a clear distinction of treatment between those with sentences of under 3 months and others. These very short-sentence cases, who with remission will serve only 2 months, must remain in their local prisons. They are kept separate from adults so far as the conditions of these prisons allow, but they can receive no training. Some may find the experience unpleasant enough to serve as an effective deterrent: for others the effect may be only the removal of that fear of prison in which lies its primary deterrent power. For the others the prospects are better; they are removed to separate establishments known as Young Prisoner Centres, where they receive the fullest training possible according to the length of their sentences. But since there were in 1951 only 179 sentences of over 12 months, this can be no substitute for Borstal training even if it were possible to reproduce Borstal conditions within a prison wall. They are released on a conditional licence to the care of the Central After-care Association. The numbers of girls are so small that special centres are not practicable.

The Criminal Justice Act made no substantial changes in the

[1] See page 75.

Borstal system. The form of the sentence, now changed from 'Borstal Detention' to 'Borstal training', implies a period of 4 years' training, of which not less than 9 months and not more than 3 years may be spent in an institution, the balance of the period being in controlled freedom under the supervision of the Central After-care Association. Training is carried out in 13 institutions for boys and two for girls: there are also one Borstal for boys and one for girls recalled for further training following unsatisfactory conduct on release.

All boys on reception go to one of two Reception Centres, where their history, character, and capacities are studied for some weeks before it is decided which Borstal is best fitted to give them the form of training they require. The boys' Borstals are diverse in character, all but four being quite open; of the 'closed' Borstals, one is in a former prison and is reserved for young men with second sentences of Borstal training and others who are found on reception, or later in their training Borstals, to be unsuitable for normal training methods. The other closed institutions are walled buildings of prison type, though much of the work is done on the farms outside the walls: they are for the more mature with the worst records, or the more unstable who could not safely be trusted in open conditions. The girls require only one closed Borstal, and one small community of about fifty in an open institution.

Open conditions, nevertheless, are essential to a system of training for freedom—a system which seeks to bring about from within changes which will endure to regulate conduct aright after the props and stays of institutional life have been removed.

The first principle therefore is character training, primarily by the personal influence of every member of the staff, then by progressive trust which demands increasing personal decision, responsibility and self-control. This means in the later stages of training a good deal of freedom to mix with others in the world outside, whether in sport and social clubs, or through the Cadet Corps and the Young Farmers Clubs. The second principle is hard work, and plenty of it, so it be directed to fitting them to be good workmen on release: the emphasis is on vocational training in skilled trades for all who can benefit by it. Then mental activity is stimulated by evening education, and the illiterate and backward are brought up to the best possible standard by regular school during the day. These influences are concentrated through the house system. The boys live in small separate communities of 50-60, with a House-master, Matron, and house staff, whose duty it is to get to know each boy as an individual, guide him through his training, and report his progress so that his fitness for release can be assessed. The closed girls' Borstal is also based on the house system.

There is no standard period of training: for some a year is enough, for others much longer may be needed—in 1951 the average period for boys was about 18 months, for girls a month or two longer. The progress of each inmate is regularly reviewed by the Institution Board, and a recommendation for release made to the Commissioners through the Board of Visitors as soon as it seems that the training has achieved the most that can be expected.

The results of this system, based on the numbers who, over a period of not less than two years from discharge, were not reconvicted or appeared after one reconviction to have settled down, give a 'success' percentage for boys before the war (1937-38) of about 79, and since the war (1947-50) of 73. For girls the figures are about 69 and 89.

At the beginning of 1954 there were 3,200 boys and 260 girls serving sentences of Borstal training.

8. ADMINISTRATION AND STAFF

The Prison Commission was established by the Prisons Act, 1877, as a Statutory Board. It is a body corporate, with power to hold land, to sue and be sued, and with the consent of the Secretary of State to exercise compulsory purchase of land. The Board today however consists *de facto* of seven persons, of whom only five are Commissioners *de lege*, this being the maximum number prescribed by the Act of 1877. The members of the Board are the Chairman, Deputy Chairman, Secretary, Establishment Officer, Director of Prison Administration, Director of Borstal Administration, and Woman Director. Commissioners are appointed by the Crown on the recommendation of the Home Secretary, and are full-time pensionable civil servants. The Chairman is appointed by the Home Secretary. Commissioners have normally been appointed from the Prison Service or the administrative ranks of the Home Office, but it is an advantage of the system that an appointment may be made from outside the Service.

The organization of the department is necessarily complicated, since it is charged with the legal custody of over 23,000 men and women, and must deal with legal and other questions and complaints arising from their condition; with their clothing and feeding; their employment and industrial training; their moral and religious training, education, and welfare; their health and medical services; the provision and maintenance of the various buildings and estates required; the recruitment, training, and management of a staff of over 6,000, and, for most of those employed in the prisons and Borstals, their clothing and housing also.

The main administrative-executive structure comprises the Secretariat, Establishment Branch, Finance Branch, and Stores and Manufactures Branch.

The functions of the Secretariat, Establishment and Finance Branches are self-explanatory. Stores and Manufactures control victualling, clothing, furnishing, stores and the placing of contracts and supply of materials for the industries of the prisons and Borstals: there is a full time Catering Adviser to advise on and inspect the catering and cooking arrangements.

The Director of Industries controls the organization and production of the workshops and farms, the industrial training of the inmates, and the finding of orders for manufactures from Government Departments and elsewhere.

The Director of Works controls the provision and maintenance of buildings, housing of prison officers, and estate management. In major new building schemes, particularly the large housing schemes undertaken since the late war, and major adaptations of new premises, the Ministry of Works takes executive responsibility: the Director however interprets the wishes of the Commissioners to the Ministry. Since the labour force of the works organization is primarily provided by the inmates of the prisons and Borstals, the works staff in the field are not only tradesmen and specialists but uniformed prison officers. At each establishment there is a Foreman of Works or Engineer in charge, with a staff of junior engineers and Trade Assistants.

The medical and psychological services are controlled by the Director of Medical Services, with an Assistant to the Director and a Chief Psychologist at Head Office. At the larger establishments there are one or more full-time Government Medical Officers, at the smaller part-time local doctors. Nine Principal Medical Officers have the oversight of groups of establishments. Prison medical officers, by virtue of their duties to report to courts on the mental condition of offenders, become recognized experts in forensic psychiatry, and Registrars of certain teaching hospitals are attached to prisons for training in this science. The psychological service, still in progress of organization, will provide Governors and Medical Officers with professional assistance in preparing reports to courts on the mental condition of offenders and their suitability for various forms of treatment, as well as in the study of prisoners for classification and training. The nursing service includes State Registered

Nursing Sisters, under a Matron-in-Chief, in the women's establishments, some male Borstals, and the surgical unit at Wormwood Scrubs. In male establishments the hospital duties are performed by prison officers, called Hospital Officers, who are trained and qualified in the work.

Education is in charge of an Assistant Commissioner working in close collaboration with the Ministry of Education, whose Senior Chief Inspector acts as Chief Education Adviser to the Home Office. A Divisional Inspector of the Ministry and a panel of Inspectors co-ordinate and inspect the work of the teachers, who are provided by the local education authorities. This Assistant Commissioner also looks after the manifold activities, including after-care, grouped under the heading of 'welfare'.

The work of the Chaplains is supervised by the Chaplain-Inspector, who advises the Commissioners generally in matters of religion. There are full-time Chaplains of the Church of England in the larger establishments, part-time in the smaller, and clergy of other denominations known as Prison Ministers are paid on a capitation basis. The full-time Chaplains are appointed with the consent of the Bishop of the diocese for a period up to seven years, after which by arrangement with the Bishops they normally return to parochial work. Thus a priest will not lose that freshness of touch which this work especially requires. At large prisons the Chaplains have the full-time help of Church Army Evangelists.

For the co-ordination of these various aspects of policy in their establishments; for the safe-custody, good order, and training of the inmates; for the efficiency and disposition of the staffs; and for the proper administration of establishments by their Governors, responsibility to the Board rests with the Directors of Prison and Borstal[1] Administration and the Woman Director. These Directors stand, under the Chairman, at the head of a hierarchial service through which the normal flow of promotion may carry a qualified officer from the lowest rank to be a Commissioner. The immediate assistants are five Assistant Commissioners, who are Inspectors under the Act of 1877 and are appointed by the Home Secretary from among the Governors. Each is responsible to his Director for the proper administration of a group of establishments, which he regularly inspects, making a written report on each visit.

Since the Directors and other members of the Board also pay frequent visits, the centre is in constant touch with the periphery; and Governors and other members of the staff are often taken into consultation on working parties or otherwise. Since there are few

[1] Including remand and detention centres.

questions arising which do not affect several interests, it is usual for questions of policy to be discussed at a monthly conference of the Board with its senior colleagues, the Board itself meeting separately as required to settle major issues. The Commissioners also attend the separate annual conferences of Governors, Chaplains and Medical Officers.

The responsible head of each establishment is the Governor. Governors, as also Chaplains and Medical Officers, are appointed by the Home Secretary, not by the Commissioners. Governors however are not normally appointed direct to the rank, the recruitment grade being Assistant Governor II. This grade may be filled through two channels. First, from suitably qualified subordinate officers of the basic grade, so far as they are forthcoming: special arrangements are made, in conjunction with the Civil Service Commission, for selecting and training such officers. Second, by open competition, following public advertisement, at a selection board held jointly by the Civil Service Commissioners and the Prison Commissioners. Selected Chief Officers of the subordinate staff may also be promoted to this rank, but are usually promoted direct to the higher grade of Assistant Governor I: this grade fills posts of deputy-governor or others of special responsibility. Assistant Governors II act as Housemasters in Borstals, and in similar posts in prisons.

The main subordinate staff, men and women, rank as Chief Officers, Principal Officers, and Prison Officers (*not* Warders), supplemented by separately recruited but established grades of trade instructors, night patrols, store men, etc. Since the prison and Borstal systems stand or fall by the humanity, integrity and competence of their staffs, the greatest care is taken in their selection. Appointment is by the Prison Commissioners, following a first stage of 'weeding out' during preliminary training at a prison or Borstal, and a second stage of testing and training at the Imperial Training School, at Wakefield, for prison and Borstal staffs, where the final selection is made by a board of the school staff presided over by a Commissioner or Assistant Commissioner. The school also provides training courses for Assistant Governors. Plans for continued 'in-service' training are at present deferred on financial grounds.

The subordinate staff have a Trade Union, the Prison Officers' Association, which forms the Staff Side of the departmental Whitley Council, and joint sub-committees of the Council are formed from time to time to discuss particular questions, e.g. housing, uniform, staff time-tables. Unresolved disputes on arbitrable questions may be remitted to the Civil Service Arbitration Tribunal. Superior officers report his progress so that his fitness for release can be assessed. The closed girls' Borstal is also based on the house system.

There is no standard period of training: for some a year is enough, for others much longer may be needed—in 1951 the average period for boys was about 18 months, for girls a month or two longer. The progress of each inmate is regularly reviewed by the Institution Board, and a recommendation for release made to the Commissioners through the Board of Visitors as soon as it seems that the training has achieved the most that can be expected.

The results of this system, based on the numbers who, over a period of not less than two years from discharge, were not reconvicted or appeared after one reconviction to have settled down, give a 'success' percentage for boys before the war (1937-38) of about 79, and since the war (1947-50) of 73. For girls the figures are about 69 and 89.

At the beginning of 1954 there were 3,200 boys and 260 girls serving sentences of Borstal training.

8. ADMINISTRATION AND STAFF

The Prison Commission was established by the Prisons Act, 1877, as a Statutory Board. It is a body corporate, with power to hold land, to sue and be sued, and with the consent of the Secretary of State to exercise compulsory purchase of land. The Board today however consists *de facto* of seven persons, of whom only five are Commissioners *de lege*, this being the maximum number prescribed by the Act of 1877. The members of the Board are the Chairman, Deputy Chairman, Secretary, Establishment Officer, Director of Prison Administration, Director of Borstal Administration, and Woman Director. Commissioners are appointed by the Crown on the recommendation of the Home Secretary, and are full-time pensionable civil servants. The Chairman is appointed by the Home Secretary. Commissioners have normally been appointed from the Prison Service or the administrative ranks of the Home Office, but it is an advantage of the system that an appointment may be made from outside the Service.

The organization of the department is necessarily complicated, since it is charged with the legal custody of over 23,000 men and women, and must deal with legal and other questions and complaints arising from their condition; with their clothing and feeding; their employment and industrial training; their moral and religious training, education, and welfare; their health and medical services; the provision and maintenance of the various buildings and estates required; the recruitment, training, and management of a staff of over 6,000, and, for most of those employed in the prisons and Borstals, their clothing and housing also.

The main administrative-executive structure comprises the Secretariat, Establishment Branch, Finance Branch, and Stores and Manufactures Branch.

The functions of the Secretariat, Establishment and Finance Branches are self-explanatory. Stores and Manufactures control victualling, clothing, furnishing, stores and the placing of contracts and supply of materials for the industries of the prisons and Borstals: there is a full time Catering Adviser to advise on and inspect the catering and cooking arrangements.

The Director of Industries controls the organization and production of the workshops and farms, the industrial training of the inmates, and the finding of orders for manufactures from Government Departments and elsewhere.

The Director of Works controls the provision and maintenance of buildings, housing of prison officers, and estate management. In major new building schemes, particularly the large housing schemes undertaken since the late war, and major adaptations of new premises, the Ministry of Works takes executive responsibility: the Director however interprets the wishes of the Commissioners to the Ministry. Since the labour force of the works organization is primarily provided by the inmates of the prisons and Borstals, the works staff in the field are not only tradesmen and specialists but uniformed prison officers. At each establishment there is a Foreman of Works or Engineer in charge, with a staff of junior engineers and Trade Assistants.

The medical and psychological services are controlled by the Director of Medical Services, with an Assistant to the Director and a Chief Psychologist at Head Office. At the larger establishments there are one or more full-time Government Medical Officers, at the smaller part-time local doctors. Nine Principal Medical Officers have the oversight of groups of establishments. Prison medical officers, by virtue of their duties to report to courts on the mental condition of offenders, become recognized experts in forensic psychiatry, and Registrars of certain teaching hospitals are attached to prisons for training in this science. The psychological service, still in progress of organization, will provide Governors and Medical Officers with professional assistance in preparing reports to courts on the mental condition of offenders and their suitability for various forms of treatment, as well as in the study of prisoners for classification and training. The nursing service includes State Registered

PART FOUR

Other Functions of the Home Secretary

Prison Rules, 1949, attempts to reconcile these difficulties. After a 'first stage' in a local prison[1] the second stage of the sentence is served in a central prison, where there is good industrial or agricultural work, full association for meals and recreation, evening education and certain privileges and amenities—including higher pay—beyond those available to a long-term prisoner.

Prisoners who remain in the second stage may earn release on a conditional licence after serving five-sixths of the sentence, thus keeping hope of improving their lot by good conduct. They pass to the supervision of the Central After-care Association, and may be recalled if they do not comply with the conditions.

There is however provision for prisoners who have responded really well, and look like maintaining their effort with some success after release, to earn that release after two-thirds of the sentence if they are selected for the third stage. This stage seeks to help re-adaptation to normal life by special vocational and social training, and a gradual tapering off of control: towards the end of the stage those who do well may be allowed to live in hostel conditions and take up ordinary outside work. Selection is made by an Advisory Board presided over by a Metropolitan Magistrate.

Section 21 also seeks to reduce the numbers of persistent offenders by taking them in good time and, instead of punishing them solely in relation to the particular offence, giving them training calculated to divert them from a life of habitual crime. To this end the courts may pass on offenders of 21 years or more who fulfil the statutory qualifications sentences of not less than 2 nor more than 4 years 'corrective training'.

Corrective training as a method of treatment does not differ from the training system already described, and is carried out in the regional training prisons for those who are found suitable for that regime. Others are trained on the same principles in separate corrective training prisons, where control and supervision are closer. The type of prison in which the sentence will be served is determined after observation in an allocation centre. Of about 1,300 men and 50 women serving sentences of corrective training in March, 1954, over 200 men and 3 women were in regional prisons, open or closed. Release on conditional licence to the care of the Central After-care Association, subject to recall on failure to comply with the conditions, may be earned when two-thirds of the sentence have been served.

[1] This may last not less than one nor more than two years, dependent on conduct.

7. THE TREATMENT OF YOUNG OFFENDERS

Before the mid-nineteenth century the penal system mitigated no horror for offenders of tender years. Certainly in 1838 the government had opened Parkhurst prison as a Government reformatory for offenders under 18 sentenced to transportation—with a junior class for those under ten years old: but the inmates would eventually be transported, unless they had been pardoned on condition of entering one of the reformatories established by private benevolence. It was not until 1854 that the courts were enabled to commit offenders under 16 to a reformatory, and then (until 1899) after not less than 14 days imprisonment.

The Prisons Act, 1865, required 'juveniles' under 16 to be kept separate and given special treatment, and by the time of the Gladstone Committee there were (on 31st March, 1894) some hundred 'juveniles' in prison and 2,226 between the ages of 16 and 20. The Committee did not approve the suggestion made to it that the imprisonment of juveniles should be prohibited, though they recommended that the age should be raised to 17, and that 'the fact of imprisonment should be the main deterrent . . . treatment should be altogether of a reformatory character'.

For the age group 16-21, however, their views resulted in the setting up of the present Borstal system. Satisfied that between these ages 'the majority of habitual criminals are made' they advised the establishment of a 'penal reformatory under Government management . . . to prevent them by strong restraint and rational treatment from recruiting the habitual class'. In 1897 Sir E. Ruggles-Brise obtained authority to establish a special prison for 'juvenile-adults', on reformatory lines, in the disused convict prison at Borstal, Kent. This experiment was however still within the prison system, and it was not until 1908 that the Home Secretary was empowered to establish 'Borstal Institutions', and the courts to commit to them direct offenders aged 16-21 under a sentence of 'Borstal detention' for 2 or 3 years.

The Criminal Justice Act, 1948, took still further the measures instituted by the Children Act, 1908, and the Children and Young Persons Act, 1933, for keeping young people out of prison. The age for complete prohibition of imprisonment was raised to 15, and for imprisonment by courts of summary jurisdiction to 17. For those over 17, the Home Secretary has power to extend the age of prohibition up to 21, by Order in Council, when satisfied that adequate methods of treatment other than imprisonment are available. The other methods provided by the Act with which the Prison Commissioners are concerned are two.

Governor summons, prorogues and dissolves Parliament in Her Majesty's name, and also gives or withholds the Royal Assent to Bills passed by both Houses.

The powers of the Crown in matters which concern the Government of Northern Ireland are exercised by the Governor on the advice of Ministers appointed by him and answerable to the Northern Ireland Parliament. Only members of the Privy Council of Northern Ireland are eligible for ministerial office, and the Ministers appointed constitute the Executive Committee of the Northern Ireland Government.

The Civil Service of Northern Ireland has in general been organized on the lines of the Civil Service in Great Britain and is controlled through the Ministry of Finance. The Civil Service Commissioners for Northern Ireland are the Minister of Finance and two permanent officials.

The Senate is composed of 2 ex-officio Senators (the Lord Mayor of Belfast and the Mayor of Londonderry) together with 24 Senators elected by members of the House of Commons according to the principle of proportional representation. The House of Commons consists of 52 members elected by a system of parliamentary franchise in accordance with the Elections and Franchise Act (Northern Ireland), 1946.

This Act gave the suffrage to adults resident in Northern Ireland who have been born there or have been continuously resident in the United Kingdom for a period of seven years ending on the qualifying date for registration. There is also a three months constituency residence qualification.

Broadly speaking, the Parliament of Northern Ireland has power to make laws for the peace, order and good government of Northern Ireland, except in respect of certain matters which are expressly reserved to the United Kingdom Parliament. These include the succession to the Crown, the making of peace or war, the armed forces of the Crown, the making of treaties, honours, naturalization and aliens, the post and telegraph services, civil aviation and, with certain limited exceptions, trade with any place outside Northern Ireland.

The Home Secretary's functions are:

(1) to act as the official channel of communication between the Governments of the United Kingdom and of Northern Ireland;

(2) to ensure that Northern Ireland's constitutional rights are not infringed and to watch Northern Ireland's interests generally;

(3) to safeguard her interests with regard to Schemes under the Agricultural Marketing Acts of the Parliament of the United

Kingdom (which in certain circumstances may be extended by agreement to Northern Ireland, although agriculture is a matter within the competence of the Parliament of Northern Ireland);

(4) to ensure that the views of the Government of Northern Ireland on matters affecting them are made known to the Government of the United Kingdom.

Questions of law and order are entirely for the Government of Northern Ireland. The Prerogative of Mercy is exercised by the Governor on the advice of Northern Ireland Ministers.

The powers conferred on the Northern Ireland Government and Parliament are necessarily limited by the provisions of the Government of Ireland Act, and from time to time need arises to extend their powers for some specific purpose. It then falls to the Home Secretary to submit the requisite legislation to the United Kingdom Parliament. For example before an agreement could be concluded between the Northern Ireland and Irish Republican Governments for the joint acquisition of all fishing rights in the tidal waters of the River Foyle and Lough Foyle, the Parliament at Westminster had to pass the Foyle Fisheries Act, 1952, to give the requisite authority to the Government of Northern Ireland. The borderline between reserved and transferred matters is not always very clear and the interlocking of responsibility can give rise to problems of some complexity. For example, the control of dangerous drugs is a matter within the competence of the Parliament of Northern Ireland, but the control of international trade (with which the control of dangerous drugs is closely linked) is not. Accordingly it may on occasions be necessary or desirable that a Bill of the Parliament at Westminster should deal both with matters within the competence of the Northern Ireland Parliament and with matters reserved to the United Kingdom Parliament. There is then a shared responsibility between the two Governments and need for close consultation. All United Kingdom Bills apply to Northern Ireland unless there is express provision to the contrary, and they have to be scrutinized to ensure that they do not infringe upon any transferred matter without the prior consent of the Government of Northern Ireland. If that Government consents to a transferred matter being dealt with in a United Kingdom Bill, care has to be taken to ensure that this is not done in such a way as to impair Northern Ireland's right to legislate on this matter if need for further legislation should arise in the future.

While the Home Secretary is the Minister primarily responsible for business between the United Kingdom Government and the Government of Northern Ireland, other Departments are concerned with various aspects of the affairs of Northern Ireland. For example, the financial relations between the two Governments concern the Treasury. Questions of trade, commerce, employment and so on concern other Ministries: and much business is done at the official level by direct contact between officials of the Northern Ireland Departments and of the corresponding United Kingdom Departments.

Personal contacts which have been established between Home Office officials and their Northern Ireland colleagues have led to mutual understanding and goodwill in the handling of thorny problems, despite occasional differences of opinion. The Northern Ireland Government have attached to the Home Office a responsible member of their Civil Service, so that close liaison may be maintained both with the Home Office and with other Departments of the United Kingdom Government. The Home Office has found this arrangement most helpful.

2. DEPENDENCIES OF THE CROWN

The Channel Islands and the Isle of Man are dependencies of the Crown—outside the United Kingdom—which are distinguished from the colonial and other overseas dependencies by their proximity to Great Britain and by the history of their relationship with the Crown of England.

Recognition of these distinctive features possibly accounts for the decision taken in 1801 to separate government business connected with these islands from government business connected with the Colonies. In that year business connected with the Colonies was transferred from the Secretary of State for the Home Department to another Secretary of State; but no change was made as regards business connected with these islands. Today such business remains with the Home Secretary as one of the varied functions discharged by his predecessors in the days when there were only two—or sometimes three—Secretaries of State.

The distinction between these ancient dependencies and the Colonial dependencies was exemplified in recent years by a special provision in the British Nationality Act, 1948 (Chapter X). In that Act the words 'citizens of the United Kingdom and Colonies' are used as a brief, collective designation of those British subjects who are not citizens of one of the self-governing countries of the Commonwealth: but as a Channel Islander or a Manxman cannot properly be called a 'citizen of the United Kingdom and Colonies', such a person is authorized by the Act to call himself a 'citizen of the United Kingdom, Islands and Colonies'.

Because of the proximity of these Islands to Great Britain they are included by the Interpretation Act within the 'British Islands', and for the purposes of the Merchant Shipping Acts and the Post Office Acts trade with the Islands is classed as 'home' trade and postage to and from the Islands as 'inland' postage.

The Channel Islands and the Isle of Man have their own systems of local administration, and their own legislative assemblies. The Crown is represented in Jersey, Guernsey and the Isle of Man by Lieutenant Governors. The Islands have their own Courts of Law with full civil and criminal jurisdiction, but *habeas corpus* writs run in the Islands and there is a prerogative right to grant leave to appeal to the Judicial Committee of the Privy Council. The Home Secretary reviews capital cases arising in the Islands, and is responsible for advising on the Prerogative of Mercy in these and other cases; in considering them he consults the Lieutenant Governor.

In practice a large measure of responsibility for the conduct of their domestic affairs is left to the Island inhabitants, and the Islands have separate fiscal systems; but the Sovereign is responsible for the appointment of the chief officers of the local administrations, and for giving by means of Orders in Council the force of law to the legislative proposals of the insular assemblies. The primary responsibility for advising Her Majesty on these matters falls on the Home Secretary; but his advice as regards Orders in Council is given in his capacity as the member of the Privy Council specially charged with responsibility for the affairs of the Island, and it is his duty before giving such advice to consult any other Minister who may be concerned.

As these dependencies are outside the United Kingdom, Acts of the United Kingdom Parliament do not apply to them unless they are so applied by express provision or by necessary implication. Acts of Parliament are so applied from time to time for special reasons, but this procedure is exceptional and is normally adopted only after consultation with the insular authorities. The Home Office keeps a careful watch on United Kingdom Bills which may affect the Islands, to ensure that they do not infringe their constitutional liberties. The insular assemblies have long been accustomed to initiate legislative measures and to petition the Sovereign in Council to give such measures the force of law; and it is the practice of Parliament to refrain from legislating on matters with which these assemblies can properly deal, unless there are overriding reasons for doing so. A United Kingdom Act which it is intended shall apply to the Islands often contains provisions which require modifications to make them consonant with the insular administrative systems, or with the method of dealing with offences in the insular courts; the Act then provides for its extension to the Channel Islands and the Isle of Man by means of Orders in Council 'with such exceptions, modifications and adaptations, if any, as may be specified in the Order'. This procedure is very suitable from the constitutional point of view, as well as being useful on grounds of practical convenience.

The relations between the United Kingdom Government and the Islands are often ill understood. From time to time the Home Secretary is asked by people in Great Britain or by residents in the Islands to intervene in matters which have been or can be dealt with by the insular assemblies; and it is sometimes difficult to make complainants understand that such intervention would be inconsistent with the constitutional practice of leaving to these assemblies the major responsibility for regulating the internal affairs of the Islands.

3. THE CHANNEL ISLANDS

The Channel Islands consist of the Bailiwicks of Jersey and of Guernsey. The Bailiwick of Guernsey includes all the inhabited Islands except Jersey.

The Islands became dependencies of the Crown, not because an English sovereign acquired jurisdiction over them, but because in 1066 their Duke acquired jurisdiction over England. At that date the Channel Islands were part of the Duchy of Normandy, and when 137 years later King John lost the mainland territory of Normandy, the Islands remained in allegiance to him and to his successors.

Each Bailiwick has a Lieutenant-Governor appointed by the Queen, usually for a period of five years. In each Bailiwick there is the Bailiff, appointed by the Crown, who presides over meetings of the States (the insular legislature) and over the sittings of the Royal Court. Each Bailiwick has an Attorney-General assisted by a Solicitor-General—these officers also being appointed by the Crown. In Guernsey the States maintain a unified Civil Service, controlled by an officer known as the States Supervisor.

The Home Secretary advises the Queen on the appointment of the Lieutenant-Governors, the Bailiffs and the Law Officers, and appointments to Crown livings are made by the Queen on the recommendation of the Home Secretary.

Insular legislation is submitted to the Queen-in-Council and the duty of considering what advice shall be given to Her Majesty falls primarily on the Home Secretary. Jersey and Guernsey follow different procedures for this. Jersey, in pursuance of a long-standing claim to direct access to the Privy Council, sends laws to the Privy Council Office, which refers them to the Home Office. Guernsey on the other hand submits laws through the Home Office. The result is the same. The Home Office, having received the advice of the Lieutenant-Governors and the Insular Law Officers, then scrutinizes the law. If it deals with a subject falling within the field of another Department the views of that Department are sought. If the law raises a point of unusual difficulty the Home Office normally either consults the English Law Officers or suggests to the Privy Council Office that they should be consulted. The Home Office does not advise refusal to ratify a measure submitted by the States unless there is some important objection of principle such as repugnancy to the principles of British justice, or infringement of an international agreement. In practice a refusal to recommend ratification is extremely rare, and in recent years has almost always arisen in respect of some technical flaw not noticed by the Insular Authorities. Nevertheless the scrutiny has to be thorough, since past experience shows that on occasion important questions of constitutional principle can arise. Uniformity with English practice is not insisted on, but departures from this are usually brought to the attention of the Insular Authorities, so that they may be aware of them, should the occasion for an amending law ever arise. On occasion the Home Office may have to defend the insular proposals against criticism from other Departments who may not be aware of conditions in the Islands. Occasionally a body of Islanders may submit a petition opposing an insular Bill, usually on the ground that it damages their private interests. Thus in 1950 a law continuing the Export of Tomatoes Law, 1949 (which provided for compulsory bulk marketing of tomatoes) was the subject of a petition by sections of the industry. When a petition of this kind is submitted to the Privy Council, the usual course is for the Lord President to ask the Home Secretary to enquire into the complaint and make recommendations.

This right of appeal is greatly valued as a safeguard of local liberties not merely by individual islanders or groups of islanders but by the States themselves, who may for example appeal to the Privy Council against any Order in Council which they may contend to be inconsistent with constitutional practice, or with some privilege granted to them by Royal Charter. Such appeals have from time to time been heard by special Committees of the Privy Council composed both of Ministers and of judicial members of the Council, and it has been the practice to treat such appeals as covering questions of policy as well as of law. In the past Orders in Council have on occasions been withdrawn or modified as a result of such appeals. Recently it has been the practice to consult the insular authorities before an Order in Council is made, and occasions for such appeals have not arisen; but the fact that in the last resort there is a right of appeal to a Committee of the Privy Council is a reason why the Channel Islanders generally prefer the procedure of applying legislative requirements to them by Order in Council rather than by direct enactment.

As the constitutional channel of communication between the United Kingdom Government and the Insular Authorities, which maintain no representation in the United Kingdom, the Home Office often has not merely to forward representations from the Islands but to support their case and explain their difficulties. Important matters, particularly those which involve a conflict of legitimate interest between the Islands and the United Kingdom, are sometimes discussed at meetings between representatives of the interested Departments and delegations from the Islands. These matters cover a wide range—for example food, civil aviation, and postal matters—and take up a good deal of the time of Home Office officials.

In the Bailiwick of Guernsey, Alderney and Sark maintain their own legislatures—in Alderney the States, and in Sark the Chief Pleas. In Sark respect for the feudal head of the Island is still strong, and the inhabitants cling resolutely to the simple life and thus contrive to carry on with little legislation or taxation. Alderney was evacuated in 1940 before the Germans arrived and turned it into a combination of fortress and concentration camp. The occupation put an end to the Island's principal industry—granite quarrying—and created new problems. Many houses were destroyed or damaged, and the stones marking the boundaries of land holdings were removed. Alderney's own resources were too limited to enable her people to set the Island to rights without help, and the United Kingdom Government had to assist in various ways, for example by rebuilding houses and rebounding the land. Guernsey generously accepted responsibility for important services, and agreed to meet any deficit in the Island's budget; in return for this Alderney agreed to pay taxes at Guernsey rates. With this help Alderney has made considerable progress, and there is reason to hope that new industries recently attracted to the Island will firmly establish themselves and bring some measure of economic stability. But in the meantime the Home Office has the duty of helping the Alderney authorities in their work of rehabilitation.

4. THE ISLE OF MAN

Until the end of the 16th century English, Scottish or Irish visitors were treated as 'aliens' in the Kingdom of Man. This little kingdom was from the end of the 9th century ruled for over 300 years by

Norse settlers. The Norse gave way to the Scottish kings in 1263, and for the next 130 years suzerainty over the island was disputed by the Kings of England and Scotland. By the time of Henry IV the claim of the English Crown was established, and Henry granted the island with its 'regalities' to Sir John Stanley and his heirs. Sir John's descendants—the Earls of Derby—were Lords of Man until in 1736 the inheritance passed to the Duke of Atholl. In 1765 the Government of Great Britain purchased the 'regalities', and sovereignty over the island was revested in the Crown by Act of Parliament.

The internal affairs of the island are regulated by laws enacted in a local assembly known as Tynwald, and submitted to Her Majesty for confirmation by Orders in Council. Tynwald is a body comprising the Lieutenant-Governor, his Legislative Council and the House of Keys. The Legislative Council is composed of the Lord Bishop of Sodor and Man, two Deemsters (judges), the Attorney General, two members appointed by the Lieutenant-Governor and four members elected by the House of Keys. The House of Keys is an ancient body of twenty-four members who are now elected by universal, adult suffrage. The consent of the Lieutenant-Governor, of the Council and of the Keys is required to all legislative measures which are submitted by Tynwald to Her Majesty in Council.

The Lieutenant-Governor is appointed by the Crown on the recommendation of the Home Secretary for a period of seven years. Unlike the Lieutenant-Governors of Jersey and Guernsey he has executive responsibility for some of the public services, such as the police and prison services; and he is responsible for initiating proposals for raising and disbursing the public revenue. Those for raising revenue require the consent of Tynwald, as do proposals for expenditure, except on reserved services for which the Lieutenant-Governor has executive responsibility. It is, however, established practice that Tynwald shall be consulted on all proposals for expenditure; and there is a standing body of members of Tynwald, known as the Executive Council, with whom the Governor confers before making proposals for the raising or expenditure of money. The majority of members of the Executive Council are Chairmen of the Boards appointed by Tynwald for the administration of the public services which are not administered by the Lieutenant-Governor.

In the 18th century the Isle of Man was an entrepot for the smuggling trade, and the object of buying out the Lords of Man and revesting their sovereign rights in the Crown was to enable the Government and Parliament of Great Britain to control the insular customs, which provided the main revenue of the island. As a result of the revesting the revenue of the island accrued to the Exchequer, and the Treasury became responsible for the expenses of the insular Government. In response to protests from the Keys and to recommendations from Lieutenant-Governors who recognized the needs of the island, large changes were made in the nineteenth century. By an Act of the United Kingdom Parliament in 1866 the finances of the island were separated from those of the United Kingdom, and the Customs revenues collected in the island were appropriated to insular purposes, subject to an annual payment of £10,000 to the Exchequer and to payment of the costs of collection by the Customs Department; and by an Act of 1887 liberty was conferred on Tynwald to fix the insular customs and excise duties, subject to confirmation by Acts of the United Kingdom Parliament. In practice the responsibility for deciding what revenue shall be raised in the island and how it shall be spent is left to the insular authorities, but these Acts place a formal responsibility on the Treasury to supervise the island finances, and the raising and expenditure of money requires Treasury approval.

CHAPTER XVI

The International Work of the Home Office

Scope of international work — International conventions and treaties — United Nations Organization — Social, Narcotics, and Human Rights Commissions — Other international work.

*

1. THE SCOPE OF INTERNATIONAL WORK

THE Home Office is the Department concerned with home affairs: international work is the responsibility of the Foreign Office. How then does international work come within the sphere of the Home Office?

International work has always involved, and involves increasingly at the present time, the consideration of questions of domestic policy. The Foreign Office cannot itself have expert knowledge of such questions, and consequently it has to consult the Government Departments concerned. Many of these questions, ranging from wide problems concerning human rights and liberties to more specialized questions such as the international control of narcotics, touch the work of the Home Office: and it follows that the Home Office must devote considerable time to advising the Foreign Office on such matters; to studying the effects on domestic policy of projected international treaties and conventions; to preparing briefs for United Kingdom representatives at international conferences—some of whom are Home Office officials; and in general to helping to determine the policy of Her Majesty's Government.

For convenience of description this work may be divided into two categories: first that arising out of the Department's concern with international conventions and treaties, and second that arising out of this country's membership of (and consequent obligations towards) the United Nations and other international bodies.

2. INTERNATIONAL CONVENTIONS AND TREATIES

The oldest, though no longer the largest, category of Home Office international work is that concerned with the negotiation of bilateral treaties. Extradition treaties (Chapter XII) are a conspicuous example: they are almost exclusively the business of the Home Office, but many other kinds of treaty contain particular provisions which are of special interest to the Home Office. Consular conventions, relating to the powers and privileges of consuls, and commercial treaties providing for the entry and establishment of nationals of one country in the territory of the other, are examples.

The function of the Home Office in advising, at the various stages of the treaty negotiations, what provisions should be proposed or accepted, frequently calls for a nice balancing of opposing interests. Treaties which secure benefits for United Kingdom nationals abroad usually confer corresponding benefits on foreigners in this country, and this may involve some limitation on the exercise of the Home Secretary's powers relating to the control of aliens. Conversely, not to admit foreigners in this country to certain benefits entails a corresponding limitation on the benefits to which United Kingdom nationals may be entitled abroad. Again, the granting of privileges or immunities to particular classes of persons may deprive the rest of the community of the right to redress in respect of acts of the privileged persons. It is often necessary to resolve by discussion conflicts of interest between the Home Office and other Government Departments concerned; and it is also the Home Office function to see that account is taken of the interests of Northern Ireland, the Channel Islands and the Isle of Man.

Since the second world war many treaties which concern the Home Office have been negotiated or are still under negotiation, and the work involved is substantial.

Once a treaty has been concluded its observance may require the passage of legislation in this country before it can be ratified, or it may involve some modification of existing administrative practice. Sometimes, particularly in the case of multilateral conventions, it may involve the assumption of new duties by the Home Office. Once the necessary legislation has been passed, or the changes in administration made, the task of the Home Office in carrying out those provisions of treaties or conventions which are its concern no longer falls under the strict head of international work, since it now arises out of provisions of our domestic law, the administration of which is the responsibility of the appropriate Division of the Home Office. But some of the work arising out of treaty obligations entered into by Her Majesty's Government is itself international in character. For example, the conventions on the control of narcotic drugs impose obligations on Her Majesty's Government which are translated into requirements of our own law by the Dangerous Drugs Act and the Orders made thereunder; but the conventions also require signatory countries to send various reports, including an annual report on the working of the conventions, to the Secretariat of the United Nations, and annual and quarterly statistics to the Permanent Central Opium Board. Similar duties fall on the Home Office under other conventions, such as those relating to the suppression of traffic in women.

3. THE UNITED NATIONS

The second type of international work, and by far the largest in volume, arises from the study given by the many international organs now in existence to subjects which are the domestic responsibility of the Home Office. The United Nations provides the major part of this work, although there are also many aspects of the activities of the Council of Europe, the Brussels Treaty Organization, and the North Atlantic Treaty Organization, which engage the attention of the Home Office.

The Charter of the United Nations proclaims as one among the 'Purposes of the United Nations':

> 'To achieve international co-operation in solving international problems of an economic, social, cultural or humanitarian character, and in promoting and encouraging respect for human rights and for fundamental freedoms for all . . .'

One of the principal organs set up by the Charter is the Economic and Social Council; and it is the Council which concerns itself with activities directed to the fulfilment of this high purpose. To assist it in its task the Council has appointed a number of Commissions dealing with economic and social questions. These Commissions include the:

Social Commission
Narcotics Commission
Human Rights Commission
Status of Women Commission
Population Commission
Statistical Commission
Transport and Communications Commission

on all of which Her Majesty's Government is represented.

It is from the first three of these Commissions that the bulk of the international work of the Home Office arises, although from time to time the activities of the other Commissions mentioned call for study.

4. THE SOCIAL, NARCOTICS AND HUMAN RIGHTS COMMISSIONS

The Social Commission advises the Council on social questions of a general character, and in particular on all matters in the social field not covered by the 'specialized agencies' (e.g. the World Health Organization, the International Labour Organization, and the United Nations Educational, Scientific and Cultural Organization). The Social Commission makes proposals to the Council for practical measures and is in particular responsible for initiating and carrying out work on international conventions in this field.

On the Social Committee of the League of Nations (whose work has been taken over, with considerably wider range, by the Social Commission of the United Nations) the United Kingdom was represented by a Home Office official; and this tradition has been continued in the Social Commission. The subjects of special interest to the Home Office with which the Commission deals are the welfare of children and young persons, the prevention of crime and the treatment of offenders, the suppression of traffic in women, social aspects of migration, and refugees. In undertaking its studies the Commission must rely mainly on information supplied by Governments, and the Home Office is from time to time asked to supply particulars about the law and practice in England and Wales.

Until recently there was another international organization concerned with the prevention of crime and the treatment of offenders—the International Penal and Penitentiary Commission. On this the United Kingdom was represented by the Chairman of the Prison Commission, who was principally concerned with penal questions, and also by the Assistant Under-Secretary of State in charge of the Children and Probation Divisions, whose main interest was juvenile delinquency and probation. The functions of this body have now devolved, by an arrangement made with the United Nations, upon a group of experts, consisting for the time being of those who represented their Governments on the I.P.P.C. This group advises the Social Commission on questions relating to the treatment of offenders.

The Narcotics Commission helps and advises the Council in exercising supervision over the application of the various international conventions on narcotic drugs; it also considers whether any changes are necessary in the machinery for the international control of these drugs, and is responsible for preparing and submitting to the Council any further draft conventions on the subject which it may consider desirable.

Since the control of narcotic drugs is a responsibility of the Home Office (Chapter VIII), the Home Office is the Department primarily responsible for advising Her Majesty's Government as to the policy to be followed in the many matters which come within the scope of the Narcotics Commission, and the United Kingdom representative on this Commission is a Home Office official. The Commission is the successor of the Opium Advisory Committee of the League of Nations. On this body, and at the conferences which drew up the principal international conventions for the control of narcotic drugs, Her Majesty's Government was represented by the late Sir Malcolm Delevingne, Deputy Under-Secretary of State in the Home Office. He is generally recognized as one of the main architects of the system set up by these Conventions, which remain among the most solid and successful achievements of the League of Nations.

The Human Rights Commission concerns the Home Office very closely. For several sessions the Commission has been engaged in preparing a draft international covenant on Human Rights; and it is also concerned with the study of such questions as freedom of information (on which a number of projects for conventions have been prepared), the protection of minorities, and the prevention of discrimination on grounds of race, sex, language or religion. The Home Office, as the traditional guardian in this country of the liberty of the subject, is deeply concerned in all the work of the Commission which relates to civil liberties, and it has a major interest in the formulation of the civil rights in the draft covenant, many of which involve questions of the provisions and procedures of the criminal law. A Home Office official represented the United Kingdom at the session of the Human Rights Commission in 1952.

5. OTHER INTERNATIONAL WORK

The Status of Women Commission assists the Council in promoting women's rights in political, economic, social and educational fields, and the Home Office is concerned here with questions relating to the legal and civil status of women in this country. The work of the *Population Commission* and the *Statistical Commission* affects the Home Office because these Commissions, in studying migratory movements, need information from the records of immigration authorities. The *Transport and Communications Commission* is concerned, among other matters, with the simplification of passport and frontier formalities.

In addition to these standing Commissions of the Economic and Social Council, the Council and the General Assembly have set up from time to time *ad hoc* bodies to study particular problems. An *ad hoc* committee was recently set up to draft a convention relating to the status of refugees; on this committee, and at the subsequent conference of plenipotentiaries which drew up the Convention in its final form, the United Kingdom was represented by Home Office officials. Another United Nations *ad hoc* committee recently appointed is at the time of writing exploring the possibility of setting up a permanent international criminal court, and the Home Office is naturally closely concerned with the related questions both of policy and procedure.

The work of the 'specialized agencies' mentioned above also concerns the Home Office in some of its aspects: for example, the activities of the International Labour Organization, so far as they relate to the employment of children and young persons, or employment in non-industrial premises.

The Council of Europe is also active in many fields in which the Home Office is the Government Department concerned in this country. It has studied such questions as human rights (on which a convention has been opened for signature by member States), the standardization of passports and the abolition of visas; and the possibility of concluding a multilateral convention on the reciprocal treatment of nationals, and a multilateral extradition treaty, is now being explored.

Sporadic work arises for the Home Office from international activities outside the United Nations and the Council of Europe. An example is the conference of plenipotentiaries which was summoned by the Swiss Government in 1949 to revise three Red Cross Conventions (dealing with the relief of wounded and sick in armies in the field, the treatment of prisoners of war, and the adaptation to maritime warfare of the principles of the Geneva Convention of 1906) and to draw up a convention for the protection of civilian prisoners in time of war. The Home Office was specially concerned with the last subject, though it was also concerned with many aspects of the revision of the three existing conventions, and it was represented at the conference by three members of its staff, one of whom was Deputy Leader of the United Kingdom Delegation.

CHAPTER XVII

The Home Secretary as Residuary Legatee

The Queen's Pleasure — Redress of grievances — Regulation of working conditions — Elections — Private bills — Byelaws — Burials, consecration of burial grounds, cremation — Summer time and calendar questions — Protection of animals — The Cruelty to Animals Act, 1876 — Wild birds' protection — Charitable collections — Taxicabs — Fairs — Private Members' legislation — Marriage guidance.

*

1. THE QUEEN'S PLEASURE

IN this chapter an attempt will be made to describe the wide range of miscellaneous duties which fall to the Home Secretary as the Minister responsible for all home affairs which do not come within the jurisdiction of any other Minister. They derive, as do all his other duties, either from his position as the successor of the King's Secretary or from Statute. A bare recital of them all would be as tedious as the genealogical trees in Genesis.

In former days the Home Secretary was the sole channel through which the Sovereign communicated with his subjects; he also published State Intelligence. It is as a survival of this duty that even today he posts outside the Home Office the bulletins announcing Royal births, the Sovereign's condition when seriously ill or the death of the Sovereign, that he informs the Lord Mayor of London, the Governor of Northern Ireland and the Lieutenant-Governors of Jersey, Guernsey and the Isle of Man of a Royal birth or the death of the Sovereign, and directs the preparation of Special Supplements to the *London Gazette* recording such events. Now that the Sovereign can speak to her peoples all over the world through the medium of broadcasting the Home Secretary's opportunities of conveying messages from the Queen to her peoples are much less than they were in Queen Victoria's reign, when his predecessors published the Queen's message to her subjects on the Jubilees of 1887 and 1897. But still today it was the Home Secretary to whom the Queen sent her messages of sympathy with the sufferers from the floods of January and February, 1953, and her thanks for all who assisted in the work of rescue. As the channel of communication between the people and the Crown it fell to him in 1952 to lay before the Queen the large number of addresses and messages of condolence on the death of King George VI which he received from local authorities, public bodies and private individuals all over the country, and to submit for Her Majesty's approval the reply to be sent. He it is who prepares for the Queen's consideration drafts for her replies to Messages from Parliament and to Addresses which she receives in person from the limited number of bodies which have the privilege of presenting Addresses to the Sovereign seated on the throne, or from local authorities or public institutions which she visits. He is responsible for submitting for the Queen's Sign Manual all warrants for the issue of Letters Patent creating peerages, baronetcies or granting charters of incorporation. All the documents which are associated with the appointment of a Bishop or Archbishop of the Church of England, after the Queen has approved the name submitted by the Prime Minister, are the responsibility of the Home Office—the *Congé d'Elire* which gives the Dean and Chapter permission to elect, the Letter Recommendatory which names the person to be elected, the confirmation of the election, and the restitution of the temporalities of the See which during the vacancy had reverted to the Crown.

After the Bishop or Archbishop has been consecrated the Home Secretary administers the following Oath:

> 'I . . . . now elected confirmed and consecrated Bishop of . . . . do hereby declare that your Majesty is the only Supreme Governor of this Your Realm in Spiritual and Ecclesiastical things as well as in Temporal; and that no Foreign Prelate or Potentate has any jurisdiction within this Realm; and I acknowledge that I hold the said Bishopric, as well the Spiritualities as the Temporalities thereof, only of Your Majesty. And for the same Temporalities I do my homage presently to Your Majesty. So help me God.
>
> GOD SAVE QUEEN ELIZABETH.'

This oath the prelate takes with his hands placed inside the Queen's hands before he is enthroned and the temporalities of the See are restored to him. The Home Secretary advises the Queen on appointments to Crown Livings in the Channel Islands and the Isle of Man, and at Investitures he presents Knights Bachelor to receive the accolade of Knighthood at Her Majesty's hands. He advises the Queen on the exercise of her Prerogative as the Fountain of Honour on such matters as the grant of the title 'Royal' or of Her Majesty's title to a society or institution, the raising of a borough to the status of a city, the grant of the dignity of Lord Mayor to the chief magistrate of a city, permission to use the Royal Arms or the Royal Cypher and the award of the Albert, Edward and Queen's Police and Fire Service Medals. And he is responsible for the arrangements at the Cenotaph on Remembrance Day when each year those who lost their lives in the defence of their country in two world wars are commemorated.

2. THE REDRESS OF GRIEVANCES

Milton, in *Areopagitica,* said:

'When complaints are freely heard, deeply considered and speedily reformed then is the utmost bound of civil liberty attained that wise men look for.'

The Home Secretary is concerned with the redress of grievances or wrongs in three ways.

First, he receives petitions to the Sovereign pleading for a remedy to a wrong or for help in some private distress. If they concern his Department they are carefully considered and laid before the Queen with a suggested reply for him to send on behalf of Her Majesty: if they concern another Department they are by Her Majesty's command transferred, on the Home Secretary's advice, to that Department: if they relate to a personal difficulty about which nothing can be done by the Crown the petitioner is told that the Secretary of State was unable to advise Her Majesty to issue any commands in the matter.

Secondly, he is concerned with the redress of grievances because of his responsibility for the large number of people who for one reason or another are entrusted to his care. He receives petitions, memorials and complaints from such people, or on their behalf, on all sorts of subjects. Since he is responsible for their custody, a high standard of care and consideration must be given to all their petitions; and as we have seen in Chapter XI he must also see to it that the law which in general serves a good purpose shall not have harmful consequences in some particular case—should it do so he will advise the Crown, as the ultimate source of natural justice in the Realm, to exercise the Prerogative of Mercy.

But it is not only from or about persons for whose custody he is responsible that the Home Secretary receives complaints or petitions. Complaints reach him on a wide range of points relating to matters which are either his specific concern as Home Secretary or come to him because they are not the business of any other Minister. All these are investigated so that the truth may be ascertained and matters found to be wrong put right.

authority. But now, although there is close liaison between t Director of Public Prosecutions and the Home Office on crimi matters, the Home Secretary is not responsible for the work and does not give instructions to, the Director.

The Home Secretary is responsible for appointing the Direc of Public Prosecutions and the Assistant Directors, and the Direc makes an annual return of his prosecutions to the Home Secret for submission to Parliament; but the Director acts in his day-day work under the general superintendence and direction of Attorney General, and it is the Attorney General who makes re lations (which have to be approved by the Home Secretary and Lord Chancellor) regulating his duties. It is in the changing cont of these regulations that the significant alteration in the relati between the Home Secretary and the Director, mentioned in last paragraph, is to be found. The regulations which were ma in 1886 under the Prosecution of Offences Acts provided that amc the cases in which it was to be the duty of the Director of Pub Prosecutions to prosecute were cases 'where an order in that beh is given to the Director by the Secretary of State. . . .' When regulations were repealed and replaced by a new set of regulati in 1946, this particular provision was not repeated. Nowadays i well recognized and has frequently been stated in Parliament t the Home Office is not a prosecuting authority.

8. CORONERS

Coroners are independent judicial officers, but the Home Sec tary has some responsibility for certain aspects of their work, a he is the Minister primarily responsible for any legislation affect them.

Coroners are appointed by county and certain borough coun and no confirmation of their appointment is needed from a Minister, although notice that the appointment has been made m be given to the Home Secretary. The Lord Chancellor (or in County of Lancaster the Chancellor of the Duchy) has power remove any coroner from his office for inability or misbehavi in the discharge of his duty, and if circumstances should a requiring him to consider whether to exercise this power, th circumstances would ordinarily be brought to his notice by Home Office. The Lord Chancellor has power to make ru regulating the procedure at inquests and post-mortem examinatic but such rules require the concurrence of the Home Secretary. T Home Secretary is responsible for fixing the salaries of coror in case of disagreement between a coroner and the local author roners are required to make to him statistical returns of their uests and verdicts. Alterations in county coroners' districts uire his approval and he can direct that the number of county oners shall be increased if changes in the districts seem to him call for an increase. An inquest can be held only by direction of Home Secretary in those cases where a body has been destroyed for some other reason no body can be found.

It has long been accepted that it is for the Home Secretary to ue general guidance or information to coroners by means of cular letters, for example about the effect of new legislation, and oners often ask the Home Office for advice on questions of law procedure.

9. CRIMINAL STATISTICS

The Home Secretary lays before Parliament each year a volume ing the criminal statistics for England and Wales. The statistics lude a return of offences furnished by the police, detailed particu- s of the proceedings before the various criminal courts, the urn submitted to the Home Secretary by the Director of Public osecutions, and statistics of extradition cases, Broadmoor patients, es in which the Prerogative of Mercy has been exercised, and es in which legal aid has been given.

10. RESEARCH

The Criminal Justice Act, 1948, gave power to the Home Secre- y to meet the cost of research into the causes of delinquency l the treatment of offenders. In present financial difficulties, it s so far been possible to make only a very modest use of these wers, but a few useful enquiries have already been initiated and addition certain facilities have been provided for research nced from sources other than public funds. Much remains known about delinquents and delinquency; and this provision in Criminal Justice Act at any rate indicates that it is recognized t research, as well as day-to-day practical experience, may throw t on the causes of crime and the best ways of dealing with nders.

11. THE HOME OFFICE NOT A MINISTRY OF JUSTICE

t will be seen from the foregoing that the functions of the Home retary fall far short of those of a 'Minister of Justice'. This pter has outlined the more important of the Home Secretary's ious and extensive responsibilities for the administration of cost of registration and elections was necessary. The Local Government Board was made responsible: in 1921 these duties were transferred to the Home Secretary.[1]

Of the Home Secretary's constitutional responsibilities, not the least important is his responsibility for election law. The nature and scope of this responsibility are commonly misunderstood. It is often supposed that the Registration and Returning Officers are the Home Secretary's subordinates, and even that he can review the validity of an election. In fact these officers are answerable only to the law, and the result of an election, or the validity of any proceedings connected with an election, can be questioned only in the courts.

Under the Representation of the People Act, 1949, which consolidated previous Acts, certain clerks of local authorities are Electoral Registration Officers and Acting Returning Officers ex-officio. In these capacities they are not responsible to their local authorities, nor can the Home Secretary dismiss them or discipline them in any way. Their duties are laid on them in detail by the law, and if any of them or any assistant is, without reasonable cause, guilty of any act or omission in breach of his duty, he commits a criminal offence and is liable on summary conviction to a fine of £100. Thus these officers have a personal and independent responsibility under the law, free from even any appearance of political interference. The Home Secretary cannot, and does not try to, interfere in the way in which individual Registration and Acting Returning Officers discharge their duties.

Nevertheless, the Home Secretary's actual responsibility in this field is very real and very important. Above all, it is his responsibility to see that the electoral law is effective, workmanlike and fair. The importance of this is very great, for public confidence in the electoral system is part of the foundations of parliamentary democracy. Election law is a subject of perennial interest, and tradition, the nature of his office, and the needs of the case demand that the Home Secretary's approach to it should be free of partisan consideration. It is he who prepares and is responsible for all legislation relating to the representation of the people in Parliament.

Questions may arise at all levels, from the fundamentals of the electoral system to the wording and arrangement of a form for use in connection with the registration of electors; and at all levels it is customary to bring the principal parties into consultation. Such fundamental questions as whether proportional representation should be introduced do not fall to be settled by any individual Minister or Department, but it is scarcely conceivable that any Government

[1] S.R.&O. 1921, No. 959.

would seek to make a change except after ample discussion between the principal political parties. The traditional method of considering such questions, as also questions of major political importance at a lower level, such as the amount that a candidate may spend on his election expenses, or the principal rules governing the conduct of an election campaign, has now become a Speaker's Conference. Less important or more technical questions, such as improvements in methods of registration, or such reforms of the procedural rules for holding an election as were made by the Representation of the People Act, 1948, are customarily considered by a departmental committee appointed jointly by the Home Secretary and the Secretary of State for Scotland, on which the political parties as well as the Registration and Acting Returning Officers are represented. Day to day questions of practice and procedure, amendments of forms and so on, are discussed more informally at meetings of an advisory conference which includes the Chief Agents of the principal parties, representative Registration and Acting Returning Officers and officials of the Government Departments concerned. At all times the object is to secure the greatest possible degree of general agreement before introducing any change.

The result of these discussions may be legislation in Parliament, or the revision of subordinate rules and regulations, or it may be merely a circular giving guidance to Registration or Acting Returning Officers. In each case the primary responsibility falls to the Home Secretary. In day to day administration, as already explained, the Home Secretary has little executive responsibility. In this field, however, informal relations are particularly close between the Home Office, the Registration and Acting Returning Officers, and the Stationery Office, which gives much technical help, especially over the arrangements for printing the register. Both through the advisory electoral conference already mentioned and in other ways, there is constant contact of an advisory, consultative and informative nature.

In addition, the Home Secretary has some specific powers and duties under election law. Thus, as regards parliamentary elections, it is his duty under the House of Commons (Redistribution of Seats) Act, 1949, to present to Parliament, and to seek parliamentary approval for orders giving effect to, reports of the Boundary Commissions for England, Wales and Northern Ireland recommending alterations of constituency boundaries. He makes regulations, subject to approval by Parliament, prescribing the dates for postal voting applications and the procedure of postal voting. The appointments of deputies to Registration and Acting Returning Officers

out of the Home Secretary's statutory powers to release on lice
persons serving sentences of life imprisonment, and his power
release certain prisoners and Borstal inmates on licence anc
restore lost remission. Another class comprises a variety of c
arising out of the Home Secretary's powers under the Prison
1952,[1] in particular to commute to imprisonment the unexpired
of a Borstal sentence if the inmate is reported by the Boarc
Visitors of his institution to be incorrigible or to be exercising a
influence on other inmates; to authorize (after consultation with
court concerned) the transfer to Borstal of a person under 21
tenced to imprisonment; or to transfer a prisoner or Borstal inn
to a prison or Borstal in Scotland. Every such case is consid
carefully on its merits. Another large class comprises the irresp
sible offenders, insane or mentally defective, who drift through
courts and whose subsequent disposal sometimes presents gr
problems to the Home Office; and the Home Office deals with
another class of individual case arising out of its concern
extradition proceedings. Some of the problems concerning t
last two classes are discussed in the following paragraphs.

5. BROADMOOR PATIENTS AND MENTAL DEFECTIVES

Reference has already been made in Chapter XI to persons cha
with murder who are found by the jury to be insane on arraignn
and unfit to plead, or guilty but insane. In both classes of
(whether or not the charge is a capital one) the court orders
individual's detention during Her Majesty's Pleasure. Such pers
were formerly known as criminal lunatics, but the Criminal Jus
Act, 1948, changed their name to 'Broadmoor patients'.

Those who are certified as insane after being sentenced to d
also become Broadmoor patients. Like the two classes of 'Que
Pleasure' patients referred to in the last paragraph, they are li
to detention for an indefinite period.

Another class of Broadmoor patients consists of the prisoner
Borstal inmates, who are certified insane during the currenc
their sentences. The Home Secretary is empowered to order
removal to a mental hospital. Their liability to be detained ther
Broadmoor patients remains until the sentence expires.

Broadmoor patients who are dangerous or violent, or have
charged with serious crimes, are normally moved by the H
Secretary's order to Broadmoor Institution at Crowthorne, B

[1] These powers were formerly exercised under the Criminal Justice
1948.

'e. He orders the removal of the others to the appropriate local ıtal hospital.

\ prisoner or Borstal inmate who has become a Broadmoor ient can be returned to prison or Borstal to complete his sen- ce if he is certified as sane. More difficult questions arise over discharge of Broadmoor patients liable to detention for an in- nite period. Broadmoor Institution is administered by the Board Control, and other mental hospitals are administered by Hospital nagement Committees under the Regional Hospital Boards, but decision whether a Broadmoor patient may properly be dis- rged is the responsibility of the Home Secretary.

This is a weighty responsibility. Discharge in the case of those cerned in the more serious offences is normally conditional in first instance, and is to the care of a friend or relative who ertakes responsibility for the patient. The Home Secretary will horize discharge in such cases only if, after taking medical advice making enquiries into home surroundings, he considers that re is a reasonable likelihood of the patient's settling down in con- ons in the outside world without serious risk of a further break- vn. The period for which those who are discharged have been ained must inevitably vary widely. Where a Broadmoor patient s before the courts on a very serious charge, the Home Secretary not normally feel that he can authorize discharge until there has n a substantial period of observation. Some patients unfor- ately can never be regarded as fit for discharge, but every case periodically examined to see whether discharge, or transfer to other hospital, can properly be considered.

The number of cases involved may be illustrated by the figures for 2. During that year, 63 persons were received at Broadmoor titution and 121 Broadmoor patients (most of whom had been tified after conviction) were received at local mental hospitals. the end of 1952, 1,013 Broadmoor patients were detained, 897 them at Broadmoor Institution. Of this total of 1,013, 597 had n detained over five years, including 224 who had been detained over 20 years.

ome prisoners and Borstal inmates may be found, after convic- 1, to be certifiable as mental defectives and may be removed by ler of the Home Secretary to an institution for mental defectives. e arrangements are made in consultation with the Board of ntrol. A person who has been removed by the Home Secretary's ler to an institution for mental defectives cannot without the me Secretary's consent be discharged during the time for which would have been liable to be detained in prison or Borstal. If for boroughs throughout England and Wales under section 24 of the Local Government Act, 1933, and by the Londo County Council and the Metropolitan Borough Counci under section 146 of the London Government Act, 1939.

(b) Byelaws for the regulation of the seashore and promenad which may be made by borough councils and district counci under sections 82 and 83 of the Public Health Acts Amend ment Act, 1907.

(c) Byelaws made by borough councils and district counci under section 164 of the Public Health Act, 1875, for th regulation of public walks and pleasure grounds.

Other byelaws for which the Home Secretary is responsib include those for the regulation of commons, open spaces, villag greens, parking places, taxicabs, pleasure boats and public bathin together with many byelaws made by local authorities under Loca Act powers.

Local authorities are invited to submit their proposals for byelaw to the Home Office in draft in the first instance, so that they may b examined in detail before they are formally adopted by the Counci These drafts are examined to ensure first, that the byelaw is *intr vires*, and secondly that it passes the legal tests of 'certainty' an 'reasonableness'.

In considering the *vires* of a byelaw, whether a byelaw does c does not exceed the power given by the Statute which authorizes to be made, account has to be taken of any restrictions imposed b that Statute. A byelaw may extend or add to the general law; it mus not conflict with the general law. Thus, if the general law ha imposed a penalty for a certain offence, a byelaw may not impose different penalty. The courts have laid down certain general prir ciples in deciding as to the 'certainty' or 'reasonableness' of byelaw A byelaw must specify as definitely as possible both the acts whic it is intended to prohibit, and the conditions under which they a prohibited. It is equally important that the byelaw should b expressed in plain and intelligible language.

Practically every new byelaw involves a fresh interference wit private freedom of action and the creation of a new criminal offenc and in each case the Home Secretary must be satisfied that the loca authority have reasonable grounds for their action. The question i each case is whether the general disadvantage of multiplying restric tions and criminal offences is outweighed in the particular instanc by the convenience to the community resulting from the byelaw. T a large extent it is a question of local circumstances, and cannot b determined by any fixed rule.

Sometimes there is a genuine conflict of local interests which it is not always easy to resolve equitably. Thus it may be argued that the flying of model aircraft, properly regulated, is not merely an innocent amusement but a hobby of considerable educational value and one which it is in the public interest to encourage. But it is a noisy pastime and disturbs the peace and quiet which is one of the main attractions of public parks in crowded areas. To forbid the hobby is harsh on the enthusiast and may be detrimental to education. To allow it is to impair the enjoyment by most ratepayers of an amenity for which they pay. If there are many open spaces in the neighbourhood the answer is a compromise. But if the town has only one park of any size in a congested industrial area the problem is difficult indeed.

The Home Office issues series of model byelaws for the guidance of local authorities desiring to make byelaws under certain statutes. Local authorities are asked to follow the models unless there is a particular reason for departing from them. Where no model byelaw exists, the Home Office is prepared to assist in framing a suitable byelaw.

When the form of a byelaw has been agreed between the local authority and the Home Office, the local authority proceed to comply with the statutory requirements laid down in section 250 of the Local Government Act, 1933. At least one month before application for confirmation of the byelaw is made, notice of the Council's intention so to apply must be given in one or more newspapers circulating in the area to which the byelaw applies, and for at least a month after the date of the publication of the newspaper containing the notice a copy of the byelaw must be deposited at the offices of the Council for inspection by the public at all reasonable hours. These provisions furnish an opportunity to persons interested, if they so desire, to make objections to the Home Secretary before the byelaw is confirmed. The local authority then submit to the Home Office evidence of compliance with these requirements, together with sealed copies of the byelaw for confirmation by the Home Secretary, who fixes the date upon which it is to come into operation.

7. BURIALS, CONSECRATION OF BURIAL GROUNDS, CREMATION

Until 1906 the Home Secretary was the central authority under the Burial Acts but in that year Parliament transferred to the Local Government Board his jurisdiction in matters of sanitation, and left him authority in ecclesiastical matters and to authorize exhumations.

Under the Burial Act, 1857, which was passed to stop body

snatching from burial grounds, it is a criminal offence to remove a body from its place of burial without a licence from the Secretary of State or an ecclesiastical faculty. Every year he issues some 250 licences to private individuals who wish to reinter the body of a relative elsewhere—for example, to remove it from a public to a private grave: the licences contain conditions designed to ensure privacy and strict sanitary precautions. In the case of every burial ground maintained by a local authority under the Burial Acts, 1852-1906, the Home Secretary's approval is required to the consecration of any part of the ground according to the rites of the Church of England and his sanction to the allotment of any portion of ground for the exclusive use of a particular denomination such as the Roman Catholics or the Jews. The Burial Act, 1900, requires the approval of the Home Secretary to every table of fees to be taken by ministers of religion for their services at interments in burial grounds provided under the Burial Acts or the Public Health Interment Acts. He has however no responsibility for, or jurisdiction in connection with, the fees payable in parish churchyards.

The introduction of the practice of cremation and the decision in the case of *Rex v. Price* (1884) that disposal of a corpse by burning was not a criminal offence led to the introduction of the Cremation Act, 1902, which charged the Home Secretary with the duty of making regulations governing the practice of cremation. The original regulations of 1903 were largely based on the practice of the London Cremation Company and were designed to secure as far as possible that cremation should not be used to conceal crime. The regulations were amended in 1930 in a number of minor respects. A Committee which sat recently to review the operation of the regulations did not recommend any relaxation of the essential safeguards of the regulations of 1903 but suggested[1] some modifications in their practical working in view of the increase of recent years in the use of cremation as a method of disposal: the annual number of cremations in Great Britain has risen from 16,312 in 1938 to 79,607 in 1949, and in 1953 it exceeded 116,000. Some of the Committee's proposals were implemented in the Cremation Act, 1952.

8. SUMMER TIME AND CALENDAR QUESTIONS

The first world war saw the introduction of Summer Time in the interest of the townsman. Double Summer Time was introduced during the last war in the interests of production and the war effort. For years there was controversy between urban and agricultural interests as to the duration of Summer Time: by the Summer Time Acts of

[1] Cmd. 8009, July 1950.

1922 and 1925 it was to begin on the day following the third Saturday in April (if that day were Easter Day on the day following the second Saturday) and to end on the day following the first Saturday in October.

During the war, by Defence Regulation, Summer Time continued all the year round: in the years 1941-1945 and 1947 Double Summer Time was introduced for some months.

The Summer Time Act, 1947, provided for the period of Summer Time to be fixed each year by Order in Council; if no period was so determined then Summer Time would be in force for the statutory period prescribed by the Acts of 1922 and 1925. Each year it falls to the Home Secretary after consultation with his colleagues, when the conflicting needs of agriculture and of fuel and power are considered, to propose what the period of Summer Time shall be. In the years 1947 to 1952 the powers of the Act of 1947 were used, but in 1953 Summer Time was in force for the statutory period.

In 1923 the League of Nations Committee for Communications and Transit appointed a Committee to consider the reform of the Calendar. This Committee reported in 1926 and dealt separately with the reform of the Calendar and the fixation of Easter. On the latter issue it did not make any definite proposal: it stated the results of its inquiries which showed that most of the churches were disposed to agree if all the churches adopted a fixed date simultaneously; that the Papacy would, if the fixing of Easter could be shown to be of universal benefit, submit the question to the next Oecumenical Council; that the Jews had no objection; and that educational and commercial interests favoured a fixed Easter.

A private member introduced in 1928 a Bill which became the Easter Act, 1928, which fixed Easter on the first Sunday after the second Saturday in April. The Act was to be brought into operation by an Order in Council which was to be laid before Parliament in draft form for affirmative resolutions. Before the draft Order was made 'regard shall be had to any opinion officially expressed by any Church or other Christian body'.

No Order in Council has been made bringing the Act into force because the Vatican have taken the line that a General Council of the Church must first be called and there is no present prospect of such a meeting, and the Anglican Church would only accept a fixed Easter if it were accepted by the other Christian communities.

Linked up with the isolated question of the fixation of Easter is the wider issue of Calendar reform, the substitution for the Gregorian calendar of a calendar in which any date falls on the same day of the week in every year. It falls to the Home Secretary to advise the United Kingdom delegation to any international conference when this matter comes up for discussion and to deal with it in the House of Commons or through the Home Office spokesman in the House of Lords. Although we are accustomed to four weekly rationing periods and the use of the thirteen month calendar in many fields for statistical purposes there is little evidence in the United Kingdom of any real interest or support for such a calendar in substitution for the Gregorian calendar.

9. PROTECTION OF ANIMALS

The Home Secretary has a general responsibility for the law relating to the protection of animals; the laws dealing with the slaughtering of animals for food or pest extermination are not his concern. The Protection of Animals Acts, 1911-1927, contain the general law relating to cruelty to animals in England and Wales: they make it a criminal offence to cause unnecessary suffering to any domestic or captive animal. In the last thirty years they have been supplemented by a large number of Acts, all introduced as Private Members' Bills, which give special protection to particular species or classes of animals, for example the Performing Animals (Regulation) Act, 1925, the Protection of Animals (Cruelty to Dogs) Act, 1933, the Docking and Nicking of Horses Act, 1949, and the Pet Animals Act, 1951. During the 1948-49 Session of Parliament, seven Bills dealing with the protection of animals and birds were introduced by Private Members. One of these, the Protection of Animals (Hunting and Coursing Prohibition) Bill would have made it a criminal offence to cause, procure, assist at or take part in, for the purposes of sport, the hunting of any deer, otter or badger or the coursing of any hare or rabbit. The Bill was rejected on Second Reading after a very full debate. Shortly afterwards a Motion was tabled calling upon the Government to set up an appropriate body to examine the law relating to cruelty to wild animals. The Government set up a Committee under the chairmanship of Mr. J. Scott Henderson, Q.C., which in 1951 presented a most comprehensive report.[1]

The Home Secretary's only executive function under the law relating to cruelty to animals is that placed on him by the Performing Animals (Regulation) Act, 1925, of maintaining, for inspection at all reasonable times, a central record of all persons registered with a local authority, in accordance with Regulations which he made, as exhibitors or trainers of performing animals.

[1] Cmd. 8266.

10. THE CRUELTY TO ANIMALS ACT, 1876

The Home Secretary is the Minister responsible for the administration of the Cruelty to Animals Act, 1876, which imposes a stringent control on all experiments likely to give pain if performed on living vertebrate animals. This subject is one of the most controversial with which he has to deal.

No experiment of this kind may be performed without a licence or, with very rare exceptions mostly related to veterinary field investigations, on premises which have not been approved by the Home Office. If the experiment is not performed entirely under anaesthetics, or if being so performed the animal is not immediately killed at the conclusion, or if horses, asses, or mules are used, special certificates are required in addition to a licence. Almost all experiments on cats and dogs also require special certificates. The Home Office issues licences, allows certificates and registers premises. A staff of medically qualified Inspectors advises on the technical aspects of all applications, inspects registered places, usually without warning, instructs licensees and applicants for licences in the requirements of the Act, and scrutinizes publications describing experiments performed under the Act. Difficult cases which have an element of severity or marked novelty are referred to an Advisory Committee composed of distinguished doctors and surgeons under the chairmanship of a High Court judge.

11. WILD BIRDS' PROTECTION

The Home Office is the central authority in the long series of Acts dating from 1869 to 1939 relating to the protection of wild birds.

The Act of 1880, the oldest unrepealed Act of the series, established, with provision for exceptions, a close time for all birds during the breeding season; the Act of 1894 empowered the Secretary of State to make orders protecting their eggs. Bird life varies so widely in different parts of the country that these and subsequent Acts empower the Home Secretary to make orders on the application of County and County Borough Councils extending or varying the close time, protecting specified birds or specified eggs for the whole year and establishing bird sanctuaries. The Acts also prohibit various methods of capturing birds which involve cruelty.

The Home Office is assisted in the administration of the Acts by an advisory committee, on which sit representatives of the principal bodies concerned with the study and preservation of bird life, along with representatives of sporting interests. The Home Office and the

Committee have been fortunate in a succession of distinguished chairmen including the late Viscount Grey of Fallodon.

The Committee considers drafts of local orders: from time to time it has also taken up the question of whether the law should be revised and placed on a different basis. Apart from the general close season and the power to create local sanctuaries, the existing Acts proceed on the principle of extending more or less protection to named species of birds according to need. In theory no doubt this principle is sound, because it avoids the unnecessary creation of criminal offences. In practice it leads to the maximum confusion, because to discover the law in any particular locality it is necessary to study long lists of birds, and these lists vary endlessly from place to place. The alternative principle, for which there is growing support, is that all birds should be protected at all times and in all places, except named species from which protection is specifically withheld or withdrawn. The advantage of this in point of simplicity is beyond question. Private Members' Bills incorporating this principle were introduced into both Houses of Parliament during the Parliamentary Session 1953-54, one becoming the Protection of Birds Act, 1954.

12. CHARITABLE COLLECTIONS

Parliament has charged the Home Secretary with responsibility for the control of street collections and house to house collections for charitable purposes. Under the Police, Factories, etc., (Miscellaneous Provisions) Act, 1916, the police authority (which is the Home Secretary in respect of the Metropolitan Police District) may regulate street collections; these regulations are subject to confirmation by the Home Secretary. Under the House to House Collections Act, 1939, a licence is ordinarily required from the police to hold a collection from house to house for charitable purposes, but under the Act the Home Secretary may by Order exempt a person from this local requirement. Regulations made under the Act require, *inter alia*, prescribed information on expenses, proceeds, and the application of the proceeds to be furnished to the police, or to the Home Secretary in exempted cases. The accounts in these latter cases are checked in the Home Office and inquiry is made when it appears that administrative costs are too high.

13. TAXICABS

The Home Secretary is vested with power to regulate taxicabs in the Metropolitan Police District and he authorizes any alterations in fares. Certain of his functions he delegates to the Commissioner of

Metropolitan Police. Local authorities outside the Metropolis can make byelaws under the Town Police Clauses Act, 1847, for regulating taxicabs in their districts; these byelaws are subject to the approval and confirmation of the Home Secretary.

14. FAIRS

Before 1871 a fair, whether granted by charter or held by prescriptive right, could not be abolished: before 1873 its date could not be altered. The Fairs Acts of 1871 and 1873 empowered the Home Secretary, subject to certain consents, to abolish a fair or alter its date. Occasion for the use of either of these powers very rarely arises nowadays.

15. PRIVATE MEMBERS' LEGISLATION

It is because his range of responsibilities is so wide and because he has to deal with all matters of home affairs which are not the responsibility of some other Minister, that the Home Secretary has to deal with so many Private Members' Bills. In every Session at least half the Bills so introduced concern the Home Office. Their subjects range from amendments of the Children Act to the prohibition of hunting and coursing: from the registration of architects to the registration of hairdressers: from proposals to amend the law relating to adoption to proposals to prohibit tied houses in the drink trade. In all these instances and in many others, it falls to the Home Secretary to examine the Bill, to assist the House of Commons by giving the views of the Government on the measure generally and the desirability of giving it a Second Reading: and if it is given a Second Reading to have the drafting of the Bill critically examined in consultation with Parliamentary Counsel to secure that by amendments during the Committee stage it may be made a watertight and workmanlike measure and not, as is sometimes the case—inevitably because the author has not at his disposal the skill of the expert government draftsman—a Bill full of gaps and imperfections.

16. MARRIAGE GUIDANCE

The Report of the Departmental Committee on Grants for the development of Marriage Guidance[1] recommended that Exchequer aid should be given for an experimental period (which began in 1949), towards the cost of marriage guidance work undertaken by three voluntary societies, the National Marriage Guidance Council, the Catholic Marriage Advisory Council and the Family Welfare Association. This help takes two forms: annual grants are made

[1] Cmd. 7566, 1948.

towards the central administrative expenses of each society, and the cost is met of selecting and training men and women for work as marriage guidance counsellors under the auspices of the societies. The Marriage Guidance Training Board, appointed by the Home Secretary and composed of representatives of the voluntary societies and of the Home Office, the Ministry of Health and the Ministry of Education, considers schemes of selection and training submitted by each of the societies and recommends what payments should be approved. The work connected centrally with this project falls to the Probation Division of the Home Office.

CHAPTER XVIII

Staffing, Finance and Common Services

The Home Office in history — The Department today: Establishment and Organization Division — Finance — Common services — Conclusion.

*

1. THE HOME OFFICE IN HISTORY

THE First Report of the Commissioners appointed by Act 25 Geo. 3 cap. 19 'to enquire into the Fees, Gratuities, Perquisites and Emoluments which are or have been lately received in the several public Record Offices therein mentioned' (Cmd. 309/1806) gives a picture of the Home Office as it was shortly after its establishment. In 1785, when the Commissioners were making their enquiries, the staff of the Home Office consisted of the Secretary of State, two Under-Secretaries, a Chief Clerk, four Senior Clerks, six Junior Clerks, two Chamber Keepers and a Necessary Woman.

To the Home Office was annexed a subordinate Office for Plantation Affairs consisting of an Under-Secretary and three Clerks. There were attached to the Home Office and the Foreign Office jointly a Gazette Writer and his Deputy, a Keeper of State Papers, a Clerk and Transmitter of State Papers, two Commissioners for methodizing and digesting the State Papers, a Secretary for the Latin Language, two Decypherers and sixteen Messengers.

The Commissioners reported:

> 'The attendance of the efficient Under-Secretaries is constant and unremitting: that of the Chief Clerk is likewise constant; and the other Clerks, though not always employed, are in daily attendance and are expected to be ready for the execution of any business on which their superiors may think necessary to employ them.'

The expenses of the Home Office were defrayed from various sources, partly from the Civil List, partly from the Post Office revenue, from the Cordatum Fund in Ireland, from Fees, from Gratuities and various minor sources of revenue such as profits from franking newspapers.

In 1784 the gross receipts of the Secretary of State were £8,497 10s. 2d. Out of these emoluments he paid in bills for coals, candles and turnery ware for the use of the office, £314 10s. 0d.: in salaries to various officers in the Home Office and the Plantation Office £1,694 12s. 0d. His net emoluments were £4,767 2s. 2d.: the total expenses of the Home Office for the year ending 1784 were £15,639 12s. 9½d.

The one woman employed in the office was the Necessary Woman. Catherine Drinkwater in her evidence to the Committee on November 28, 1785, said:

'She is deputy to Mrs. Emmet the Necessary Woman; and has been so for nearly three years; her business is to take care of the apartments, to clean them and light the fires, etc., for which purpose she, at her own expenses, keeps two female servants, and finds towels, dusters, soap, whiting and sand, etc., for the use of the office.

'She receives a salary from Mrs. Emmet of 28 guineas a year: besides which she receives small presents at Christmas from the Secretary of State, the Under Secretaries and Clerks, which amounted in the year 1784 to between £5 and £6; also half a guinea from the Coal Merchant; she has the remainder of the tallow candles used by the Clerks, old pens and loose paper, which amounted in the year 1784 to between £30 and £40, but from particular circumstances she thinks the produce of that year was more than common. This is the whole of her net receipt of every kind by virtue of her office. She has apartments and coals and candles for her own use.'

The Commissioners after examining every member of the staff concluded their Report on the Home Office in the following terms:

'From what we have been able to collect, the general business of the office is scarcely sufficient to furnish full employment for the Clerks at present borne upon the establishment; and we consider their present number as rather to be justified by the propriety of having fit persons always in readiness upon any extraordinary pressure of business, than from the degree of the employment which the office affords. If they were reduced to eight . . . Your Majesty's service might not suffer from such reduction.'

On August 5, 1875, the Home Office moved to its present main office in Whitehall. Fifteen months later, on November 7, 1876, the following Office Instruction on the Conduct of Business in the Home Office was issued:

'Letters arriving here, after registration, are minuted by the heads of departments with the proposed answers; which minutes, being revised and approved by the Under-Secretary of State, are extended by Clerks of the Upper Division into the form of letters for signature; which, after being examined by the head of the department are approved and signed by the Secretary of State or the Under-Secretary of State as the case may be, and sent to the Registry to be copied into books and despatched by Clerks of the Lower Division, assisted by copyists.

'In cases of important letters which require drafts to be made for approval before being written out for signature, the drafts, when approved, are now sent to be copied by Clerks of the Lower Division as are also drafts of limited circulars and forms to be filled up.'

The total staff of the Department, including Messengers, at the date of that Instruction was thirty-four, of whom four belonged to a class that was to be abolished as vacancies occurred.

2. THE HOME OFFICE TODAY: ESTABLISHMENT AND ORGANIZATION DIVISION

Today there are more than 3,000 non-industrial and 2,000 industrial staff employed by the Home Office spread over more than forty Divisions and Branches, eleven Regional Headquarters and a variety of other premises including Immigration Offices, Police Training Schools, Forensic Science Laboratories, Civil Defence Schools, Wireless Depots and Civil Defence and Fire Service Stores all scattered throughout the country.

The wide range of the Home Secretary's multifarious duties has been indicated in Chapter I; but reference to the organization chart will show that as a general rule the sphere of each of the Assistant Under-Secretaries of State forms a natural and homogeneous whole. The exception is the group of general divisions which include the large and miscellaneous collection of subjects described in Chapter XVII.

The functions of some Departments of State readily lend themselves to devolution to a regional organization; but most of the Home Secretary's wide and varied duties do not. A notable exception to this has already been mentioned in Chapter VI—for Civil Defence purposes England and Wales are now divided into eleven Regions with a Principal Officer in each as the representative of the Home Secretary. He is responsible for securing the implementation within his Region of the policy of the Home Secretary in relation to Civil Defence. Another exception is the Children's Branch Inspectorate (Chapter VII) which is also partly 'regionalized', being organized into six Regions with headquarters in North and South London, Birmingham, Leeds, Manchester and Cardiff.

The tasks of organizing the work of all these units and of managing the staff are the responsibility of the Establishment and Organization Division. At its head is an Assistant Secretary with the title of Establishment Officer, and one of the Under-Secretaries is as Principal Establishment and Organization Officer directly responsible to the Head of the Department for its activities.

The Division's control of staff throughout the Office is immediate and at first hand. Nevertheless the structure of the Department presents certain problems in the execution of routine establishment work. The office is comparatively small, but as we have seen its long history has made it responsible for an extraordinary number of diverse subjects and services, many of which have no direct relation one with another. There are small administrative divisions and large executive branches; technical, specialist and executive branches; inspectorates; a heterogeneous collection of regional headquarters, schools and stores and a commercial undertaking in Carlisle. In any of these units an officer of a general service class may find himself placed for a time. Amid this diversity a primary task of the Establishment Division is to secure that no unit should appear to itself to become isolated from the main body. This is done, as far as possible, by interchange of staff; by assimilating new types of work to the existing general service class structure wherever possible; by centralized promotion; and by the provision of suitable 'background' training to new entrants and others. Integration comes too in the transactions of the Departmental Whitley Council, where the staff associations, without neglecting their special interests, learn to cooperate with the official side in promoting the efficiency of the Department and the well-being of the staff. Relations between the two sides are extremely good and most matters are dealt with in an informal way outside the Whitley Council.

3. FINANCE

The Permanent Under-Secretary of State is responsible for the accounting of six Parliamentary Votes, viz.:

Class III, Vote 1—Home Office.
" " " 2—Home Office (Civil Defence Services).
" " " 3—Police, England and Wales.
" " " 5—Child Care, England and Wales.
" " " 6—Fire Services, England and Wales.
" " " 7—Carlisle State Management District.

During the financial year 1954-55 these six Votes provide for gross expenditure amounting to £72,691,690 towards which receipts of £4,548,360 are authorized to be appropriated in aid of the Votes, leaving a net expenditure of £68,143,330.

Of this gross expenditure of £72 million the Exchequer grants to local and other authorities for services with which the Home Office is concerned account for approximately £54 million, allocated roughly as follows: Civil Defence Services, £3¾ million; Police £33½ million; Child Care, Approved Schools and Remand Homes, £9·4 million; Fire Services, £4·4 million; Probation Expenses, £·8 million; Magistrates' Courts, £2·2 million and School Crossing Patrols £¼ million (fines, fees, etc., collected at Magistrates' Courts amounting to £1·1 million are appropriated in aid of the Vote). All claims by local authorities for Exchequer grant are examined by the District Auditors of the Ministry of Housing and Local Government, and their reports are available to assist the Home Office in examining claims.

The allocation of the remaining £18 million is roughly as follows: Home Office Vote, £3 million, the bulk of which is disbursed in salaries and wages; Civil Defence Services Vote, £12½ million, providing mainly for the purchase of equipment and materials, and for the expenses of the training establishments; the Police Vote, £1 million, consisting mainly of the expense of maintaining the common police services; and the expenses of the Carlisle State Management District, £1½ million.

The Vote for the Carlisle State Management District is for a token sum of £100 only. As a result of the decision not to adopt the system of State management in new towns, provision is limited to trading in the Carlisle State Management District, where trading receipts exceed the expenditure. As this service is a trading concern, an annual Profit and Loss Account and Balance Sheet giving the result on a commercial basis of the trading operations has to be prepared for submission to Parliament.

The Permanent Under-Secretary of State has been nominated by the Treasury to be the Accounting Officer of the Home Office. He is personally responsible to Parliament, through the Public Accounts Committee of the House of Commons, for the financial administration of the Parliamentary Grants for the services under the control of the Department.

The work of the Finance Division is (*a*) to assist the Accounting Officer in carrying out his responsibilities to Parliament, through the Public Accounts Committee; (*b*) to maintain such controls over payments and receipts as are necessary for proper administration, including financial control before expenditure takes place, and for the prevention of fraud and irregularities; and (*c*) to provide, in conjunction with the Administrative Divisions, material for the preparation of the Parliamentary Estimates and Appropriation Accounts, and for keeping under continuous review the out-turn of expenditure in relation to the Estimates.

There is consultation between the administrative divisions and the Finance Division on all questions of policy involving financial considerations. In matters where it is necessary to seek Treasury approval to expenditure the Finance Division is associated with the administrative Divisions in any correspondence or discussions with the Treasury.

4. COMMON SERVICES

Registries, etc.

The Registries, whose main duties consist of the filing and recording of correspondence and the custody of papers, are organized on a decentralized basis serving either single divisions or groups of divisions—according to their size—in the various Home Office buildings, the whole being under the control of a Chief Registrar. Noting of precedents and decisions and the weeding and destruction of papers are other important functions performed by Registry staff.

Registries are never an end in themselves: they are only a means to facilitate the work of the Department; but upon their efficiency in registering papers and producing them when required depends to a great extent the smooth working of the office.

The typing staff in the Home Office are employed in 'pools' serving particular Divisions. In addition, most senior officials have personal assistants who are qualified as shorthand writers.

The office keepers and messengers, without whom the business of the office could scarcely be carried on, are mostly ex-servicemen, the majority of whom are established civil servants.

The Legal Adviser's Branch

It will be apparent from what has been said in preceding chapters that much of the work of the Home Office concerns the law, and especially constitutional and criminal law; and the importance to the Department of legal advice need scarcely be stressed.

In so far as it is possible to generalize it may be said that the interests of the Home Office are such that important policy decisions usually have a legal aspect and often raise problems of constitutional propriety. For this reason the members of the Legal Adviser's Branch are not so much an inquiry bureau giving specific answers to particular questions as counsel in one set of chambers whose main work is to give opinions on matters which raise points of law and of interpretation. In addition, they themselves draft subordinate legislation, assist in the preparation of instructions for Bills and play an important part in the discussions with Parliamentary Counsel as to the form and content of the legislation he is drafting for the Department.

The Statistical Branch

Statistics are needed in the Home Office to help in formulating new policy and in judging the effect of measures that have been adopted; they are also required to satisfy the reasonable demands of Parliament, research workers, and the public generally, for information about the Department's work.

Under the general guidance of the Statistical Adviser the Statistical Branch provides a centralized service for the collection and analysis of data and the tabulation of statistical information on behalf of the administrative divisions of the Home Office and the Prison Commission. The Branch is divided into three sections:

(i) The *Criminal* section, which is responsible for preparing the annual Command Paper *Criminal Statistics, England and Wales* and certain supplementary tables which have restricted circulation to libraries and research workers; the annual *Return of Offences relating to Motor Vehicles* for presentation to Parliament; certain tables for inclusion in the annual Report of the Prison Commissioners, which is also laid before Parliament; and tables about persons placed on probation.

(ii) The *General* section, which prepares statistics relating to:

The Children's Department.
The Aliens Division.
Dangerous Drugs.
Liquor licensing and drunkenness.
The Annual Report of Her Majesty's Inspectors of Constabulary.
Experiments on living animals.
Betting and Lotteries.

These are not generally published in the form in which they are prepared, but are often incorporated in Annual Reports on their work produced by the administrative divisions. As already stated in Chapter XVI, statistical returns relating to dangerous drugs are sent to the Permanent Central Opium Board.

(iii) The *Machine* section, which contains a number of punched card accounting machines used to sort and tabulate data mainly for the Criminal section.

The Statistical Adviser, in addition to giving directions of a general nature to the Statistical Branch, advises on research projects bearing upon the Department's multifarious interests and on various other matters that have a statistical aspect.

The Scientific Adviser's Branch

The Scientific Adviser's Branch was set up in 1939 as a branch of the war-time Ministry of Home Security. Reference has already been made in Chapter VI to its work in advising on the scientific aspects of civil defence: the Branch also advises other administrative Divisions of the Home Office on scientific matters.

The Architect's Branch

The Home Office is brought into touch with building projects in several ways, in particular through its responsibilities in relation to the police, the fire service, local authority children's homes, approved schools, remand homes and probation homes and hostels. The Architect's Branch examines building plans and advises on their technical details, on building contracts, costs, and similar matters.

Research bulks largely in the work of the Architect's Branch. Stress is laid on the need for economy, and research has been carried out into the use of new materials and original designs in an attempt to lower building costs. The Branch co-operates with the administrative divisions of the Home Office in developing 'model' plans for—for example—children's homes; and by a nice balance of economy in the use of materials combined with a reasonable standard of amenity, it has been possible to draw up 'standard' plans which lower by more than fifty per cent the estimated cost per head of providing accommodation for children in local authority children's homes. Research with similar objects is being carried out upon the designs of police and fire stations. The Branch has executive functions also, and is responsible for the whole of the drawings, specifications and bills of quantities required in any alterations to the public houses and hotels in the State Management District (Chapter VIII) and for designing new public houses there as they are required.

The Communications Branch

The help given by Home Office Wireless Depots to local police authorities in providing the police forces with wireless facilities has already been mentioned in Chapter IV. Both the fire and civil defence services rely to a great extent on wireless communications, and similar work is done for them also. The Wireless Depots, of which there are nine, are responsible for installing wireless equipment in vehicles employed by the users (for example in police cars), and for installing main transmitting stations. They also maintain and repair the equipment.

All work connected with 'lines' communications—telephones, teleprinters and air raid warning siren systems—is the responsibility at headquarters of a small lines section; and Civil Defence Regional Offices also contain a Regional Communications Officer who advises local authorities on the day-to-day problems of civil defence communications.

The Communications Branch at the Home Office, in addition to controlling the provincial Wireless Depots and issuing technical instructions to the Regional Communications Officers, has specific duties of its own. It is responsible for obtaining wireless equipment from trade sources ('lines' equipment is supplied and maintained by the Post Office) and it collaborates with other Departments and with manufacturers in the development of improved and new equipment for the use of the police, fire and civil defence forces. A Test and Development section is responsible for testing the equipment when it is received from the manufacturers, and for initiating the development of new equipment in the light of experience gained in the field.

Supply and Transport Branch

The Supply and Transport Branch is the handmaiden of the Civil Defence and Fire Service Departments. It is responsible for the provision, storage, maintenance and issue of civil defence and auxiliary fire service supplies, and for the repair and maintenance of Home Office vehicles and the transport used by the W.V.S.

Although much of the work of the Branch is directly linked with defence preparations and the storage of supplies that would be needed in time of war, its value in peace time was strikingly demonstrated during the disastrous floods in February, 1953, when some ten million sand bags were issued from Home Office stores, together with 40,000 blankets, 100,000 feet of hose, pumps, stretchers, gum boots and other articles urgently required, including 40 pairs of thigh boots for use in Holland.

Public Relations Branch

This Branch is one of the newest and smallest branches of the Department. It was started in 1936, partly to relieve busy officials of the duty of replying to enquiries from journalists and others about their work, and partly to provide a better service of news and information to the press and the B.B.C. The duties of the Branch soon widened, and they now cover the whole range of the Department's publicity. The Branch keeps the Home Office informed of news and views on Home Office subjects and provides a link between the Home Office on the one hand and the public on the other both directly and also indirectly through the press and the B.B.C.

5. CONCLUSION

The wide and varied duties of the Home Secretary make special demands on the staff who assist him in discharging them. The work of the Home Office is concerned with fundamental questions of government, such as the delicate balance between personal freedom and the maintenance of an ordered community, the conflicting demands of justice and mercy, or the distinction between harmless indulgences and unbridled excess. For this work, qualities of judgment are needed, which require not only intellectual ability but integrity of character and a real appreciation of the principles of democratic government, in the sense in which we understand it. The Home Office is also responsible for the organization of large services, work which requires executive ability, energy, resourcefulness and the ability to work in harmony with local authorities and voluntary organizations. Above all, the Home Office deals with questions which affect intimately the lives of thousands of individuals, each of them a human being who is entitled to expect that his problems will be considered with sympathy and respect.

The Home Secretary's responsibilities are a subject of constant interest in Parliament; the preparation of Bills, the consideration of proposals for legislation, and the drafting of answers to letters and questions from Members of Parliament, form a large part of the work of the administrative staff. Although politics, in a party sense, is a field on which the civil servant must never trespass, the senior members of the staff cannot give the Home Secretary a full measure of assistance without an intelligent and realistic understanding of Parliamentary technique and procedure, and considerable knowledge of the published programmes of the several political parties.

The tasks to be performed are so varied that there is no common pattern of Home Office official: some types of work develop abilities which may not be as useful in other branches of the office; but two qualities, above all others, are called for: adaptability, so that members of the staff may move from one branch to another without impairing the efficiency of the Department, and, most important of all, humanity and a liberal outlook in the very widest sense of that word. The Home Office official has no motto; if he should ever feel the need of one, he could do worse than adopt the well-known words of Terence:

'Homo sum: humani nihil a me alienum puto'

SECRETARIES OF STATE FOR THE HOME DEPARTMENT FROM 1782

Rt. Hon. William, Earl of Shelburne, afterwards Marquess of Lansdowne	27 Mar.	1782
Rt. Hon. Thomas Townshend, afterwards Lord Sydney	17 July	1782
Rt. Hon. Frederick, Lord North, afterwards Earl of Guilford	2 Apr.	1782
Rt. Hon. Thomas, Lord Sydney, afterwards Viscount Sydney, *again*	23 Dec.	1783
Rt. Hon. William Wyndham Grenville, afterwards Lord Grenville	5 June	1789
Rt. Hon. Henry Dundas, afterwards Lord Melville	8 June	1791
Most Noble William Henry, Duke of Portland	11 July	1794
Rt. Hon. Thomas, Lord Pelham, afterwards Earl of Chichester	30 July	1801
Rt. Hon. Charles Philip Yorke	17 July	1803
Rt. Hon. Robert, Lord Hawkesbury, afterwards Earl of Liverpool	12 May	1804
Rt. Hon. George John, Earl Spencer	5 Feb.	1806
Rt. Hon. Robert, Lord Hawkesbury, *again*	25 Mar.	1807
Rt. Hon. Richard Ryder	1 Nov.	1809
Rt. Hon. Henry, Viscount Sidmouth	11 June	1812
Rt. Hon. Robert Peel, afterwards Sir Robert Peel	17 Jan.	1822
Rt. Hon. William Sturges Bourne	30 Apr.	1827
Most Hon. Henry, Marquess of Lansdowne	16 July	1827
Rt. Hon. Robert Peel, *again*	26 Jan.	1828
Rt. Hon. William, Viscount Melbourne	22 Nov.	1830
Rt. Hon. John, Viscount Duncannon, afterwards Earl of Bessborough	19 July	1834
Rt. Hon. Henry Goulburn	15 Dec.	1834
Rt. Hon. Lord John Russell, afterwards Earl Russell	18 Apr.	1835
Most Hon. Constantine Henry, Marquess of Normanby	30 Aug.	1839
Rt. Hon. Sir James Robert Graham, Bart.	6 Sept.	1841
Rt. Hon. Sir George Grey, Bart.	6 July	1846
Rt. Hon. Spencer Horatio Walpole	27 Feb.	1852
Rt. Hon. Henry John, Viscount Palmerston	28 Dec.	1852
Rt. Hon. Sydney Herbert, afterwards Lord Herbert of Lea	8 Feb.	1855
Rt. Hon. Sir George Grey, Bart., *again*	28 Feb.	1855
Rt. Hon. Spencer Horatio Walpole, *again*	26 Feb.	1858
Rt. Hon. T. H. S. Sotheron-Estcourt	28 Feb.	1859
Rt. Hon. Sir George Cornewall Lewis, Bart.	18 June	1859
Rt. Hon. Sir George Grey, Bart., *again*	23 July	1861
Rt. Hon. Spencer Horatio Walpole, *again*	6 July	1866
Rt. Hon. Gathorne Hardy, afterwards Earl of Cranbrook	17 May	1867
Rt. Hon. Henry Austin Bruce, afterwards Lord Aberdare	9 Dec.	1868
Rt. Hon. Robert Lowe, afterwards Viscount Sherbrooke	9 Aug.	1873
Rt. Hon. Sir Richard Assheton Cross, G.C.B., afterwards Viscount Cross	21 Feb.	1874
Rt. Hon. Sir William Vernon Harcourt	23 Apr.	1880
Rt. Hon. Sir R. A. Cross, G.C.B., afterwards Viscount Cross, *again*	24 June	1885
Rt. Hon. H. C. E. Childers	6 Feb.	1886
Rt. Hon. Henry Matthews, afterwards Viscount Llandaff	3 Aug.	1886
Rt. Hon. Herbert H. Asquith, afterwards Earl of Oxford and Asquith	18 Aug.	1892

Rt. Hon. Sir Matthew White Ridley, Bart., afterwards Viscount Ridley	29 June	1895
Rt. Hon. Charles Thomson Ritchie, afterwards Lord Ritchie	12 Nov.	1900
Rt. Hon. Aretas Akers-Douglas, afterwards Viscount Chilston	11 Aug.	1902
Rt. Hon. Herbert John Gladstone, afterwards Viscount Gladstone	11 Dec.	1905
Rt. Hon. Winston Leonard Spencer Churchill, afterwards Sir Winston Churchill, K.G., O.M., C.H., D.L.	19 Feb.	1910
Rt. Hon. Reginald McKenna	24 Oct.	1911
Rt. Hon. Sir John Simon, K.C.V.O., K.C., afterwards Viscount Simon, G.C.S.I., G.C.V.O., O.B.E.	27 May	1915
Rt. Hon. Herbert Louis Samuel, afterwards Viscount Samuel, G.C.B., G.B.E.	12 Jan.	1916
Rt. Hon. Sir George Cave, K.C., afterwards Viscount Cave	11 Dec.	1916
Rt. Hon. Edward Shortt, K.C.	14 Jan.	1919
Rt. Hon. William Clive Bridgeman, afterwards Viscount Bridgeman	25 Oct.	1922
Rt. Hon. Arthur Henderson	23 Jan.	1924
Rt. Hon. Sir William Joynson-Hicks, Bart., afterwards Viscount Brentford	7 Nov.	1924
Rt. Hon. John Robert Clynes	8 June	1929
Rt. Hon. Sir Herbert Samuel, G.C.B., G.B.E., afterwards Viscount Samuel, *again*	26 Aug.	1931
Lieut. Col. The Rt. Hon. Sir John Gilmour, Bart., D.S.O., afterwards G.C.V.O.	1 Oct.	1932
Rt. Hon. Sir John Simon, G.C.S.I., K.C.V.O., O.B.E., K.C., afterwards Viscount Simon	7 June	1935
Rt. Hon. Sir Samuel Hoare, G.C.S.I., G.B.E., C.M.G., afterwards Viscount Templewood	28 May	1937
Rt. Hon. Sir John Anderson, G.C.B., G.C.S.I., G.C.I.E., afterwards Viscount Waverley	4 Sept.	1939
Rt. Hon. Herbert Morrison, afterwards C.H.	4 Oct.	1940
Rt. Hon. Sir Donald B. Somervell, K.C., O.B.E.	28 May	1945
Rt. Hon. James Chuter Ede, afterwards C.H.	3 Aug.	1945
Rt. Hon. Sir David Maxwell Fyfe, Q.C., afterwards Viscount Kilmuir, G.C.V.O.	27 Oct.	1951
Rt. Hon. Gwilym Lloyd-George	19 Oct.	1954

PARLIAMENTARY UNDER-SECRETARIES OF STATE FOR THE HOME DEPARTMENT

Thomas Order		1782
Evan Nepean		1782
Henry Strachey		1782
Hon. John Thomas Townshend		1783
Hon. G. North		1784
Charles Greville		1796
William Wickham		1798
Edward Finch Hatton		1800
Sir George Shee, Bart.		1800
Reginald Pole Carew		1803
John Henry Smyth		1804
Charles Watkins William Wynn	19 Feb.	1806
Hon. Charles Cecil C. Jenkinson, afterwards Earl of Liverpool	10 Oct.	1807
Henry Goulburn	27 Feb.	1810
Rt. Hon. John Hiley Addington	21 Aug.	1812
Henry Clive	21 Apr.	1818
George Robert Dawson	17 Jan.	1822
Spencer Perceval	30 Apr.	1827
Thomas Spring Rice, afterwards Lord Monteagle	16 July	1827
William Yates Peel	5 Apr.	1828
Sir George Clerk, Bart.	5 Aug.	1830
Hon. George Lamb	22 Nov.	1830
Henry, Viscount Howick, afterwards Earl Grey	13 Jan.	1834
Edward John Stanley, afterwards Lord Stanley of Alderley	23 July	1834
William Gregson	3 Jan.	1835
Hon. Fox Maule, afterwards Earl of Dalhousie	18 Apr.	1835
Edward Adolphus, Lord Seymour, afterwards Duke of Somerset	15 June	1841
Hon. Henry John Thomas Manners Sutton	3 Sept.	1841
Sir William Marcus Somerville, Bart.	5 July	1842
Sir Denis le Marchant	22 July	1847
Sir George Cornewall Lewis, Bart.	15 May	1848
Hon. Edward Pleydell Bouverie	9 July	1850
Sir William George Hylton Jolliffe, Bart., afterwards Lord Hylton	27 Feb.	1852
Rt. Hon. Henry Fitzroy	28 Dec.	1852
Hon. William Francis Cowper	16 Feb.	1855
William Nathaniel Massey	13 Aug.	1855
Gathorne Hardy,† afterwards Earl of Cranbrook	26 Feb.	1858
George Clive	18 June	1859
Henry Austin Bruce,† afterwards Lord Aberdare	14 Nov.	1862
Hon. Thomas George Baring, afterwards Earl of Northbrook	25 Apr.	1864
Edward H. Knatchbull-Hugessen, afterwards Lord Brabourne,	25 May	1866
Somerset Richard Lowry, Earl of Belmore	10 July	1866
Sir James Fergusson,* Bart.	1 Aug.	1867
Edward H. Knatchbull-Hugessen, *again*	10 Dec.	1868
George John Shaw-Lefevre,* afterwards Rt. Hon. Lord Eversley	11 Jan.	1871
Henry Selfe Page Winterbotham	17 Mar.	1871
Sir Henry Selwin Ibbetson, Bart., afterwards Lord Rookwood	25 Feb.	1874

Sir Matthew White Ridley,† Bart., afterwards Viscount Ridley	6 Apr.	1878
Arthur Peel, afterwards Viscount Peel	23 Apr.	1880
Leonard H. Courtney*	1 Jan.	1881
The Earl of Rosebery	8 Aug.	1881
Sir John T. Hibbert,* K.C.B.	7 June	1883
Sir Henry H. Fowler,* G.C.S.I., afterwards Rt. Hon. Viscount Wolverhampton	12 Dec.	1884
Charles B. Stuart-Wortley,* afterwards Rt. Hon. Lord Stuart of Wortley	30 June	1885
Henry Broadhurst	6 Feb.	1886
Charles B. Stuart-Wortley,* *again*	4 Aug.	1886
Herbert J. Gladstone,†* afterwards Rt. Hon. Viscount Gladstone	19 Aug.	1892
George W. E. Russell*	12 Mar.	1894
Rt. Hon. Jesse Collings	3 July	1895
Hon. Thomas Horatio A. E. Cochrane	11 Aug.	1902
Herbert Louis Samuel,†* afterwards Rt. Hon. Viscount Samuel, G.C.B., G.B.E.	12 Dec.	1905
Charles Frederick Gurney Masterman*	8 July	1909
Ellis Jones Griffith,* K.C., afterwards Sir Ellis Griffith, Bart.	17 Feb.	1912
Cecil Harmsworth	4 Feb.	1915
William Brace*	31 May	1915
Rt. Hon. Sir Hamar Greenwood, Bart., K.C.	14 Jan.	1919
Sir John Lawrence Baird, Bart., C.M.G., D.S.O., afterwards Lord Stonehaven	10 July	1919
Lieut. Col. The Hon. George Frederick Stanley,* C.M.G.	1 Nov.	1922
Godfrey Lampson Tennyson Locker-Lampson*	13 Mar.	1923
Rhys John Davies	23 Jan.	1924
Godfrey Lampson Tennyson Locker-Lampson,* *again*	10 Nov.	1924
Capt. Douglas Hewitt Hacking,* O.B.E.	9 Dec.	1925
Lt. Col. Sir Vivian Leonard Henderson, M.C.	10 Nov.	1927
Alfred Short	11 June	1929
Hon. Oliver Stanley,* M.C.	3 Sept.	1931
Rt. Hon. Douglas Hewitt Hacking, O.B.E., *again*, afterwards Lord Hacking	23 Feb.	1933
Capt. Harry F. C. Crookshank*	2 July	1934
Capt. David Euan Wallace,* M.C.	19 June	1935
Geoffrey William Lloyd*	28 Nov.	1935
Osbert Peake*	24 Apr.	1939
Earl of Munster*	1 Nov.	1944
George Harold Oliver	5 Aug.	1945
The Hon. Kenneth Gilmour Younger*	14 Oct.	1947
Geoffrey de Freitas	2 Mar.	1950
David Treharne Llewellyn	5 Nov.	1951
Sir Hugh Lucas-Tooth, Bart.	4 Feb.	1952
Lord Lloyd, M.B.E.	25 Nov.	1952
Lord Mancroft, M.B.E., T.D.	18 Oct.	1954

* Subsequently sworn of the Privy Council after appointment to the Home Office.

† Subsequently Secretary of State.

PERMANENT UNDER-SECRETARIES OF STATE

Scrope Bernard 1789
John King 1792
John Beckett, junr., afterwards Sir John Beckett, Bart. 19 Feb. 1806
Henry Hobhouse 28 June 1817
Samuel March Phillippes 16 July 1827
Rt. Hon. Horatio Waddington 15 May 1848
Hon. Sir Adolphus Liddell, K.C.B. 14 Aug. 1867
Sir Godfrey Lushington, G.C.M.G., K.C.B. 25 July 1885
Sir Kenelm Edward Digby, G.C.B., K.C. 7 Jan. 1895
Sir Mackenzie Dalzell Chalmers, K.C.B., C.S.I. 9 Sept. 1903
Sir Edward Troup, K.C.B., K.C.V.O. 1 Feb. 1908
Rt. Hon. Sir John Anderson, G.C.B., afterwards Secretary of State and Viscount Waverley, G.C.B., G.C.S.I., G.C.I.E. 13 Mar. 1922
Sir Robert Russell Scott, K.C.B., C.S.I., I.S.O. 29 Mar. 1932
Sir Alexander Maxwell, G.C.B., K.B.E. 26 Jan. 1938
Sir Frank Newsam, K.C.B., K.B.E., C.V.O., M.C. 1 Oct. 1948

HOME OFFI

(A

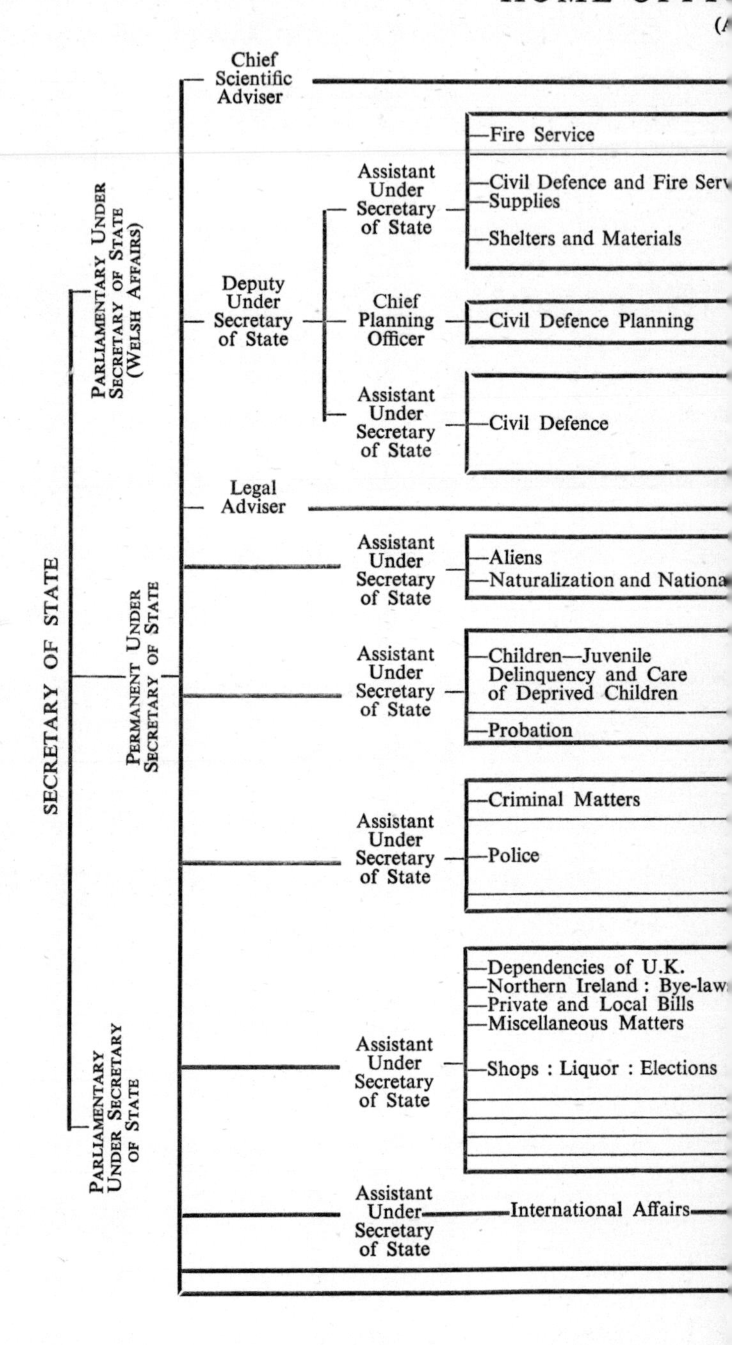

Chief Scientific Adviser
Fire Service
Assistant Under Secretary of State
Civil Defence and Fire Serv
Supplies
Shelters and Materials
Parliamentary Under Secretary of State (Welsh Affairs)
Deputy Under Secretary of State
Chief Planning Officer
Civil Defence Planning
Assistant Under Secretary of State
Civil Defence
Legal Adviser
Assistant Under Secretary of State
Aliens
Naturalization and Nationa
Secretary of State
Permanent Under Secretary of State
Assistant Under Secretary of State
Children—Juvenile Delinquency and Care of Deprived Children
Probation
Criminal Matters
Assistant Under Secretary of State
Police
Dependencies of U.K.
Northern Ireland : Bye-law
Private and Local Bills
Miscellaneous Matters
Assistant Under Secretary of State
Shops : Liquor : Elections
Parliamentary Under Secretary of State
Assistant Under Secretary of State
International Affairs

RGANIZATION CHART

ne, 1954).

ientific Adviser's Branch

Division —— Fire Service Inspectorate
Division —— Fire Service College
Division

pply and Transport Branch —{ Civil Defence Stores; Fire Service Stores and Workshops

Division
Division

Division
Division

Division
Division
Division

aining Division —— Civil Defence College and Schools
vil Defence Regional Offices

gal Adviser's Branch

Division —— } Immigration Branch —— Immigration Offices
Division —— }
Division

Division
2 Division
3 Division
ildren's Department Inspectorate
Division —— Probation Inspectorate

Division
Division
Division —— { Police College; Police Training Centres; Forensic Science Laboratories
Division
.M. Inspectors of Constabulary

Division —— { Inspectors under the Cruelty to Animals Acts; Dangerous Drugs Branch —— Drugs Inspectors
Division —— Explosives Branch —— Explosives Inspectors
Division —— { Carlisle and District State Management; Women's Voluntary Services
stablishment and Organization Division
rchitect's Branch
ommunications Branch —— Provincial Wireless Depots
iblic Relations Branch
atistical Branch

Division

inance Division
edical Adviser

NUMBERS OF HOME OFFICE STAFF

(As at June, 1954)

	Treasury Classes			Professional and Technical	Others
	Administrative	Executive	Clerical and Typing		
Scientific Adviser's Branch	—	3	7	17	—
K Divisions; Fire Service Inspectorate; Fire Service College	11	22	24	26	4
Supply and Transport Branch	—	35	116	47	68
O and Q Divisions	3	11	8	—	—
P Divisions	6	11	5	—	—
J Divisions	13	24	14	5	—
T Division; Civil Defence Staff College and Schools	3	6	33	71	11
Civil Defence Regional Offices	—	53	95	21	10
Legal Adviser's Branch	—	1	2	8	—
B Divisions; Immigration Branch; A2 Division	10	425	185	—	6
D Divisions; Children's Department Inspectorate	11	34	53	71	17
N Division; Probation Inspectorate	3	7	7	9	1
C Divisions	8	9	10	—	—
F Divisions; Inspectors of Constabulary	13	28	20	6	2
Police College and Police Training Centres	—	12	56	1*	6
Forensic Science Laboratories	—	—	12	63	4
A1 Division; Cruelty to Animals Inspectorate; Dangerous Drugs Branch	4	6	15	8	—
E Division; Explosives Branch	3	10	14	5	—
H Division	3	3	3	—	600†
Establishment and Organisation Division	2	21	46	—	4
Architect's Branch	—	—	3	20	—
Communications Branch	—	1	10	27	1
Wireless Depots	—	—	27	101	9
Public Relations Branch	—	1	2	4	—
Statistical Branch	1	6	12	—	12
International Division	1	1	2	—	—
Finance Division	—	75	55	—	5
Officekeeping	—	—	—	—	152
Registries	—	25	112	—	52
Secretariat	14‡	1	9	—	—
Typists	—	3	170	—	—
Cleaners	—	—	—	—	60
TOTALS:	109	834	1,127	510	1,024

* Commandant of Police College; all other Commandants and instructional staffs are seconded police officers (total 142).

† State Management staff (all grades—but excluding part-time staff).

‡ Includes Assistant Under-Secretaries of State.

INDEX

GEORGE ALLEN & UNWIN LTD
London: 40 Museum Street, W.C.1

Auckland: 24 Wyndham Street
Sydney, N.S.W.: Bradbury House, 55 York Street
Cape Town: 58–60 Long Street
Bombay: 15 Graham Road, Ballard Estate, Bombay 1
Calcutta: 17 Chittaranjan Avenue, Calcutta 13
New Delhi: 13–14 Ajmeri Gate Extension, New Delhi 1
Karachi: Haroon Chambers, South Napier Road, Karachi 2
Toronto: 91 Wellington Street West
São Paulo: Avenida 9 de Julho 1138–Ap. 51

BRITISH GOVERNMENT SINCE 1918

Lord Campion, D. N. Chester, W. J. M. Mackenzie
W. A. Robson, Sir Arthur Street, J. H. Warren

'On the subjects the book treats no better qualified set of authors could have been assembled . . . a symposium that is stimulating and informative because the authors range where they will and concentrate mainly on interpretation and on bringing the less familiar rather than the commonplace to notice. What they jointly produce in consequence is as lively and full an account as has yet appeared of some of the leading problems of our time.'
—*Manchester Guardian.*

Demy 8vo. 2nd Edition. 16s. net

★

PARLIAMENT—A SURVEY

Lord Campion, L. S. Amery, D. W. Brogan
J. J. Craik Henderson, Sir Arthur Salter, H. E. Dale
Ivor Thomas, F. W. Lascelles, E. C. S. Wade
Sir Cecil Carr, A. L. Goodhart, G. M. Young

'A survey such as this is valuable—indeed essential.'—The Rt. Hon. Walter Elliot in the *Daily Telegraph.*

'One of the best commentaries on our political system we have had in recent years. The book is calmly objective, balanced in its criticisms, temperate in its apprehensions, and cautiously modest in its proposals.'—*Political Quarterly.*

Demy 8vo. 2nd Impression about 25s. net.

★

GEORGE ALLEN AND UNWIN LTD